ORGANIZE FUNDRAISING

HAVE A PURPOSE

VOLUNTE

ACTIVE CITIZEN

WRITE A LETTE

You Can Make A Difference

ORGANIZE A CLEAN

BE INFORMED

BE EMPOWERED

ANGELO BOLOTTA
MARC KEIRSTEAD
JILL COLYER
CATHY COSTELLO
SHANE PISANI

CONTRIBUTING AUTHOR:
TRACEY McBRIDE

SPEAK OUT

SIGN A PETITION

OXFORD
UNIVERSITY PRESS

OXFORD

UNIVERSITY PRESS

70 Wynford Drive, Don Mills, Ontario M3C 1J9
www.oup.com/ca

Oxford University Press is a department of the University of Oxford.

It furthers the University's objective of excellence in research, scholarship,
and education by publishing worldwide in

Oxford New York

Auckland Cape Town Dar es Salaam Hong Kong Karachi
Kuala Lumpur Madrid Melbourne Mexico City Nairobi
New Delhi Shanghai Taipei Toronto

With offices in

Argentina Austria Brazil Chile Czech Republic France Greece
Guatemala Hungary Italy Japan Poland Portugal Singapore
South Korea Switzerland Thailand Turkey Ukraine Vietnam

Oxford is a registered trade mark of Oxford University Press
in the UK and in certain other countries

Published in Canada
by Oxford University Press

Copyright © Oxford University Press Canada 2006

ISBN-10 0195424069
ISBN-13 9780195424065

Publisher: Janice Schoening
Managing Editor: Monica Schwalbe
Developmental Editor: Nancy Christoffer
Copyeditor: Geraldine Kikuta
Photo Research and Copyright Permissions: Paula Joiner
Cover design: Brett Miller
Page Layout: PageWave Graphics Inc.
Cover images: l) © Royalty-Free/CORBIS/MAGMA;
(c) CP/Lethbridge Herald(Ian Martens), (r) CP(Chuck Stoody).
Illustrations pages 2, 62: Scot Ritchie Illustration
Maps pages 151, 169, 179: Crowle Art Group

1 2 3 4 — 09 08 07 06   Printed and bound in Canada

CONTENTS

Chapter 3
Canada's Legal System   62

Chapter 4
Municipal Government and You   98

Chapter 5
Hear My Voice: Public Issues and Civil Action   122

Chapter 6
The Global Citizen Today   148

Putting It All Together 184

When you see this icon on pages in this book, go to the *Active Citizen* on-line resource centre at www.oup.com/ca/education/companion and click on the cover. You can also go to the site directly at www.oup.com/ca/education/companion/activecitizen.

INTRODUCTION

Being an Active Citizen

Have you ever thought that you'd like to make a difference but just didn't know how? Many of you know that in a democratic society people can influence changes if they know what to do and care enough to do it. A key purpose of this course is to teach you how to change the things that you don't like in a democratic society.

There are plenty of opportunities to improve our democratic society. To be an effective participant you need to:

1. *Be informed.* Learn the rules and procedures of collective decision making. Find out your responsibilities and rights as a valued member of a group or community. Know who has the power to make changes.
2. *Be purposeful.* Be clear about what you believe would make things better. Learn how to convince others that what you would like to see happen is a good thing for the community. Communicate this information to the right people, people who can help you to get the job done.
3. *Be active.* Roll up your sleeves and work at making good things happen. Network with others who support your cause.

Remember these three qualities for effective participation. You will be hearing much more about them throughout this book.

Citizenship education should not only be practical, but also current. It should acknowledge important local, regional, national, and global concerns. The authors of this book have attempted to create a practical toolkit with a fresh approach to citizenship and civics.

The design of this text enables practising citizens, like your teacher, to effectively pass the torch of citizenship to you—the next generation of informed, purposeful, and active citizens. You will be the politicians, decision-makers, and agents of change in the future. If your generation is not up for this challenge, then all Canadians will be at a disadvantage. Throughout human history, diversity has led to division and conflict. In multicultural Canada, we are trying to show the world that diversity can be a source of strength and creativity.

Teen's letter a perfect lesson

Father rescued by missives via Amnesty International

Students asked to write on behalf of persecuted Colombian

By Tess Kalinowski,
Education Reporter

Barbara Yebuga, 18, did something last week that few teenagers would dream of—she brought her family to high school.

She stood proudly with her brother and sister before a special assembly as her mother, Irene, told her schoolmates what their family owes to an Amnesty International letter-writing campaign, known as an Urgent Action.

The letters once saved Barbara's father, John Yebuga, said Irene.

The family is still grieving John's death at age 56 in January from cancer, but they went to Our Lady of Mount Carmel High School last Friday to offer living proof that, together, Barbara's 1800 schoolmates could help save a stranger's life just by taking a few minutes to write a letter.

And they urged students to do just that—write a letter asking the president of Colombia to protect Yolanda Becerra, a threatened women's rights advocate there.

Figure 1-11 Irene Yebuga watches as daughter Barbara writes a letter as part of an Amnesty International campaign.

In 1982, his vocal objections landed him in a Sudanese prison, Amnesty sources say. The next day Irene lost her job.

Yebuga spent a year in prison while his pregnant wife tried to care for her daughters. Finally, after smuggling out a letter to Amnesty supporters, they were able to pressure the Sudanese authorities into freeing him. Meanwhile, a group of Canadian Amnesty supporters brought his case to the ...

The students were among about 7000 students from 10 Mississauga public and Catholic high schools who wrote letters on Becerra's behalf.

"We need to be a voice for the voiceless. We may not be able to help everyone, but one is better than none." Barbara said...

Her parents fled Uganda in the late 1970s, toward the end of dictator Idi Amin's bloody regime. They went to a refugee camp in Sudan, where John Yebuga took an administrative job. But the camp was run by Amin's former henchmen, who also had ties to Sudanese officials. Yebuga saw them stealing relief supplies from starving people.

1. What personal qualities do John and ...
2. How successful was this Urgent Actio...
3. Why is the support of young people ...

Active Citizen

10

...attention of the student council?

...students take to find out how other students felt and how ... was selected?

What difficulties would the student council face in making its music selection? Brainstorm a student concern at your school and follow the same steps to develop your case study. What powers does your student council have and what restrictions are placed on it? Do you feel the restrictions are justified? Explain.

KEY LEARNINGS

In this chapter you will explore the following topics:
* the structure and function of Canada's federal and provincial governments
* what is involved in electing governments in Canada
* the various roles involved in the political process
* the civic literacy skills of detecting bias and accessing reliable resources

Chapter 2: How ...

9. ...? given that power? Justify your choices and explain how each change would represent an improvement. Summarize your work in a video report, newscast, photo essay, or a PowerPoint presentation.

Culminating Performance Task: Making a Difference

The purpose of this textbook is to prepare you to be informed, purposeful, and active citizens. Each chapter contains knowledge and provides opportunities to practise useful civic literacy skills.

This culminating performance task asks you to put the knowledge and skills you have learned in this chapter to effective use. It provides you with an opportunity to make a difference and to learn from the experience.

Before you carry out a sound action plan, you need to do some research and some clear thinking.

Your teacher will provide a time frame for the individual components and an assessment rubric. This process and rubric will provide valuable constructive feedback along the way.

Reminders at the end of Chapters 3, 5, and 7 will help you to stay on task. Conferencing with your teacher will also help you get the most out of the time and effort that you are putting into this culminating performance task. Keep a portfolio to document and assess your steps and all outcomes.

Kristop was born biliary a... carry bile bile build... Children two years...

Before Kristopher system out liver ...

Making the Textbook Work for You

This book presents information and ideas in many ways: the written text, photographs, tables, graphs, diagrams, and maps. There are also a number of features throughout the book.

Key Learnings These appear at the beginning of every chapter to let you know the main learning points in the chapter.

Key Terms When a term appears in boldface in the text, its definition appears in the margin beside it. This is to help you understand important terms as you read.

Literacy Hints These margin tips will help you develop and use the literacy skills we all use to help us make sense of what we are reading and viewing.

Civic Skills Power These citizenship and social studies skills include skills in the areas of research and inquiry, critical and creative thinking, communication, decision making, conflict resolution, and teamwork. These features give you a chance to practise the skills yourself.

Checkpoint These questions appear throughout the chapters to help you make sure you understand what you have read.

People Power These short biographies are about people who have made a difference in various areas of citizenship. Some are well-known people from Canada and around the globe. Others are students like you who have made a difference.

Going to the Source: Charter of Rights and Freedoms

...below are excerpts from the *Charter of Rights and Freedoms*. Because the Charter is part of our Constitution, none of these rights can be taken away by the government.

Fundamental Freedoms
2. Everyone has the following fundamental freedoms:
a) freedom of conscience and religion;
b) freedom of thought, belief, opinion and expression, including freedom of the press and other media of communication;
c) freedom of peaceful assembly; and
d) freedom of association.

Democratic Rights
3. Every citizen of Canada has the right to vote in an election of members of the House of Commons or of a legislative assembly and to be qualified for membership therein.

Mobility Rights
6. (1) Every citizen of Canada has the right to enter, ... and leave Canada.

specific offence;
b) to be tried within a reasonable time;
c) not to be compelled to be a witness in proceedings against that person in respect of the offence;
d) to be presumed innocent until proven guilty according to law in a fair and public hearing by an independent and impartial [unbiased] tribunal;
e) not to be denied reasonable bail without just cause;
f) except in the case of an offence under military law tried before a military tribunal, to the benefit of trial by jury where the maximum punishment for the offence is imprisonment for five years or a more severe punishment;
g) not to be found guilty on account of any act or omission unless, at the time of the act or omission, it constituted an offence under Canadian or international law or was criminal according to the general principles of law recognized by the community of nations [meaning the accused should not be found guilty unless an act is committed against Canadian or international law];
h) if finally acquitted of the offence, not to be tried for it again and, if finally found guilty and punished for the offence, not to be tried or punished for it again; and

For links to sites on HIV/AIDS in Africa

...x school boar... another. The fec... Labelling Act. Ad... of factories when...

HIV/AIDS in Af... How much do you... about what this dise... not know as much a... like Africa. A 10-year... page 153. As you read... she feels about her life... she wrote it, it contains...

Informed to Be Effective

For many Aboriginal people citizenship is based on a sense of kinship or family relationship to their larger community or nation. Many see their relationship with Canada as being one of nation to nation. They negotiate with Canada on land claims and resource issues on a nation-to-nation basis. Aboriginal people who are registered under the Indian Act are also considered Canadian citizens. What issues do you think this raises for Aboriginal people and others?

grandparents or guardians are ... of the family. They are recognized as t... their age, experience, financial resou... Nonetheless, government laws pro...

Throughout history all civiliza... citizens involved in those govern... have evolved over time. Officials ... or absolute rule by one person o... be separate and balanced. ... the entire community. Some appl... Nations, Métis, and Inuit have gov... regions. In Canada, every level of go... well-being of citizens.

CHECK
1. Which points on the timeline show... a say in how they were governed?
2. What are the rights and responsi...
3. What is the purpose of a democr...
4. How would you define democrac...

Issue Analysis These features allow you to analyse specific public issues or concerns. They are often presented in Pro/Con format. Each one includes questions for you to think about where you stand on the issue.

Going to the Source Here you will find primary sources and documents. You have an opportunity to analyse them through the focus questions.

In the News This feature allows you to interpret civics topics currently in the media.

Informed to be Effective In this feature you will find helpful information that allows you to be an effective citizen.

Web Links These icons in the margins tell you that if you go to the *Active Citizen* website, you will find web links to more information on key topics.

Chapter Review Each chapter ends with a summary that highlights, in point form, key information presented in the chapter. It also includes activities that ask you to reflect on, synthesize, and apply your learning about the chapter's main topics.

Culminating Performance Task You will have a chance to apply what you have learned by completing a culminating performance task. You will find information in Chapters 1, 3, 5, and 7 to help you complete this task.

COMMUNITY AND THE COMMON GOOD

The Real Survivors

You and your best friend have just won an all expenses paid vacation to the Fiji Islands. These islands are sometimes called "paradise on Earth." Unfortunately, on your way to paradise, your small plane crashes onto a deserted tropical island.

Only five people survived—you, your friend, and three strangers. The crew perished. Everything was lost in the fire that followed the crash. You only have the clothes you are wearing. All communications systems were destroyed, so it looks as though you are going to be stranded for a while.

Figure 1-1 The Real Survivors

Here is what you are dealing with:

- The island is three kilometres long and two kilometres wide.
- It contains a freshwater spring.
- It has abundant tropical vegetation, fruits, nuts, and vegetables.
- The ocean surrounding the island has a variety of fish.
- There are no dangerous mammals on the island, but there are unknown varieties of lizards and snakes.

Literacy Hint

Visualizing. Use the details in the scenario to get a mental picture of the island.

You cannot count on being rescued quickly. You'll have to set up a peaceful and orderly community to provide for all your needs. Organize yourselves into groups of five survivors. Appoint roles for group members and assign specific duties, as follows:

- taskmaster—keeps members focused on task and remaining time
- recorder—takes notes during your decision-making process
- reporter—lists in order of importance the statements made by group members and later reports the thinking behind group decisions
- reviewer—seeks clarity and meaning in what is being stated by members
- gatekeeper—makes sure all members contribute.

As a group, determine what plans and rules you need to make together to ensure everyone survives until you are rescued. Plans should include: food and shelter, sharing responsibilities, and rules of behaviour.

As a class, compare the decisions each group made. Then, identify which concerns and decisions were common to all groups.

1. What were the most important features of survival plans?
2. What did this **simulation** reveal about you and about your group?
3. What insights did this simulation give you about people living together?

simulation: a model imitating real or assumed conditions

KEY LEARNINGS

In this chapter you will explore the following topics:
- the need for communities to make decisions in a democratic way
- the beliefs and values involved in democratic citizenship
- responses at the community level to civic issues
- how societies can be organized to pursue goals
- the civic literacy skills of distinguishing fact from opinion and of processing information

Community Living Is Not a Spectator Sport

community: a group of people who have joined together to pursue common needs and goals

common good: what is best for the community and all its members because it promotes dignity, security, and prosperity

social trade-off: giving up personal freedom to achieve social harmony

bylaw: a law or rule passed by a municipal council and applicable only to that municipality

Could any of us survive alone? Since the beginning of human existence, people have chosen to live together in **communities** to deal with the challenges that threaten their survival. The basic necessities of life—food, clothing, shelter, security, and companionship—can all be obtained more easily through community living.

Many First Nations have teachings about the importance of living together in strong communities. Think about this teaching, for example. A single twig or arrow can be broken easily. If you bind five twigs or arrows together, they are much stronger. Once there were five separate nations of Mohawk, Oneida, Onondaga, Cayuga, and Seneca. They united to form the Haudenosaunee (Iroquois) Confederacy. It has been said that a Chief from each nation was to bring one arrow. The five arrows were then bound together. This bundle of arrows symbolized strength in unity.

The Give-and-Take of Community Living

Living together in a community has both costs and benefits. People in a community need to recognize that they may have to give up some personal freedom to serve the **common good**. Living together may mean we have to give up personal preferences, accept routines, and follow rules that we don't always fully understand or appreciate. For instance, your parents might want to spray their property regularly to get rid of insects and weeds. But if your community has imposed a ban on pesticides to protect residents with allergies, your parents would have to stop spraying for the common good.

The Social Trade-off

This understanding of the common good is the basis for an important **social trade-off** that all communities must address. Some things may have to be sacrificed to achieve other things. For example, most urban communities have a rule or **bylaw** about loud noise after a certain time at night, because it disturbs neighbours. The rights of one citizen, say to enjoy music, have been adjusted to protect the rights of others to not be disturbed. The common good means that we seek the most good for the greatest number of people.

Your school community, like most others, includes many people with different personalities, interests, and viewpoints. These differences provide variety, but they can also lead to arguments. If not handled properly, arguments can lead to conflict. All communities need to have processes in place to settle disputes, to make common decisions, and to teach young people how to be contributing citizens.

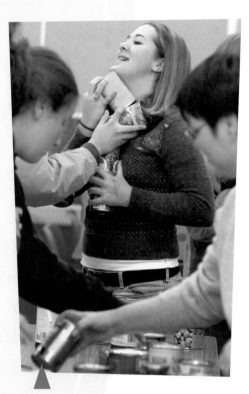

Figure 1-2 How have these students from Peterborough Collegiate and Vocational School decided to make a difference? How does this example demonstrate the strength of a community?

It is important for individuals to feel a sense of belonging and commitment to their community or society. It is just as important for the society to show that it cares for the well-being of all members. Society does this by promoting human dignity, security, personal growth, and prosperity.

As a member of a community, you will at some point come up against a situation that is difficult to accept. Think about these possibilities:

- An employer demands that you work extremely late hours on school nights.
- A bylaw forces you to get rid of a family pet considered to be dangerous.
- Your community lacks clean drinking water.
- A school rule (that you feel is unfair) requires you to take your spares in the library only and not in the cafeteria.
- There's a crosswalk near your school where students have been hit by speeding motorists.
- A student at your school likes to bully or take advantage of others.

The possibilities are endless. How will you know what to do to make a difference?

There is no perfect community. Different communities around the world experience different problems. What kind of community do you feel that you are living in? Are the rights and needs of all members being dealt with fairly? Do community members feel safe and secure? Are they left to provide for their own needs? Study the following four images taken from four different communities around the world. What problems of community living do these images reveal?

Literacy Hint

Make a Connection. What does the word "community" mean to you? Write a sentence or two to describe a community to which you belong. Next consider the situations listed in the text. What is your response to each one?

Figures 1-3 to 1-6 These are uncommon scenes in Canada today, although they happen in areas around the world. What will it take to prevent them from happening in your community?

Figure 1-3 Evidence of racially motivated mass murder is uncovered in Rwanda.

Figure 1-4 A politician is assassinated by a car bomb in Lebanon.

Figure 1-5 A police officer guards the halls of El Sereno Middle School in East Los Angeles.

Figure 1-6 A young boy stands amid the rubbish that surrounds his home at Quayaquil's Dump in Ecuador.

What Is Citizenship?

To answer the question of how you can make a difference, we need to think about what citizenship means. One early concept of **citizenship** originated in the city state of Athens around 500 BCE. In ancient Athens, all free male citizens were guaranteed freedom of speech, equality before the law, and membership in the state assembly. City states have evolved into larger multi-city nations. As Figure 1-7 shows, today we are citizens of local, regional, national, and global communities.

A **citizen** is more than a resident or an inhabitant. A citizen has responsibilities to the community or group. In return, the community has specific responsibilities toward its members. **Civics** looks at how a society chooses to strike a balance between individual freedom and collective needs and goals, such as:

- peace
- security
- order
- responsible government.

It is also the study of how decisions are made about public issues or concerns.

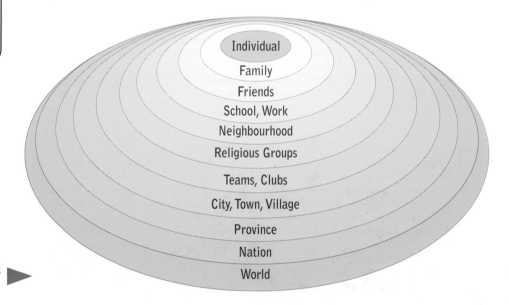

Figure 1-7 Different Levels of Citizenship

As you saw in the Real Survivors simulation, effective community living means members must have rules to live by. Many of these rules may be unwritten and based on traditional practices. Some of the more important or complicated rules may be recorded into a code of law or behaviour. Whether

citizenship: the responsibilities, duties, and rights of a member of a state or nation

citizen: a member of a state or nation, with certain rights and responsibilities

civics: the study of the duties and rights of citizenship

Literacy Hint

Nuggets or dotted points can make information easier to read and understand by breaking it down into smaller chunks.

written or unwritten, the most important thing is that the group practise these rules, ideally without force. These rules cover:

- how members are to treat one another
- how duties or chores will be divided among the group
- how disputes will be settled
- how offenders will be dealt with
- how the group will pursue its goals and ensure its future.

Literacy Hint

Access Your Background Knowledge. Try to think of a rule that could be made for each situation listed here.

In small communities, such as a classroom, people know one another. When issues arise, we can often resolve them through open and informal discussion. In larger and more complicated communities, like our multicultural country, we often use a more impersonal approach. With many different viewpoints and conflicting wants, we need a more formal and binding decision-making process.

To make matters more complicated, most of us belong to more than one community. For example, besides being a member of the classroom and school communities, you may also belong to a specific ethnocultural community. You may be a member of a social club, a service organization, or a labour union. Different levels of community exist at the same time. Figure 1-8 below gives an example of some of the communities one person might belong to.

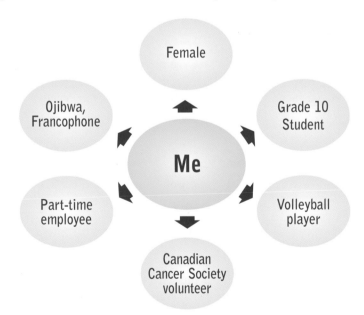

Figure 1-8 How many communities do you belong to? Create your own organizer like the one shown here.

No matter how many communities you belong to, the following holds true: Responsible citizenship is not a spectator sport. It requires action—informed and purposeful action. Figure 1-9 on the next page shows some forms that active citizenship can take in a community.

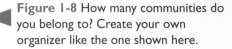

CHARACTERISTICS OF HEALTHY COMMUNITIES

Quality or Characteristic	School Example	Local Example
A common identity, goal, or purpose helps to bond people together	The student council raises money to buy new uniforms for school teams.	A community decides to organize a breakfast for local children.
People want to belong to the community and they value the common good	Students report a health and safety concern to the school administration.	Residents attend a meeting to organize a Neighbourhood Watch program.
Needs and challenges are addressed together or collectively	Administration, staff, and students combine efforts to plan the school's 25th anniversary celebrations.	Local officials organize a public meeting to discuss the need for more shelters for homeless people.
All members assume personal responsibility for the common good and in turn receive equal rights and benefits	School board officials meet to hear community members regarding the need for a new science lab and gymnasium.	A recycling program is started to reduce the amount of solid waste being generated by the community.
Responsibilities are seen to come before rights	A student is suspended from school for failing to get a required inoculation of hepatitis vaccine.	A young driver's licence is suspended because of successive dangerous driving convictions.
A decision-making process is in place to ensure that there is peace and harmony	A principal invites the school advisory council and the student council to provide input regarding the adoption of a code of behaviour.	Residents are invited to a public meeting to present their concerns regarding a drug rehabilitation centre being proposed for the community.
A conflict resolution process is in place to quickly address disputes	A vice-principal is required to settle a dispute between two students, both claiming to own the same MP3 player.	A municipal hearing is called to settle a property dispute between two neighbours involving a shared driveway.

Figure 1-9 Is your community a healthy one?

You Can Make a Difference

There are many ways you can become involved in responsible citizenship. Your actions could make a simple but important difference in your community. Or you could aim your sights even higher.

Miranda Brar, a 13-year-old Grade 7 student from Orangeville, Ontario, suffers from severe allergies. She developed soreness in her limbs, dizziness, and head congestion that lasted for days. Her family doctor said the reactions could have been caused by exposure to pesticides. Miranda gathered 300 student signatures supporting a ban of pesticides. She then presented the petition to the mayor of Orangeville.

 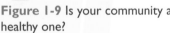

People Power

Kristopher's Wish

Kristopher Knowles lives in Sarnia, Ontario. He was born with an incurable liver disease known as biliary atresia. This disease destroys the ducts that carry bile from the liver to the small intestines. As bile builds up in the liver, liver tissue is destroyed. Children with this disease rarely live more than two years.

Before his first birthday, doctors operated on Kristopher. They created a new bile drainage system out of a piece of his intestine. Since his liver was already badly damaged, he was immediately placed on the transplant waiting list. Over the past 10 years, Kristopher has undergone several additional surgeries to save his life. It is very easy for someone in this situation to give up in frustration.

Currently, about 4000 Canadians are waiting for an organ transplant. Kristopher is a member of this community. For years, Kristopher had a wish—that every person on the waiting list receive a new organ. On January 8, 2004, assisted by the Step-By-Step Organ Transplant Association, Kristopher began a cross-Canada journey to promote organ donations.

During Kristopher's Wish Campaign, he visited over 200 cities and towns and one secondary school in each community. During his walks his message reached over half a million students: "Don't take your organs to heaven. God knows that we can use them here on earth." By the time he completed his journey on December 16, 2004, to a hero's

Figure 1-10 Kristopher Knowles (carrying the Torch of Life) completes the last kilometre of his cross-Canada journey. He is accompanied by students from Cardinal Carter Academy for the Arts in Toronto.

welcome, he had generated over 800 media stories drawing attention to his cause.

Despite his personal illness Kristopher Knowles dared to make a difference. "No one knows what Kristopher's future will hold," reflects Kristopher's father. "All we know is he has the most incredible will to live."

1. What motivated Kristopher to take action? Which community was he intending to serve?
2. What personal risks did Kristopher take by going on his cross-Canada journey?
3. What can you do to support Kristopher's Wish?

Teen's letter a perfect lesson

Father rescued by missives via Amnesty International

Students asked to write on behalf of persecuted Colombian

**By Tess Kalinowski,
Education Reporter**

Barbara Yebuga, 18, did something last week that few teenagers would dream of—she brought her family to high school.

She stood proudly with her brother and sister before a special assembly as her mother, Irene, told her schoolmates what their family owes to an Amnesty International letter-writing campaign, known as an Urgent Action.

The letters once saved Barbara's father, John Yebuga, said Irene.

The family is still grieving John's death at age 56 in January from cancer, but they went to Our Lady of Mount Carmel High School last Friday to offer living proof that, together, Barbara's 1800 school-mates could help save a stranger's life just by taking a few minutes to write a letter.

And they urged students to do just that—write a letter asking the president of Colombia to protect Yolanda Becerra, a threatened women's rights advocate there.

Figure 1-11 Irene Yebuga watches as daughter Barbara writes a letter as part of an Amnesty International campaign.

About 7000 students from 10 Mississauga high schools wrote letters on Becerra's behalf.

"We need to be a voice for the voiceless. We may not be able to help everyone, but one is better than none," Barbara said....

Her parents fled Uganda in the late 1970s, toward the end of dictator Idi Amin's bloody regime. They went to a refugee camp in Sudan, where John Yebuga took an administrative job. But the camp was run by Amin's former henchmen, who also had ties to Sudanese officials. Yebuga saw them stealing relief supplies from starving people.

In 1982, his vocal objections landed him in a Sudanese prison. The next day Irene lost her job.

Yebuga spent a year in prison while his pregnant wife tried to care for her daughters. Finally, after smuggling out a letter to Amnesty supporters, they were able to pressure the Sudanese authorities into freeing him. Meanwhile, a group of Canadian Amnesty supporters brought his case to the attention of immigration officials here, and on Oct. 18, 1984, the Yebuga family landed in Canada.

"...It took my husband courage and risk to speak up for people who could not speak for themselves," Irene Yebuga said. "It took one man to speak up for so many people."...

Of the 469 urgent actions done by Amnesty International last year, 49 per cent had a positive outcome,...

"Idealism and the drive for human rights starts when you are young. This is when we can catch you so you will continue this when you're an adult," said Dr. Shobana Ananth, Amnesty's event co-ordinator in Mississauga.

Source: *Toronto Star*, Mar. 1, 2005, p. B2.

1. What personal qualities do John and Barbara Yebuga have in common?

2. How successful was this Urgent Action campaign?

3. Why is the support of young people important to Amnesty International?

Seven months passed without any response. Miranda and her friends decided to take further action. They brought a second petition with 460 adult signatures to a town council meeting. One councillor had this reaction: "We don't have enough kids involved in the political process. The more we have, the better off we'll be." The town's environmental advisory committee has since recommended a bylaw. It will either ban pesticides in the months of July and August, or eventually ban them outright.

Any student can make a difference in his or her community. But first that student has to choose to act. What's your passion? Or, what's your excuse?

Figure 1-12 Orangeville students, including Miranda Brar, front, speak out against the unnecessary use of pesticides at a town council meeting. Why do you think that so few young people get involved in the political process?

CHECKPOINT

1. **Using your own words, explain the terms "citizenship" and "civics."**
2. **Explain the social trade-off that exists in society between individual interests and the common good.**
3. **Outline seven characteristics that you feel make a healthy community or society. Defend your views.**

Your School: A Society in Miniature

The Ties That Bind

Your school is a mini-society with its own identity, customs, and story—in other words, its own **culture**. School *identity* is easy to find. Often mascots, logos, crests, and uniforms are used to represent this identity. The real sense of identity comes from the common purpose that brings community members together—in this case education. This common purpose provides a sense of belonging, often seen in the form of school spirit or pride. It is also seen in *customs* and traditions, such as commencement, grad proms, student council elections, and school spirit assemblies.

To uncover the *story* of your school, a bit more work is required. Those who have come before you may have left behind records to help tell this story. **Artifacts**, such as photos, documents, yearbooks, trophies, awards, and videos, can help tell this unfolding story. What artifacts can you find in your school? Are they stored or on display?

culture: the beliefs, language, customs, ceremonies, arts, institutions, social relations, and other human endeavours characteristic of a particular community, people, or nation

artifacts: material evidence of a distinct community and its shared values and culture

Should We Have Separate Schools for Black Students?

Ontario has had separate private high schools for males and females for a very long time. The idea of separate schools for Black students was first proposed in 1991 by the Royal Commission on Learning in Ontario. School boards were urged to set up separate schools to deal with the lower graduation rates among Black students. Each time this issue resurfaces, emotional arguments are stirred up on both sides of the debate. Below are four examples, taken from an article in the *Toronto Star*. Each person was asked, "Should Ontario further explore the idea of Black-only schools?"

Literacy Hint

Read down each column first to get a sense of one person's views on the topic. Then, read each listed item across the two columns to understand the debate.

YES

Figure 1-13 Christopher Spence became director of education for the Hamilton-Wentworth District School Board in 2004. He is an accomplished educator, author, and community leader.

- Definitely there were times for me feeling awkward in class, going through lessons and seeing people of African descent depicted in a certain way that was not always positive. ... Let's be honest, when you take a look at Black students in the public school system, success has been elusive...

- I had an opportunity, about 10 years ago, to visit two all-Black schools in Detroit. And I have to say that there was no sense of segregation there, but rather a sense of support. There was a sense of racial pride and identity.

- Research shows that, when people have choices and they make a decision to go to [a particular] school, parents get more involved. They monitor their children's work and success and at the end of the day, they're more satisfied with the children's schooling.

NO

Figure 1-14 Lincoln Alexander became Canada's first Black Member of Parliament in 1968. He has also served as Lieutenant-Governor of Ontario from 1985 to 1990.

- In the school system at that time (the late 1930s) there were few, if any, Black teachers, no Black principals, no Black anything. And yet many of us, countless hundreds of us, were able to go to school ... to learn. We worked twice as hard, which we all still do, but we always made it.

- Now it seems to me that every time the Blacks get into trouble they want to blame somebody except themselves.

- We don't need any Black images, or Black this or that. You go to school to learn. You're in a country that is primarily White. There will always be those (Blacks) who are able to compete, and they understand what they have to do: Work hard, have confidence in yourself and do the best you can...

YES

Figure 1-15 Rosemary Sadlier is an author and president of the Black History Society.

NO

Figure 1-16 Austin Clarke is an award-winning author and poet. He has worked as a journalist and as a civil rights activist.

- I was (originally) discouraged from entering a university-bound program ... I was advised that I should take a non-university bound program because, 'Didn't I want to be a secretary?'... And in that high school there were only about 10 African Canadians in a school of about 1400 students ...

- If [through education] what we are doing is trying to prepare students, to give them all the skills that they would need to be part of and involved in a global economy, how can you then forget that some of them have a background, a history and an experience that is not part of the mainstream?

- Segregation already exists. ... We have already segregated our society with (social and economic) barriers. So you're not creating a segregated school. The segregation ... is already there.

- The question is more complicated than it seems. The stories we hear about Black children and school are ones that become important because of difficulties these students have. You hear the bad stories. It's obvious that there are Black kids in Toronto schools who do very well.

- ...when a Black person... is in this Black [school] community ... he is cut off from the bigger community, in which he has got to live and serve when he graduates from this alternative school.

- Education is not White or Black. Education is the assessing of certain facts and techniques that will make your life easier because you have that knowledge. I don't think that it detracts from a person's Blackness to go to a school that is predominantly White.

Source: *Toronto Star*, February 5, 2005, p. A20.

1. Identify the strongest point made by each person.

2. Assess each of the arguments presented to determine whether:

   a) opinions are supported with factual evidence

   b) the arguments are persuasive.

3. With which position do you agree most? Explain why.

4. Is there any cultural group in your society that might benefit from this type of school structure? Develop one argument in favour of separate schools for this group.

Rules That Protect

Your school community has different people with diverse backgrounds, interests, viewpoints, and ambitions. This diversity can enrich your school. It can also lead to disagreement and conflict. The greater the variety of opinions and viewpoints, the greater is the potential for conflict.

Like all communities, schools need rules to help people live together peacefully. Rules establish procedures that deal with individual needs, while respecting the common good. They can also set standards for behaviour as well as the consequences for unacceptable behaviour.

Rules protect the rights of community members and help keep schools safe for staff and students. One common rule is that all visitors must first report to the main office. Another common rule is that students who resort to violence to settle a dispute will be suspended. In a responsible society, there are always consequences for unacceptable behaviour. Consequences are meant to discourage inappropriate behaviour.

Literacy Hint

This topic has two parts: "The Ties that Bind" and "Rules that Protect." What are some connections between this subtopic and "The Ties That Bind" on page 11?

Figure 1-17 What rules of behaviour might students have to follow in a hallway or a cafeteria? Why would those rules exist?

CHECKPOINT

1. Name the three strongest ties that you have to your school community.
2. What is an artifact? Why are artifacts important to a community?
3. Why do school communities need rules?

Am I a Good Citizen?

Now that we've looked at your school as a mini-society, let's explore your personal role within it. Rules help people live together peacefully in an effective community. There is more to being a good citizen, however, than just following rules. Are you a giving member of your school community? Or are you a taking member? To answer this question we need a model for good citizenship. Is your behaviour law-abiding, reliable, respectful, and responsible? This is an important start, but it is only a start.

Am I a Good Citizen of My School Community?

1. Am I a law-abiding community member?

Law-abiding citizens do not see themselves as being above the rules. They do not pick and choose the rules they will follow or ignore. Such an attitude cannot work in a healthy society. Allowing yourself the right to break a rule means you grant others the right to break rules too. Then, in the end, there are no rules.

In a healthy society no one can be granted the right to be above the law. No one can take the law into his or her own hands. When laws are no longer seen as valid by a majority of community members, the laws must be updated or cancelled. The **rule of law** is an important protection in any healthy society.

In a school community, law-abiding citizens are respectful of others. They are on time for class and they respect due dates. They value **learning skills**, which include the ability to:

- work independently
- be an effective team player
- organize resources, time, and effort
- stay on task and produce quality work
- show initiative.

These important skills are assessed by all teachers and reported on provincial report cards. Law-abiding citizens are reliable, respectful, and responsible. Which qualities and skills do you think employers look for when interviewing students for part-time work? Which qualities and skills do you think will help you to be a leader in your community?

2. Am I a reliable, respectful, and responsible community member?

A team member is expected to be reliable and show up for each game, be respectful of teammates and opponents, and be a responsible player. These are qualities that are important in every community. What three qualities do you look for first in your classmates?

Figure 1-18 Why should people not be allowed to ignore this rule and skateboard where they want to? List three examples of school rules that work the same way.

rule of law: the principle that no government or person is above the law

learning skills: a set of skills assessed by all teachers and reported on provincial report cards

Informed to Be Effective

Many schools have student councils to act on behalf of the students. Most student councils require students to have solid grades before they can run for council. In addition, candidates cannot have a suspension on their student record. Outside of secondary school, other opportunities may be closed to you if you have a record of irresponsible behaviour.

Figure 1-19 Canadian employers look for a core set of marketable skills in the candidates they consider for employment. What are these valuable skills?

Reliability is an important quality in any community. In a school community, reliability means you can depend on, trust, and have confidence in others.

Respect is an important quality in any community where diverse personalities and viewpoints come together. School communities reflect this diversity. Respect is the most common action verb found in the code of conduct for schools. How important do you consider respect to be? Can you recall an incident at school where you felt disrespected? How did it make you feel?

Taking responsibility for one's actions requires self-discipline and self-assessment. Discipline is acquired through community living—first as a responsible family member and then as a contributing member of other communities.

3. Am I an informed member of the community?

Just as you need to know information for each class to be effective, a good citizen must be in the know. Members of a community must be aware of what is going on around them. Understanding their surroundings will help them identify what to do and what to avoid.

- Do you have a practical understanding of current issues and rules and how they are made and changed?
- Can you see the reasons for these rules and the shared values that these rules represent?
- Do you know how decisions are made and revised within the community?
- Do you know who the most powerful people are?
- Can you figure out what is likely to happen next for given situations in your community?

Figure 1-20 According to the cartoonist, what happens when you ignore your surroundings?

Source: Peanuts: © United Features Syndicate, Inc.

4. Am I a purposeful community member?

Have you ever thought that you'd like to make a difference, but just didn't know how? To be effective, a good citizen must be purposeful with defined goals to pursue. Members of a community must be aware of their own identities, beliefs, moral purpose, and community responsibilities. They need to reflect on who they are, where they are coming from, and what they would like to achieve.

- Do you have a strong sense of community identity?
- Do you have a good sense of where you are going and what you will need to get there?
- Do you have a good sense of how the school community—with its diverse values, viewpoints, and goals—can work and grow?
- Do you see yourself as a community giver or a taker?
- Are you part of the problems or part of the solutions in your community?

5. Am I an active community member?

To be effective, a good citizen must have basic community-building skills. He or she must also be willing and able to apply those skills for the greater good. Basic community-building skills are sometimes referred to as **civic literacy skills**. They include skills in the areas of research and inquiry, critical and creative thinking, communication, decision making, conflict resolution, and teamwork. These individual skills are presented in the Civic Skills Powers found throughout this book.

- Are you willing to spend time and energy to make a difference?
- Do you have an action plan? Do you see yourself as acting alone or with others?
- Do you have the skills and devotion needed to succeed?
- Do you have the mind to imagine, the heart to care, the courage to try, and the will to succeed?
- Who can help you?

civic literacy skills: skills in the areas of research and inquiry, critical and creative thinking, communication, decision making, conflict resolution and teamwork used for community building

Figure 1-21 Amanda Doris, right, is an 18-year-old co-op student at Ajax High School who is making a difference. She spent a four-month placement working with Girls Incorporated of Durham. She focused mainly on their Operation SMART program, which encourages girls in the areas of Sciences and Engineering. After her co-op term ended, Amanda continued to volunteer with Girls Incorporated. Amanda has also been actively involved with her student council, the school community council, and her school's Culture of Peace program.

CHECKPOINT

1. **What are the important qualities of a good citizen in a school community?**
2. **Why is the rule of law important in your school community and in society?**
3. **Explain what is meant by civic literacy skills.**

Processing Information

Find the Main Ideas

In any book chapter, there are many ideas. How do you decide which ideas are the important or main ones? The chapter itself provides many clues:

- The *chapter title* names one or more key ideas. The title of this chapter mentions the idea of community and also the goal of a common good—a situation that protects the rights and freedoms of the greatest number of people.
- *Subtitles* in the chapter may also reveal the main ideas. Find two subtitles in this chapter that confirm and extend the idea of community.
- *Words in boldface* define main ideas or key terms. For example, on page 4, you will find a definition of the idea of "community."
- *Tables or charts* reveal aspects of a main idea. How does Figure 1-9 on page 8 help you to understand the idea of community?
- *Short stories* may be used to illustrate main ideas. Find one in this chapter and explain to a partner how that story helps you to understand what it means to be a member of a community.
- *Pictures and captions* provide evidence to support main ideas. Working with three others, choose two photos each, examine them, and then explain to each other how these photos prove how you can be part of a community or contribute to the common good.
- A *summary* at the end of each chapter highlights important information.

Making a Web

One way to get the picture of a main idea is to web it as you read or reread parts of the chapter. Begin with a circle

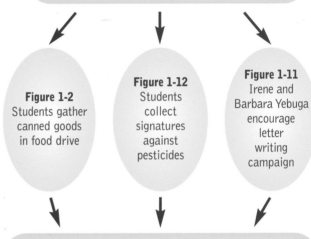

Community: a group of people who have chosen to unite in pursuit of common needs and goals.

Figure 1-2 Students gather canned goods in food drive

Figure 1-12 Students collect signatures against pesticides

Figure 1-11 Irene and Barbara Yebuga encourage letter writing campaign

Drawing a conclusion about the main idea of these photos: Students working together on needs and goals have the power to make a difference for the common good.

 **Figure 1-22**

or rectangle at the top of your page with what you think is the main idea. Add your definition right below. Then attach other circles naming or describing photos, stories, or other details that provide evidence or supporting details for this main idea. Figure 1-22 shows a sample web based on some of the photographs in this chapter.

You Try It

Choose four other photographs, subtitles, or stories from this chapter and web them under the definition of community. Then draw a conclusion about the message these photos, subtitles, or stories give you about the idea of community.

Challenges of Community Living

People in communities do not always agree on what should be done. Nor do they always agree on what their share of the work or the rewards should be. Self-interest can lead to conflict. Disputes need to be resolved before matters get worse. And difficult decisions need to be made together to best serve the common good. In a school community, when you involve people in the decisions that affect them, you are likely to get more commitment to follow through.

Sharing Decision-Making Power

When conflicts arise, the community faces difficult decisions. Different viewpoints on what is best for the community and how to prioritize tasks complicate group decision making. Community living is challenged by individuals who take from the community but do not contribute. Some individuals put their own interests ahead of the common good. Others take matters into their own hands to get what they want. These individuals provide a further challenge. Decision making is often affected by who has the most **power**. Some communities have instituted practices that limit the ability of individuals to place their own interests ahead of the group.

Who has the most decision-making power in your school? Who has the most power in your civics class? Why is this power granted? Should there be any limits on this power? Why?

How does power affect decision making? Let's assume that the school advisory council has raised $10 000 for school improvements. Should it be used to purchase

- a new sound system for the auditorium
- a new floor for the gym
- a new exhaust system for the science lab
- a digital imaging centre for the library?

Each improvement is needed, but there is not enough money to do more than one. How should the community make this difficult decision?

One way would be for the school principal to make this decision. When a single person or small group has the power to decide, it is called rule by authority or **autocracy**. As a class, find an example of a decision that was made this way in your school community. When an autocracy bans all forms of opposition to gain absolute power, it is called a **dictatorship**. Can you explain why your school is not a dictatorship?

Figure 1-23 Why are firefighters an essential component of any community?

power: the ability to direct others to achieve what you want

autocracy: a system in which a single person or authority has the power to make decisions

dictatorship: a system where a single ruler seizes absolute power by banning all opposition

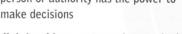

vote: the act of expressing an opinion by a show of hands or ballot; used to make a decision such as passing a resolution or electing a candidate to office

democracy: a system of decision making that uses a majority vote of members or of elected representatives to make decisions

consensus: a system of decision making based on one common agreement supported by all members

Literacy Hint

Use a three-column chart to summarize the three ways of making community decisions—direct, representative, and consensus.

Another option is to share the decision. A matter put to a free **vote** is called rule by majority or **democracy**. In our decision-making example, members of the school community would be invited to vote for their preferred use of the raised funds. To arrive at a majority decision, additional votes might be needed, each time dropping the least popular project from the list of choices. This is an example of *direct* democracy. Democratic decision making is said to be *representative* when individuals are elected to make decisions on behalf of a larger group. A student council is an example of representative democracy. As a class, find an example of a school decision that was made by each type of democratic process.

Another way to share the decision would be to discuss the options to arrive at a common agreement. This would be an example of rule by **consensus** or collaborative decision making. Historically, consensus was the preferred decision-making process of the Iroquois Confederacy. It is still used by many First Nations today.

In this decision-making example, members of the school community would be invited to a series of meetings to discuss the benefits and limitations of each option. They would aim to find one option that all members can support. To reach consensus, community members must change their focus. The key question shifts from *what do I prefer* to *what can I live with*. When a class decides to discuss four field trip options to agree on one choice, this is an example of decision making by consensus. As a class, find another example of a school decision that was made by consensus.

Figure 1-24 How would you feel if you didn't vote in a student election and the candidate you liked the best lost by one vote? Make your vote count.

A Civil Society

Societies have created formal systems and structures called **governments** to deal with the complex challenges. Caring for those who live with poverty, who are ill or most vulnerable, education of youth, and enforcement of rules and regulations are examples of social challenges. Civil societies use governments to:

government: the rule or authority over a country, province, or district

- organize essential services (like public transportation, education, and health care)
- make and enforce the rules of civil or orderly behaviour (like laws and processes to deal with law breakers)
- keep the peace (by resolving disputes and preventing conflicts)
- make important decisions collectively (like ensuring community safety)
- establish and maintain peaceful relations with neighbouring societies.

In a **civil society** an attempt is made to respect the dignity of all members. Organizations of public servants and volunteers provide support services to those in need. The Canadian National Institute for the Blind, Kids Help Phone, and the Legal Aid Society are three examples. The rule of law is another important component.

civil society: a caring, peaceful, and supportive society where human dignity is respected

    In the next chapter you will explore more about Canada's government and the role citizens play in it.

Figure 1-25 In a civil society, we care for each other. A rescue worker from Vancouver, British Columbia, walks down a street wrecked by Hurricane Katrina in Chalmette (just east of New Orleans) September 3, 2005. How else could Canadians support victims of a disaster like this one?

Active Citizen Website

For links to sites of Civic support service organizations

CHECKPOINT

1. Explain what is meant by a civil society. What role does government play in a civil society?
2. How do autocracy, democracy, and consensus differ?
3. What is most important in a civil society in your view?

Evaluating Sources, Distinguishing Between Fact and Opinion

In a textbook or television documentary, you expect the information to be true. How can you be certain? Should you believe everything you read in a book or see in a televised documentary? Writers and reporters who do their job well check their facts. They also like to hear a story from at least two reliable sources before they believe it and put it in print. What about other sources, like the Internet, magazines, posters, and pamphlets? How can you tell if they are reliable?

There are steps that you can take to evaluate or make a judgment about photographs and stories you come across. You may decide that you need to evaluate the news story about Barbara Yebuga in this chapter, or a photograph you found on the Internet. You could start by checking the following:

- What is the source of the photo or the story? What do you know about this source? Do you consider it to be reliable?
- Can you determine who actually wrote the story or took the photograph?
- Is there another source that you can check to discover whether the story and photographs are true and real? Sometimes you can find a *primary source*—a person who actually saw an event or was part of it—to confirm the facts. Other times, you may have to rely on a *secondary source*—other books, magazines, newspapers, or the Internet—to discover whether a story or photograph truly represents an event.

Fact or Opinion?

Each person has thoughts, wishes, and goals that may be different from those of another person. These influence each person's opinions. A good judge of any situation tries to separate facts from opinions.

- Opinions are often based on emotion or on an inference—an assumption a person thinks is true without really knowing for sure.
- Facts tell the actual details of a situation—who was involved, what happened, and where and when the event occurred.

However, you have to be careful with "facts," because they may not always tell the truth of a situation. Since facts cannot speak for themselves, they need to be interpreted and presented. Facts can be changed over time and as they travel from one person to another. For example, you may hear about a fight between two people that occurred off school grounds. By the time you hear the same story the next day, it may have changed and suggest many more people were involved.

How can you check the facts? Count on reliable sources—people who can be trusted to tell you only what they know for certain. When a second source can be found to verify the facts, you can be even more certain.

You Try It

Read the story about Miranda Brar on pages 8 and 11. Create a two-column chart. Label the columns "Facts" and "Opinions." Choose details from the story and list them in one column or the other. Discuss your lists with a partner or small group to see whether you wrote the same details in the same columns. What questions do you have about this story based on your lists?

Summing It Up

- People live in communities to pursue common needs and goals together. People can belong to more than one community.

- Citizenship means having responsibilities, duties, and ultimately rights, as a contributing member of a state or nation.

- Individuals who become responsible citizens can make a difference.

- Rules and consequences are necessary to govern social behaviour. No government or individual is above the rule of law.

- Good citizens are law-abiding, reliable, respectful, and responsible. They are also informed, purposeful, and active.

- In an autocracy an individual or small group has the power to make decisions and to direct others. Where this power is absolute a dictatorship is formed.

- In a democracy, representatives are elected by a majority vote to serve as accountable decision-makers on behalf of the entire community.

- Civil societies use governments and volunteer organizations to create caring, peaceful, and supportive communities.

KEY TERMS

- simulation
- community
- common good
- social trade-off
- bylaw

- citizenship
- citizen
- civics
- culture
- artifacts

- rule of law
- learning skills
- civic literacy skills
- power

- autocracy
- dictatorship
- vote
- democracy
- consensus

- government
- civil society

Thinking: To Be Informed

1. Use a local newspaper to research examples of people your age who have made a difference. Write a brief report, using the People Power on page 9 as a model.

2. Analyse your student handbook or school agenda book to identify three examples of rules that protect the common good. Develop a rule of your own that could be added.

3. Research a community or country to determine who has power and how decisions are made (the system of government). Make a web or chart for a class discussion.

Communicating: To Be Purposeful

4. Create a visual product—cartoon strip, Bristol board display, PowerPoint presentation, or illustrated web—to compare the basic features of autocratic and democratic governments.

5. With a partner, write a code of behaviour for your civics class.

6. Design a collage of images to illustrate the caring relationship between the individual and the community in a civil society.

Applying: To Be Active

7. Identify one community that you belong to outside of school. Use Figure 1-9 to assess whether this community functions effectively.

8. Use what you have learned about community living to design a checklist or web page with FAQs. The FAQs should help people determine if they are a contributing member of the school community.

9. What three important changes would you make to your school if you were given that power? Justify your choices and explain how each change would represent an improvement. Summarize your work in a video report, newscast, photo essay, or a PowerPoint presentation.

Culminating Performance Task: Making a Difference

The purpose of this textbook is to prepare you to be informed, purposeful, and active citizens. Each chapter contains knowledge and provides opportunities to practise useful civic literacy skills.

This Culminating Performance Task asks you to put the knowledge and skills you have learned in this chapter to effective use. It provides you with an opportunity to make a difference and to learn from the experience.

There are three parts to a completed Culminating Performance Task:

- an action plan
- a brief report on how the plan was carried out
- an assessment of effectiveness.

These parts need not be written assignments. For example, the report can take the form of a photo essay, video, PowerPoint presentation, etc. The assessment can also be videotaped, audiotaped, or based on an assessment tool supplied by the teacher.

Your teacher will provide a time frame for the individual components and an assessment rubric.

This process and rubric will provide valuable constructive feedback along the way.

Reminders at the end of Chapters 3, 5, and 7 will help you to stay on task. Conferencing with your teacher will also help you get the most out of the time and effort that you are putting into this Culminating Performance Task. Keep a portfolio to document and assess your steps. Before you carry out a sound action plan, you need to do some research and some clear thinking.

Active Citizenship	Process Steps
Be Informed	1. Find a community or civic need that is important to you. 2. Research options for meeting that need and identify available supports.
Be Purposeful	3. Assess the strengths and limitations of each available option to select a manageable goal. 4. Plan a strategy, accessing the best available support.
Be Active	5. Implement your action plan. 6. Assess the plan's effectiveness and make the necessary revisions. Reflect on the intended and actual outcomes of your plan for future reference.

Sample Student Action Plans

Civics students have successfully completed tasks like the following examples:

- Martina chose to create a web page to record the history of her ethnic dance group.
- Raj and Crystal started a Students Against Drunk Driving club in their school.
- Lani, Ali, and Mara organized a fund-raising effort to support tsunami victims.
- Sarah Rose sent a letter, with supporting signatures, to the government of Thailand to protest child prostitution.
- Philip designed a poster to promote energy conservation.
- Jose, Jordan, and Jessica made a short video to promote stronger gun control laws.
- Mohamed attended a community meeting and spoke to elected officials to support a shelter for homeless youth.
- Evan, Curtis, and Stephanie cleaned up neighbourhood parkland as an Earth Day project.

Evaluation Criteria

The following criteria will be used to evaluate your work:

- **Knowledge and Understanding**
Uses civics terms, concepts, and ideas accurately.

- **Thinking**
Plans, researches, and analyses information from a variety of sources.
Uses a decision-making model effectively.

- **Communication**
Presents information clearly and in appropriate form for the intended audience.

- **Application**
Plans and implements an action plan; presents with impact or persuasiveness; makes meaningful connections.

HOW DO GOVERNMENTS IN CANADA WORK?

A Scenario: Beginning Our School Day

It's Monday morning and here you are at your locker again. Suddenly, classical music begins to blare over the PA system. This happens at the same time every morning, so you know that you have five minutes to get to your first class.

Figure 2-1 What kind of music would you like to start your day at school?

As you listen to the music you cringe and wonder who chose it. Why don't they play something decent? After all, during the last student council elections, all the candidates said they would change the music. Why haven't they done anything? Does the student council have the power to make such decisions? Since your friends feel the same way, you decide to take the issue to the student council.

In groups of four, analyse the situation and then role-play the meeting with the student council.

First, two of you analyse the constitution of the student council to determine whether the council really has the power to select the music.

Two of you work out criteria for selecting the music and decide on an equitable way of adopting various music styles.

One of you talks to either the staff representative on the council or to a school administrator to determine what criteria have been used to determine the current music.

One of you canvasses members of other classes to get their ideas about criteria for selecting the music.

In your groups, make a list of suggested alternative songs based on your findings. Each group, in turn, presents its list to the student council (the class), which votes on the selections.

Now although mornings at school may still be hard to take, at least the music is more appealing.

1. How did the issue of music come to the attention of the student council?
2. What actions did the students take to find out how other students felt and how the music was selected?
3. What difficulties would the student council face in making its music selection?
4. Brainstorm a student concern at your school and follow the same steps to develop your case study. What powers does your student council have and what restrictions are placed on it? Do you feel the restrictions are justified? Explain.

KEY LEARNINGS

In this chapter you will explore the following topics:
- the structure and function of Canada's federal and provincial governments
- what is involved in electing governments in Canada
- the various roles involved in the political process
- the civic literacy skills of detecting bias and accessing reliable resources

Canadian Governments: A Reflection of History

Like the students in our scenario, Canada's national, provincial, and municipal governments also have to make decisions about issues. The main difference is the complexity of issues and their impact on the lives of Canadians. Let's look briefly at how Canada's governments have evolved.

Canada's history has reflected the relationships among Aboriginal peoples (First Nations, Métis, and Inuit peoples) and French and English colonists. All three groups have played a major role in the development of Canada. Each had its own forms of government. The evolution of the Canadian government is a reflection of the events and personalities of the past centuries.

5th century BCE

The Greeks lived in self-governing cities. Free male citizens of Athens would gather to discuss and debate issues. Decisions were reached by consensus. Women, foreigners, enslaved people, and children were not considered citizens. Since the number of free citizens was relatively small, direct democracy could take place.

527 CE

Byzantine Emperor Justinian proclaimed the Divine Right of Kings. Ever since King David of the Old Testament was anointed by God's prophet, monarchs claimed to have the divine right to rule their people as absolute rulers. The monarchs claimed that they had received their right to govern from God and were accountable only to God.

1215

In England, King John's nobles revolted and forced him to sign the Magna Carta (Great Charter). Though it benefitted the nobles most, it also established some basic legal rights: the rule of law, which said that the king was not above the law; and habeas corpus, which gave everyone the protection of the law and the right to a fair trial within a reasonable amount of time.

1450 (approximate)

Five distinct Aboriginal nations—the Mohawk, Seneca, Oneida, Cayuga, and Onondaga—formed the Haudenosaunee (Iroquois) Confederacy. This may have been the first federated government in known history. A Grand Council of 50 representatives from the five nations met to make major decisions based on consensus.

In the photo above, Tahdodaho (right) was the last of the Five Nations warriors to accept the message of peace based on unity and the use of reason as delivered by the Peacemaker. It is said that the Peacemaker symbolically "combed the snakes" out of Tahdodaho's hair.

1642–1646

At the end of the English Civil War, the parliamentary forces defeated King Charles I and abolished the monarchy. Parliament was declared the governing body of Britain. Later in the century a constitutional monarchy was established with the monarch ruling with Parliament.

Late 18th century

The American Revolution (1775–1783) and the French Revolution (1789–1799) ended monarchical rule and established republics with elected leaders in both countries.

1849

Lord Elgin, the Governor of a united Upper and Lower Canada, accepted that the elected body was supreme. Responsible government was created. The executive branch became responsible to the elected Assemblies and followed the will of the people's representatives.

1867

Four provinces in British North America united under the *British North America Act* to form a Confederation. The Act set out the structure of the federal system. The division of power was separated between federal and provincial governments. The structure of government modeled the British system with an elected House of Commons. An appointed Senate replaced the British House of Lords.

Literacy Hint

What features of the timeline make it easy to read? You may have to read this timeline differently from a paragraph. Try reading from right to left or from top to bottom and follow the arrows for connections to the photographs.

1916, 1918

In 1916, the federal vote in Canada was given to White women over 21 years of age who were British subjects. The federal vote was given to Canadian women two years later in 1918. Women of colour, however, did not have the vote. First Nations women did not receive the right to vote in federal elections until 1960.

1929

Britain's highest judicial authority, the Privy Council, overturned a ruling by the Supreme Court of Canada. The Privy Council ruled that the term "person" refers to both males and females. Women had the right to run for public office and to be appointed to government positions. The Famous Five fought for this ruling.

The monument in the photo was unveiled in Calgary in 1999. From left to right the Famous Five are Emily Murphy, Nellie McClung (holding newspaper), Irene Parlby (standing), Louise McKinney (seated), and Henrietta Muir Edwards.

1931

The Statute of Westminster was passed by the British Parliament. It gave the former colonies the power to self-govern and the right to pass laws involving foreign affairs. The former colonies became equal members in the British Commonwealth.

1982

The *Constitution Act* gave Canada the right to make changes to its own Constitution without having to apply to the British Parliament. The Act also included a *Charter of Rights and Freedoms* that outlined the rights of Canadian citizens.

What Is the Role of Citizens?

In Chapter 1 you started to explore what it means to be a citizen. Did you know that when immigrants apply and are accepted for citizenship, they must take an oath of allegiance or loyalty?

"I [name of person] swear" [or "affirm"] "that I will be faithful and bear true allegiance to Her Majesty Queen Elizabeth the Second, Queen of Canada, Her Heirs and Successors, according to law and that I will faithfully observe the laws of Canada and fulfil my duties as a Canadian citizen."

What are the duties of Canadian citizens? Before you read the next section, take a minute to think about this question. Share your ideas with a partner.

According to the federal government, all Canadian citizens have the responsibilities shown in Figure 2-2.

Figure 2-2 What other duties did you and your partner come up with?

Although these responsibilities are important, many are not laws. For instance, how can you make someone help a neighbour who is in need? These responsibilities often rely on the good civic attitude of people. People must believe that while they enjoy rights in Canada, they also have responsibilities to the nation.

Forms of Government

As you saw in Chapter 1, Canada is a democratic country. Canada's governments are responsible to the citizens of the country. Not all countries accept democracy. Other forms of government in the world are not as responsible to the **popular will**. Authoritarian governments, for example, rely less on popular input.

Informed to Be Effective

Aboriginal peoples in Canada (First Nations, Métis, and Inuit) consist of many different nations with distinct languages and cultures. They had their own forms of government before Canada became a nation and many still honour and practise aspects of their traditional forms of government today.

popular will: the wishes of the voters

Informed to Be Effective

For many Aboriginal people citizenship is based on a sense of kinship or family relationship with their larger community or nation. Many see their relationship with Canada as being one of nation to nation. They negotiate with Canada on land claims and resource issues on a nation-to-nation basis. Aboriginal people who are registered under the Indian Act are also considered Canadian citizens. What issues do you think this raises for Aboriginal people?

Structure and Power of Governments

Your family reflects one structure of power and responsibility. Your parents, grandparents, or guardians are responsible for the safety and well-being of the family. They are recognized as the head of the family because of their age, experience, financial resources, and legal responsibilities. Nonetheless, government laws protect your rights.

Throughout history all civilizations have had governments and citizens involved in those governments. Democratic governments have evolved over time. Officials recognized that to avoid dictatorships, or absolute rule by one person or one group, powers would have to be separate and balanced. Some powers and responsibilities affect the entire community. Others apply to an area or region. Some First Nations, Métis, and Inuit have governing powers over their particular regions. In Canada, every level of government is responsible for the well-being of its citizens.

CHECKPOINT

1. Which points on the timeline show that the larger population wanted a say in how they were governed?
2. What are the rights and responsibilities of citizens?
3. What is the purpose of a democratic government?
4. How would you define democracy to a person who had lived under an authoritarian government?

What Are the Governments in Canada?

Canada is one of the world's largest nations. It spans six time zones. Yet, it has a relatively small population that is divided by geography and regional interests. Although only four provinces were involved in developing our system of government in the 1860s, it must have been a daunting task.

The politicians had some models of government to consider. In Britain the elected Parliament governed the entire nation. However, Britain was a much smaller nation. The United States had a system of state and federal governments. However, since their country had engaged in civil war, it seemed as though their federal government had too little power.

Eventually, a compromise was reached. The framers of Canada's Constitution agreed on a **federal system** of government. This system divides responsibilities between two levels. The *British North America Act* (*BNA Act*)

Literacy Hint

Picture the provinces at Confederation in your mind. Imagine how the different interests of Quebec, Ontario, New Brunswick, and Prince Edward Island would make creating the nation of Canada a difficult task.

federal system: a two-level system of governing

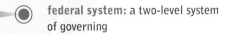

of 1867 outlined the system and separation of powers. The **federal government** addressed national issues; the **provincial government** dealt with regional concerns.

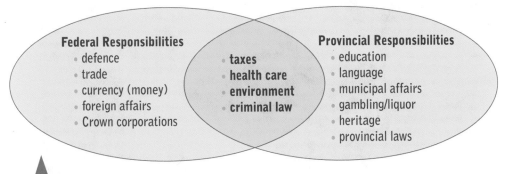

Federal Responsibilities
- defence
- trade
- currency (money)
- foreign affairs
- Crown corporations

- **taxes**
- **health care**
- **environment**
- **criminal law**

Provincial Responsibilities
- education
- language
- municipal affairs
- gambling/liquor
- heritage
- provincial laws

Figure 2-3 Some of the key federal and provincial responsibilities. Which responsibilities overlap? What might be the advantages and disadvantages of the governments sharing some responsibilities?

Canada is a **constitutional monarchy**. This means the nation has a set of guidelines called the Constitution. It outlines how the government should be organized and elected. Canada also recognizes the British monarch as its own. Being officially ruled by the British monarch may seem strange. It dates back to 1763 when Canada became a British colony after the defeat of the French.

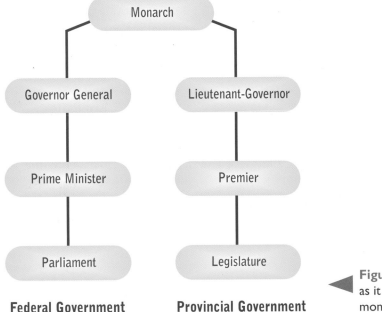

Monarch

Governor General — Lieutenant-Governor

Prime Minister — Premier

Parliament — Legislature

Federal Government — **Provincial Government**

federal government: the level of government responsible for issues of national concern, represented by Parliament in Ottawa

provincial government: the level of government responsible for provincial issues, represented by Legislative Assemblies in provincial capitals

constitutional monarchy: a nation under a monarch whose powers are restricted to those granted under the Constitution and laws of the nation

For links to sites on the organization of Canada's government

Figure 2-4 Canada's Constitutional Monarchy as it was established in 1867. Should the British monarch still play a role in Canada?

Figure 2-5 Queen Elizabeth II is greeted at the First Nations University in Regina in May 2005. She visited the province as it celebrated the centennial of its entry with Alberta into Confederation. Why would the Premiers of Saskatchewan and Alberta invite the Queen to help celebrate their anniversary?

legislative branch: the branch of government responsible for passing laws and representing the interests of the voters

bill: proposed legislation

speech from the throne: a speech written by the government that sets out the legislative program the government will present to Parliament

riding: a political division represented by a Member of Parliament or a Member of the Legislative Assembly; a constituency

Federal Level

Once a federal system was approved, the British model was adapted. The **legislative branch** has two houses—the Senate (the upper house) and the House of Commons (the lower house). This branch represents Canadian citizens. Its role is to make, change, and repeal laws. The legislative branch considers **bills** that eventually may become laws.

It was decided that members of the House of Commons would be elected. Eligible citizens in each province and territory would elect a certain number of members to the house based on population. The number could change as population rates changed. Because this system would favour the provinces with the largest population, an appointed Senate was established. This addressed the concerns of the smaller provinces and Quebec's fear of English domination. The Senate includes an equal number of Senators from each region.

Think about it this way. Suppose that senior students in your school outnumber the Grade 10s. If an issue were put to a vote, the seniors would probably win if they voted as a group. That means that the Grade 10s would always lose. Now suppose a system was set up that gave 10 representatives to each of the grades who would discuss issues that affected the entire student body. Would this system be more equitable for all grades? What are possible disadvantages?

Active Citizen

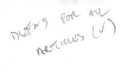

KEY POSITIONS IN CANADA'S GOVERNMENT

Position	How position is acquired	Responsibilities
Governor General	appointed by the monarch on the advice of the Prime Minister	• represents the monarch in Canada • signs bills into law • acts as the Commander-in-Chief of the Armed Forces • appoints Prime Ministers based on the results of elections • protects the integrity of the government in cases of abuse • performs ceremonial tasks such as greeting foreign dignitaries, officially appointing members of the Order of Canada, visiting foreign countries to promote Canada, and officially opening Parliament by reading the **speech from the throne**
Prime Minister	appointed by the Governor General after winning the largest number of seats in the House of Commons in an election	• Member of Parliament responsible to his or her voters • leader of a political party • head of government • identifies the needs of the nation • develops programs to meet those needs on a national level • meets and negotiates with foreign leaders • presents government bills for consideration by the House of Commons and maintains the functioning of government. Although the monarch and Governor General represent the nation, the real power in government rests with the Prime Minister.
Cabinet	members of either the House of Commons or Senate who are appointed to their positions by the Prime Minister	• head government departments, such as defence, environment, labour, foreign affairs • manage the department, answer questions about matters related to their departments in the House of Commons, and provide the Prime Minister with information and advice about their departments
Members of Parliament	elected in one of the federal **ridings** in a general election must be at least 18 years of age and a Canadian citizen	• represent the voters of their riding • debate and vote on whether bills should become laws • sit on various committees examining bills • support their party positions on issues and in debates
Senators	appointed by the Governor General on the advice of the Prime Minister must be at least 30 years old, own at least $4000 worth of property, live in the province or territory they represent, and retire at the age of 75	• read and pass bills into law • sit on various committees and examine issues of public interest such as government spending, foreign aid

Figure 2-6 How many of these government positions can you find mention of in today's newspaper?

executive branch: the branch of the government responsible for daily government affairs, which includes introducing bills that may become law

judicial branch: the branch of government responsible for interpreting and enforcing the laws passed by the legislative branch

The federal system was to be further defined with separate powers and roles for the **executive** and **judicial branches**.

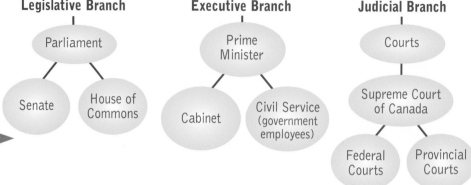

Legislative Branch
- Parliament
  - Senate
  - House of Commons

Executive Branch
- Prime Minister
  - Cabinet
  - Civil Service (government employees)

Judicial Branch
- Courts
  - Supreme Court of Canada
    - Federal Courts
    - Provincial Courts

Figure 2-7 The Branches of Canada's Government. What are the advantages and disadvantages of dividing the government in various branches?

Figure 2-8 Jeanne Sauvé was the first female to be appointed Governor General. Here she takes the oath of office as Canada's 23rd Governor General in 1984.

Figure 2-9 Prime Minister Paul Martin holds a news conference in 2005. He announces the appointment of Michaëlle Jean as Canada's first Black Governor General. She is joined here by her husband and daughter. How many female Governor Generals have there been?

Governor General

In the past, a British official was always appointed to this position. This changed in 1952 when Vincent Massey became the first Canadian Governor General. Since then the office has been held by a number of prominent Canadians. Since the Governor General is not an elected member of government, he or she is free to speak for and represent all Canadians.

Prime Minister

The Prime Minister is the leader of the political party in power. He or she is elected to this leadership at a party convention. As leader, he or she becomes the spokesperson for the party and its policies. As well as being the head of government, the Prime Minister is also an elected Member of Parliament and has the responsibility to represent the people in his or her riding. Can you imagine having so many roles that you could be negotiating a major treaty one day and trying to answer a question about a voter's pension the next?

Members of Parliament

Canada is a large country with over 31 million people. It is impossible for all citizens to actively participate in creating laws and debating issues. We rely on representatives to present our views on issues. An elected Member of Parliament, also called an MP, must balance the views of the voters with the policies of his or her political party. This can sometimes be difficult.

On some issues, the government allows members to vote according to their conscience or to reflect their voters' views. This is called a **free vote**. Members do not lose favour with the party if they do not support the government. A free vote was held when government introduced a bill to abolish capital punishment in 1976. Recently, members have supported the idea of more free votes to allow them to better represent the views of the voters.

Senate

Senators represent the various provinces/territories and cultural make-up of the nation. Currently Canada has Senators from First Nations, Asian, and Caribbean communities. There are 105 senators in the Senate with the following break down:

Province/Territory	Number of Senators
Maritimes	24
Quebec	24
Ontario	24
Western provinces	24
Newfoundland and Labrador	6
Yukon Territory	1
Northwest Territories	1
Nunavut	1

When the Senate was created in 1867, its purpose was to provide a "sober second thought" on government bills and actions. Since Senators do not need to seek re-election, they can take unpopular positions that are considered in the best interests of the nation. Today, the Senate has come under criticism by those who see it as an ineffective government body of appointed friends of the Prime Minister.

free vote: a parliamentary vote in which Members of Parliament are allowed to vote according to their conscience or to reflect the voters' views

Figure 2-10 Members of Parliament are meant to be representative of all citizens in Canada. In 2004, Steven Fletcher was the first quadriplegic person elected to the House of Commons. Melissa Anderson, on right, is Fletcher's aide.

Figure 2-11 Do you think the divisions of seats in the Senate provide smaller regions and provinces/territories with an equal voice to that of the larger provinces?

Figure 2-12 Roméo Dallaire was appointed to the Senate in March 2005. Do an Internet search to determine what qualities he possesses that might have earned him this position.

Issue Analysis

What Should Be Done to the Senate?

The Senate is a controversial branch of government. Some people think that it is time to get rid of it. Others believe it needs to be changed, or reformed. One suggested change is that Senators be elected instead of appointed. Still other people feel it should be kept in its present form. Let's examine the arguments on all sides.

ABOLISH THE SENATE

- The elected House of Commons is all our country needs to make laws.

- Rarely does the Senate change bills; therefore, it does not have a true purpose.

- It costs approximately $70 million annually to run the Senate. That money could be used for important programs such as education and healthcare.

- The Senate is not democratic. Why should people who are not elected have a say in our government?

REFORM THE SENATE (CREATE AN ELECTED SENATE)

- After nearly 140 years of existence, it is time to update the Senate.

- Rather than appointing Senators, let the provinces vote for whom they want to represent them. Unelected Senators are not accountable to the people.

- The Prime Minister may consult the provinces about the choice of a new Senator. Several times Alberta attempted to influence an appointment by holding a provincial vote. The province then tried to persuade the Prime Minister to appoint the person who received the most votes.

- To keep the ideas fresh and the energy level high, limit the terms of Senators to 10 years.

MAINTAIN THE SENATE AS IT CURRENTLY EXISTS

- An unelected Senate means that Senators are not vulnerable to pressure groups with their own agendas.

- The Senate provides an important second look at legislation without needing to satisfy all the groups involved in the issue.

- The Senate represents Canadians from various cultures and occupations and it brings their perspectives to the government.

- The Senate represents the provinces who would not be heard if the Senate were elected based on representation by population.

1. Do you think that the Senate is a useful organization? Explain.

2. What points from the chart best match your idea of an ideal Senate? Why?

3. Design a job advertisement for a Senator who you feel would be the best suited to sit in your ideal Senate. Consider what requirements there would be.

House of Commons

The House of Commons is a debating forum where the government presents its plans and ideas for running the country while the other parties (the **opposition**) oppose the government. The opposition's role is to:

- question government policies
- ensure that laws beneficial for all Canadians are passed
- keep the government accountable by making sure it does not act in an illegal manner, such as taking bribes or trying to limit the rights of minorities.

opposition: the political party or parties not in power

question period: the time when members of the House can pose questions to the government

S Speaker: elected by members, maintains order during debates

PM Prime Minster: head of the government

C Cabinet: Members of Parliament responsible for government departments

B Backbenchers: Members of Parliament, not in the Cabinet or Opposition critics, who sit in the back benches

O Leader of the Opposition: ensures the government is accountable for its actions

CL Clerk: gives the Speaker advice on procedures to be followed in the House

P Pages: students who serve the Speaker and Members of Parliament

Figure 2-13 House of Commons. Match the letters on the photo with the descriptions on the right.

The seating galleries above the floor of the House of Commons are for visitors and the press. They often remain empty during debates, but quickly fill for **question period**. This is the part of each day when the opposition holds the government accountable for its actions. Opposition members challenge Cabinet ministers to explain and defend their decisions. Usually the opposition attempts to embarrass the government by asking questions that make the government appear incompetent. As emotions get stronger, members often heckle each other. The Speaker has to frequently intervene to maintain order. Do you think members should be disciplined for such behaviour or is it all part of the political game?

Informed to Be Effective

Each year, Pages are selected to serve the House of Commons. Being a Page provides insight into how politicians and the government work. A candidate for the Page program must: be a Canadian citizen or permanent resident; have an overall academic average of at least 80 percent; be bilingual in both official languages; be a secondary school graduate and accepted at a university or college in the National Capital Region.

Judiciary

The judiciary branch of the government is made up of all the justices, or judges, in Canada. Their role is to settle disputes, interpret the law, and decide on punishments in the Canadian court system. The Supreme Court of Canada is the highest court in the country. It is made up of a chief justice and eight justices, who are appointed by the federal government. By law, three of the justices are from Quebec. By tradition, three come from Ontario, two from Western Canada, and one from the Atlantic Provinces. The Supreme Court is strictly an appeals court. It has no trial division. This court only considers cases from provincial courts of appeal and the Federal Court of Appeal. Its decision is final. The Supreme Court may also refuse to hear a case. The judiciary will be further explored in Chapter 3.

Figure 2-14 The justices of the Supreme Court of Canada. Should Members of Parliament or justices appointed by the federal government determine whether or not laws violate the Constitution?

CHECKPOINT

1. **What are the three branches of government and what are their responsibilities?**

2. **How does our Parliamentary system reflect Canada's population distribution and still protect the smaller provinces?**

3. **Why is the House of Commons seen as the most powerful government institution?**

Provincial and Territorial Governments

Canada's provincial and territorial governments function along the same lines as the federal government. Why do you think Quebec calls its legislature the "National Assembly?"

Figure 2-15 Branches of Provincial Governments

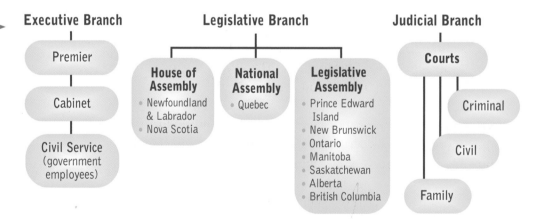

Executive Branch
- Premier
- Cabinet
- Civil Service (government employees)

Legislative Branch
- House of Assembly
  - Newfoundland & Labrador
  - Nova Scotia
- National Assembly
  - Quebec
- Legislative Assembly
  - Prince Edward Island
  - New Brunswick
  - Ontario
  - Manitoba
  - Saskatchewan
  - Alberta
  - British Columbia

Judicial Branch
- Courts
  - Criminal
  - Civil
  - Family

Active Citizen

The provincial leader is elected in the same manner as the Prime Minister. The leader of the party that wins the most **seats** becomes the Premier or Premier ministre in Quebec. Each Premier appoints a Cabinet and must answer to the opposition parties.

At the provincial level the representative of the Crown is the Lieutenant-Governor, who is appointed by the Governor General on the advice of the Premier. The duties of the Lieutenant-Governor are similar to the Governor General only on a smaller scale. They include:

seat: the right to sit as a member of a legislature, based on winning a riding in an election

- visits around the province
- opening the provincial legislature
- swearing in Cabinet ministers
- signing bills and calling elections on the advice of the Premier.

Over the last few decades, Lieutenant-Governors tended to represent different cultural and ethnic groups that reflect the social and cultural make-up of their province. In 2002, Ontario appointed James Bartleman, a member of the Manjikanig First Nation, as the province's first Aboriginal Lieutenant-Governor.

How They Work

Members in the provincial legislatures are elected and function in the same manner as at the federal level. Provincial members are called Members of Legislative Assemblies (MLAs) or Members of Provincial Parliaments (MPPs), depending on the province. The governing party introduces bills and has to answer to the opposition for the government's actions.

In the Northwest Territories and Nunavut, however, the government is run by consensus. Members who are elected to these territorial governments do not belong to political parties. After they are elected, they elect a Premier, Speaker, and Cabinet from their own members. Issues and bills are debated and passed with the agreement of all members. This is an example of consensus government that is not adversarial but seeks compromise and benefits for all citizens. It was adapted from the First Nations and Inuit systems of government.

As you explored earlier in this chapter, the provinces have responsibilities in a number of areas. Education is one area in which provinces resist any federal interference, even when it involves establishing education bursary programs. The provinces view education as an area where the youngest members of society can learn not only the basic skills but also become aware of their provincial culture and heritage. The result is different curriculums across the nation and different diploma requirements.

Figure 2-16 Paul Okalik became Premier of Nunavut in 2004. The majority of the population in Nunavut is Inuit and so they have a form of self-government in this territory. What might be the advantages and disadvantages of ruling by consensus?

Literacy Hint

Ask yourself questions about why the curriculum is different from province to province. What topics and issues would be important to a coastal province? What about a prairie province? What do you think your province should stress in its schools?

People Power

Lincoln Alexander

Occupation: Lieutenant-Governor of Ontario, 1985–1990

Fast Facts:
- born in Toronto on January 21, 1922, to West Indian immigrants
- served in the Air Force during the Second World War
- married Yvonne Harrison in 1948
- called to the bar in 1953
- appointed a Queen's counsel in 1965
- elected first person of colour to the House of Commons in 1968
- appointed Minister of Labour in 1979
- appointed Lieutenant-Governor of Ontario in 1985
- became a Companion of the Order of Canada and also of the Order of Ontario in 1992
- became chair of the Canadian Race Relations Foundation in 1996

His story: Lincoln Alexander is an example of a person who got involved in government with a goal to make a difference. He challenged those who discriminated against others. He was the first person of colour to be appointed Ontario's Lieutenant-Governor. He decided to use his office to encourage the young people of the province to establish high expectations and to work to achieve them. He also wanted to promote racial harmony. In his many visits to various schools in the province he told students of the obstacles he faced as a person of colour. He related stories of how

Figure 2-17 Lincoln Alexander presents two awards. Who in your school or community do you feel would be a worthy recipient of the Lincoln Alexander Award?

he was often taunted at school and fought back against prejudice and racism. He wanted students to know that they could make a difference.

In recognition of his contributions, the Lincoln Alexander Award was established. It recognizes young people between the ages of 16 and 25 who model racial harmony in the province of Ontario.

Quotation: Alexander has said, "Who would believe that a poor Black boy growing up in Toronto would one day become Lieutenant-Governor of Ontario?"

1. What is the main message Lincoln Alexander wanted to communicate to young people?
2. How can young individuals promote Alexander's call for racial harmony?

The relationship between the provinces/territories and Ottawa has been characterized by some as a love-hate relationship. The provinces/territories need financial assistance from the federal government in the form of **transfer payments** for areas such as health care and infrastructure. The federal government also administers the equalization program where the richer provinces contribute to the others by paying a larger share of taxes to Ottawa. In this way, all citizens have access to basic services.

The delicate nature of federal-provincial relations was illustrated in December 2004, when the Premier of Newfoundland and Labrador stormed out of a meeting with the Prime Minister. The meeting involved negotiations over the province's share of gas and oil revenues. The Premier felt the federal government was not granting a large enough share to the province and was limiting its ability to raise the standard of living for its residents. When he returned to the provincial capital, he ordered all provincial buildings to remove the Canadian flag in protest. Controversy erupted. The Prime Minister accused the Premier of insulting the nation's honour and using the nation's symbol as a bargaining ploy. The Premier replied that the federal government's attitude amounted to an abandonment of the province. Eventually, both sides agreed to meet. In early 2005, a deal was reached and the maple leaf once again flew in the province.

transfer payments: a system of payments from provinces with stronger revenues to provinces with smaller tax bases; intended to ensure equality of services for all Canadians

> ### Literacy Hint
> **Think Critically.** What do you think of the way the Premier of Newfoundland and Labrador acted? Were his actions reasonable and justifiable or not?

Figure 2-18 The Canadian flag is untied from in front of the Confederation Building in St. John's on December 23, 2004. Do you think that provincial leaders should defy the federal government? Provide reasons for your opinion.

Municipal or Local Governments

The level of government that probably has the greatest impact on you but is often the least acknowledged is municipal government. This level provides leadership and governance for towns, cities, and regions. The leaders are elected and are responsible for such things as:

- local taxes
- bylaws
- water inspection
- maintenance of roads
- garbage collection
- public libraries.

Aboriginal local governments may have additional responsibilities including housing, education, and resource development. You will explore municipal government further in Chapter 4.

CHECKPOINT

1. What are the branches of the provincial governments?
2. What responsibilities are given to provinces under the Constitution?
3. Why are municipal governments seen as having the most direct impact on citizens?

How Do Citizens Select Their Government?

In an ideal world, all citizens would give their opinions and vote on decisions. Imagine how difficult it would be if your principal wanted suggestions from every student for a new school mascot. It could take months! Wouldn't it be easier to talk to class representatives from each homeroom? Representatives could present feedback from their classmates to the principal. Similarly, it is impossible to get input from every citizen in Canada. Instead, we select representatives to make decisions on our behalf.

Canadians usually vote for individuals representing a political party. Political parties were formed when people sharing similar ideals joined together. If enough party members were elected, the party could form a government and introduce the members' ideas to the country.

Canada has two long established parties—the Liberal and Conservative parties. The New Democratic Party, which evolved from the Cooperative Commonwealth Federation (CCF), was created in 1960. The Green Party was founded in 1983 with a platform that emphasized environmental issues. The Bloc Québécois, created in 1991, only has candidates in Quebec. This party wants Quebec to separate from the Canadian federal system. The number and names of parties change from time to time, and new parties are created.

Literacy Hint

How can you discover more information on the four political parties mentioned in Figure 2-19 on the next page? See the Civic Skills Power: Detecting Bias and Frame of Reference on pages 46–47 for suggestions.

Active Citizen

KEY PARTIES AND ISSUES IN CANADA'S GOVERNMENT

Issue	Green	NDP	Liberal	Conservative
Role of Government	• strong government presence to promote healthy communities, environmentally friendly industries, and discourage waste and pollution	• more government presence in the economy and society to ensure equity of services and opportunities	• some government presence that should ensure basic services are provided to everyone	• limited government presence to reduce large bureaucracies and high government spending
Taxes	• reduce individual taxes and increase taxes on pollution-producing industries • use taxes to fund further research on environmentally friendly power sources and support government programs	• base tax rate on income, with higher-income people paying more than those with lower incomes • use higher taxes to maintain government programs	• base tax rate on income, with taxes reduced as government revenue from other sources increases	• base tax rate on income, with a focus on reducing taxes to increase the purchasing power of citizens to maintain economic growth
Health care	• increase funding for public health care • encourage healthy lifestyles	• controlled by government, fully publicly funded	• controlled by government, regulated under the *Canada Health Act*	• a possible combination of publicly funded and private health services
Environment	• improve the environment through all policies, especially the Kyoto Accord	• increase government spending on research into alternative energy sources • support Kyoto Accord through funding and laws to enforce pollution controls	• commit to limits on pollution and green house gases as set out in Kyoto Accord • fund research for alternative energy sources and address current pollution sources	• increase fines against private and industrial polluters • increase research on alternative energy sources • redirect funds from Kyoto commitments to domestic solutions
Social services	• fund basic social services with an emphasis on early education, affordable housing, safe food and water	• finance priority social programs, such as affordable housing, increased financial aid to cities, services for seniors, and daycare spaces	• finance social programs such as daycare, affordable housing, increased pensions, and services for seniors	• provide tax incentives to companies to build affordable housing and increase services to seniors

Figure 2-19 What other political parties exist in your area? What are their views on the above issues?

Detecting Bias and Frame of Reference

As you read this chapter, you are probably realizing that people feel strongly about how they are governed and who governs them. Political parties and candidates, the Senate, the Governor General, and certain issues create strong emotions in people. When you, your parents or guardians, or your friends talk about politics, your conversations no doubt contain strong emotional words. This emotional flavour that expresses the interests, feelings, and values of a person is called *bias*.

Every political candidate or political party wants your vote and will try to influence you to get it. Votes equal power when a person is elected. How do you decide whether to let a politician have power over you? You must watch and listen for the person's biases and then decide whether or not you agree with the way that candidate thinks.

A *frame of reference* is the background that influences a person's bias. That frame of reference may include many influences:

- How, when, and where a person grew up can shape his or her thinking. How might you be influenced if you were raised in a wealthy family in Vancouver as compared with a family living in poverty in Ontario? Would you have similar attitudes towards money?
- The particular interests a person develops over time because of experiences and education may affect his or her point of view. How might a person who grew up with pet dogs or cats feel differently about fur trapping in northern Ontario than someone who depends on trapping to make a living?
- The values a person acquires from parents, religion, and life experiences may sway his or her vote on issues with strong moral content. How might a person who has a relative with a disability feel about providing equal employment opportunities for the physically challenged?

Often elements of a person's frame of reference come together in such a way that the person feels most comfortable with the philosophy and points of view of a particular political party. Reread the chart in Figure 2-19 to get some sense of the frame of reference of three of Canada's political parties.

How do you detect bias and frame of reference?

1. Listen for a tone of voice and describe it. Is the person angry about injustices, enthusiastic about future plans, or cynical about progress? The tone tells you how the person feels about the topic being discussed.

2. Pay attention to the words a person uses. Are they strong words that give you a clear picture in your head? For example, "This government is *clumsy and wasteful* with our money." Do the words exaggerate a situation? Words are chosen to influence you. You must decide whether you will let your opinion be swayed by the words you hear.

3. Analyse the stories or examples a person uses. Are they meant to arouse your emotions rather than appeal to your reason and sense of logic? For example, a story about a relative who waited six hours in a hospital emergency room might influence your thinking about the effectiveness of our health care system.

4. Ask yourself questions about what a person says. For example, "Are the statements true? Do I know anything

myself that would prove or disprove these statements? Have I had any similar experiences?" Test the other person's point of view by comparing it with your own thoughts and experiences.

5. Make a judgment about the information you hear. Decide whether you will let that person influence your thinking. A democracy allows for many different points of view and biases to coexist in an orderly manner.

You Try It

Listen to a political speech, watch a political commercial, or read an editorial about government in the newspaper. Make a note of the words that convey a certain tone or point of view. Decide how the examples or situations described influence your feelings and thoughts. Write down the decision you make about the issue, party, or person when you have finished this exercise.

The Election Process

Canada is divided into over 300 ridings. The number of ridings assigned to provinces and territories is based on population. Since Ontario has the largest population, it has the greatest number of ridings. Prince Edward Island, with a population of just over 100 000, has the fewest. The largest electoral district in Canada by area is Nunavut, with over 3 million square kilometres; the smallest is Laurier–Sainte-Marie, with only 9. How large is your electoral district? The riding of Charlottetown with a population of approximately 18 600 and the riding of Willowdale with a population of over 50 000 each elect one member. Do you agree with this system?

By law, federal elections must be called at least every five years. A federal election is called when the Prime Minister advises the Governor General to dissolve the House of Commons and call an election. An election is also held if the government is defeated in a **vote of non-confidence**. This type of vote happens when a bill introduced by the government is defeated by the opposition parties. This indicates that the government can no longer govern and must seek a **mandate** from the people. This occurred in 1963 when the government of Prime Minister Defienbaker was defeated over its defence policies. A vote of non-confidence can also happen when an official confidence vote is held or when the government is defeated on a money bill such as a budget. In 1979 the budget of Joe Clark's government was defeated and an election was called.

To run for election in Canada, you must be over 18 years of age and a Canadian citizen. You will need lots of help from friends, supporters, and volunteers. You need to find a campaign location, meet as many voters as possible, hand out pamphlets, and put up signs. If you are representing an

Literacy Hint

Stop and make some predictions. List the things that you could do to convince voters to elect you. Check your predictions after you read the following paragraphs.

vote of non-confidence: occurs when a proposed bill receives less than a majority of votes in the House of Commons, defeating the government and forcing it to resign

mandate: support given to a political party or government by the electors

established political party, you will receive financial assistance from the party. You may even get a visit from the party leader.

To run for election in a Band Council on a First Nation territory, you must be a member of the community. However, anyone who is nominated can run for Chief, including non-members. Only members of a First Nation may vote in a Band Council election. These elections occur every two years. Some First Nations have been permitted by the federal government through Indian and Northern Affairs Canada to have their own local election regulations, which may provide for a longer term in office.

During an election campaign, voters get to meet their potential representatives. It is an opportunity to ask questions and make their opinions heard.

Figure 2-20 Elections provide many opportunities for people—including young people—to get involved. Here are some ideas: attend an all candidates meeting; help deliver pamphlets; make calls in support of a candidate; provide childcare for other volunteers.

The Role of the Media

Since most ridings are large, candidates rarely get to meet all the eligible voters. They must find other ways to make themselves known and present their ideas. In this age of rapid communication and technology, the media have become major players in presenting candidates in the best light. Just think how important it is to make a good first impression. What would you like people to see and remember about you when they meet you for the first time? During the election campaign, candidates and political parties spend millions of dollars on travel, advertising, and rent for election offices and rally locations. Advertisements either present the candidate in a positive light or try to cast negative images or impressions of their opponents.

If you were creating an ad for a candidate, what images would you select? In federal elections, the flag or maple leaf is often present. The leader of the party is often seen speaking to admiring voters. He or she usually has a 20–30 second speech clip that sends out a positive message on an issue. Colour, symbols, attractive visuals, and large crowds are used to make the leader look "prime ministerial."

An unfavourable light is cast on opponents by questioning their policies or using quotations from past campaigns that may seem contradictory. There has been a great deal of controversy over these ads. Do they actually help voters make up their minds? Should there be limits on these ads?

This issue came to the forefront in the 1993 election when the Progressive Conservative Party televised an ad that appeared to highlight the facial disability of the Liberal leader, Jean Chrétien. The ad presented slow moving images of Mr. Chrétien speaking that emphasized his disability. The sound track included a person saying that she felt embarrassed every time Mr. Chrétien spoke. This ad brought immediate negative feedback from many voters and many Progressive Conservative candidates. People felt this ad had crossed the line and should be withdrawn. Prime Minister Kim Campbell quickly removed the ad from the airwaves. However, the damage had been done and many observers blamed this ad as one reason for the defeat of Campbell's government.

There have also been examples where female candidates and Members of Parliament have complained that media coverage has tended to report on the

Literacy Hint

Stop and reflect on your answers to the important questions asked in the paragraphs about the media and advertising. What examples can you add of commercials or photographs you have thought to be too negative to be effective?

Active Citizen Website

For links to sites on elections in Canada

Figure 2-21 Sometimes debate can get heated, as seen in this 2004 leader's debate. Liberal leader Paul Martin (second from right) debates with Conservative leader Stephen Harper (left) as NDP leader Jack Layton (centre) and Bloc Québécois leader Gilles Duceppe look on. Who appears to look more prime ministerial? What criteria did you use to make your selection?

fashions of the candidates rather than their stand on the issues. Outspoken male candidates are described as decisive, while female candidates exhibiting similar behaviour might be characterized as pushy and arrogant. These perceptions were reinforced in the 2004 election. Belinda Stronach, a candidate for the Conservative Party, was portrayed as an attractive, blond, rich girl trying to buy her election. There were more stories written about her clothes and personal life than about her stand on the issues. Besides these obstacles, what other difficulties do you feel female candidates face compared with male candidates?

The media play an important role in elections by reporting candidates' movements throughout the campaign. Often the leaders will engage in television debates in both official languages. This provides the leaders with an opportunity to present their visions for the country. They also use it to attack the policies of their opponents. These debates may be the only time a large number of voters will see the leaders on the same stage. Debates have become such an important part of the campaign that leaders have negotiated such things as the height of the podium and acceptable format. A successful performance can give a party momentum. A poor performance can put a leader on the defensive for the rest of the campaign.

Election Day

The election campaign is a gruelling experience with party leaders travelling from one electoral district to another. There are many early mornings and late nights. It is important that the leader maintain a high profile during the election. The leader must convince Canadians to elect the most candidates from his or her party in order to form a government.

All campaign work focuses on election day, when Canadians cast their ballots. Did you know that advance polls allow people to vote who might not be able to cast their ballots on voting day? This ensures that everyone can make his or her vote count.

On election day, the polls open early in the morning and close in the early evening. Because we have six different time zones, the polls in Newfoundland and Labrador close long before those in British Columbia. Consequently, the media are not allowed to transmit results to regions where polls are still open. This gives every voter the opportunity to vote without outside factors influencing their decision. Yet, in 2004, the CTV Network felt that it had a disadvantage because the results were being shared across the Internet. The network decided to broadcast the results to all regions as they became available. How do you think the other two television networks felt about CTV's decision?

Literacy Hint
Think about your background knowledge of election day. Where have you seen polling station signs in your community? Where have your parents or guardians gone to vote?

Figure 2-22 In some countries like Australia it is compulsory for citizens to vote and fines are levied against those who do not. Do you think Canada should adopt a similar law?

Active Citizen

Issue Analysis

Should the Voting Age Be Lowered?

"Every citizen of Canada has the right to vote in an election of members of the House of Commons or of a legislative assembly and to be qualified for membership therein."
—Section 3, *Canadian Charter of Rights and Freedoms*

"Every individual is equal before and under the law and has the right to the equal protection and equal benefit of the law without discrimination based on race, national or ethnic origin, colour, religion, sex, age or mental or physical disability."
—Section 15, *Canadian Charter of Rights and Freedoms*

Figure 2-23 Eryn Fitzgerald (left) and Christine Jairamsingh (right)

Are teenagers "citizens"? Should the approximately one million 16- and 17-year-olds in Canada be permitted to vote? Eryn Fitzgerald and Christine Jairamsingh think that they should. In fact, these young women from Edmonton, Alberta, felt so strongly that they took their case all the way to the Supreme Court of Canada.

In 2001, Fitzgerald and Jairamsingh went to court in Edmonton requesting the right to vote in the municipal election. They argued that putting a limit on the voting age violates the democratic rights guaranteed to every Canadian in section 3 of the *Canadian Charter of Rights and Freedoms* (see above). The judge in the case, Justice Erik Lefsrud, was sympathetic to their argument. He acknowledged that putting an age restriction on voting is a violation of the democratic and equality rights (see section 15 above) available to all Canadians in the Charter. However, Judge Lefsrud ruled such limits are justified because they preserve the integrity of Canada's electoral system. In other words, denying the vote to teenagers is acceptable.

Some opponents questioned lowering the voting age because the lowest voter turnout in the 2004 election was for voters between 18 and 24. The head of Elections Canada listed a number of reasons why he felt the turnout was so low:

- little understanding of politics
- lack of interest
- a declining sense that voting is a civic duty
- other priorities such as working, school, social life.

Despite Judge Lefsrud's ruling, Fitzgerald and Jairamsingh did not give up. They appealed to the Alberta Court of Appeal. In May 2004, this court also ruled that the *Charter of Rights and Freedoms* does not guarantee a youth's right to vote. By January 2005, the case was appealed to the Supreme Court of Canada, but the justices refused to hear it.

Eryn Fitzgerald and Christine Jairamsingh are now old enough to vote. They will think of their experience when they fulfil their civic duty and vote in the next election.

1. What goal did Eryn Fitzgerald and Christine Jairamsingh set out to accomplish? How did the Canadian court system respond to their request?

2. Do you think that 16- and 17-year-olds should vote? Support your position.

voters' list: a list giving the names, addresses, and occupations of all those entitled to vote in a given riding

Figure 2-24 Why is it crucial that polling stations be clearly marked?

At the Polls

Election polls are located in churches, schools, legions, and other appropriate facilities in each riding. Throughout the day, voters come to the polls and take part in their most fundamental right and responsibility as a citizen. Candidates try to ensure that all their supporters who are eligible to vote get to the polls. Voters may be offered rides. People with disabilities or challenges can be assisted at the polls, and those who are unable to come to the polls can appoint someone to vote in their place.

Once you arrive at the polling station, you are directed to the proper table where a poll clerk asks you your name and checks the **voters' list** to make sure you are eligible. The names on the list are generated from tax returns. If your name is not on the list, you can still vote if you swear an oath that you are a Canadian citizen, over 18 years of age, and have lived in the riding for the past year. You are handed a ballot that an official has initialled and then you are directed to an area that provides privacy for you to mark your ballot. The names of the candidates are shown on the ballot in alphabetical order by surname along with the party the candidate represents.

Mark the circle next to the candidate of your choice, fold the ballot, and return it to the poll clerk. The poll clerk checks the initials on the outside of the ballot to ensure that it is the same ballot that was given to you. The part of the ballot on which the initial was placed is removed and you are instructed to deposit the ballot in the ballot box.

Counting the Ballots

Once the polls close the ballots are counted. Some voters may wish to express their displeasure with the candidates by marking more than one name or leaving the ballot blank. These are considered spoiled ballots and will not be counted. A voter can also refuse the ballot. Once the votes are counted the number of ballots is compared with the number of voters to ensure that no one voted more than once. In an election, every vote counts. In the 2004 federal election, one seat in British Columbia was decided by less than 20 votes. When results are this close, recounts are ordered. The election results are official after the Chief Electoral Officer certifies that the vote was fair.

On election night all party leaders and candidates anxiously watch as results come in. Party leaders look at the results from their own riding and the national results. In our Parliamentary system, the next Prime Minister is the person whose party wins the most seats in the House of Commons. This party will be given the opportunity to form a government.

People Power

It was a late night again for the School Board's trustee meeting. As presenters waited to give their reports, they took a quick look at the trustees and a young student sitting with them. What was she doing there? Not only was this student sitting at the same table as the trustees, she was also participating in the discussions. The more they listened the more impressed they became because her questions were reflective and insightful.

The young student was a student trustee who was a typical teenager in some areas but exceptional in others.

Nancy La Neve had always had an interest in promoting worthy causes. Her interest began in elementary school where she organized a pop tab campaign to raise money to help purchase a wheelchair. When she moved on to high school, she realized that she could either keep to herself in this new environment, or take a proactive role.

She had an opportunity after the horrible events of 9/11. She organized an Art Project with the theme, Promoting A Culture of Peace. She quickly came to the attention of the school administrators, who encouraged her to seek the position of student trustee. Nancy was required to write a speech, outlining her reasons for wanting the position, and to deliver it to her fellow candidates. She won.

One of Nancy's first roles was to represent her school board at the Ontario Student Trustee Association. At the meeting, she was involved in a number of committees and her peers were so

Figure 2-25 What similar organizations exist in your school or community that would allow you to follow Nancy's example?

impressed, they encouraged her to run for the position of president of the Board Council. She was successful. In that position, she presented the student perspective on educational issues to Ministry of Education officials and trustees.

Nancy's parents instilled in her a sense of hard work and leadership. Her goals have been to realize her strengths, develop a sense of leadership, and promote global citizenship. Nancy has earned the respect of her peers and trustees. She is not finished yet. As she says, "If you want change, you have to start the process."

1. What qualities does Nancy have that make her effective in promoting issues important to young people?

2. What does Nancy feel were the influences in her life that encouraged her to get involved in various issues?

3. Why is it important to have a student trustee on Boards of Education?

The Results

An election can produce two possible results: a **majority** or a **minority government**. If one party is able to capture 50 percent plus 1 of the seats in the House of Commons a majority government is elected. This means that even if all the opposition parties were to vote against the government, it will still be able to pass legislation. However, if the leading party has under 50 percent of the seats, the government elected is a minority government. In this case, the opposition parties may outnumber the governing party on a vote.

majority government: a government that has more than half of the total number of parliamentary seats

minority government: a government that has fewer seats in Parliament than the total number held by all other parties

Figure 2-26 Who is portrayed in this cartoon? What is the cartoonist saying about the 2004 minority election results?

When a minority government is elected, the leader of that party goes to the Governor General for permission to form a government. If the Governor General agrees, the leader becomes Prime Minister and forms a Cabinet. The government then goes to the House of Commons and seeks a vote of confidence. Usually the governing party meets with opposition leaders and tries to make an agreement for their support by offering to include some of their ideas in government legislation.

If the government does not get a vote of confidence, the Governor General has two options. He or she can either call upon the leader with the second largest number of seats to attempt to form a government by getting support from the other parties or the Governor General can call a new election. In some cases, the Prime Minister may seek to govern by appointing some of the opposition to the Cabinet. This would result in a **coalition government**. This was done during the First World War when Prime Minister Borden sought to unite the country after a divisive election. What are the advantages of a minority and majority government?

Making Your Voice Heard

Even though elections are often held four to five years apart, citizens can still make their views known in the meantime. One of easiest ways to make your point is to contact your local MP. This person has an office in your riding and one in Ottawa. Both are staffed with people trained to deal with **constituents**.

Many people do not get involved in the political process because they don't know who to contact, don't understand the political process, or don't have time to get involved. Remember, if you want to make a difference, you need to be informed, purposeful, and active.

If you feel that your opinion is not being heard, you can visit your MP or protest outside the constituency offices. If there are a number of people who feel the same as you do, you can organize a petition-writing campaign. You would list your concerns and ask people to sign your petition as a show of support. A member would be foolish to ignore a petition signed by many constituents.

The best way to make your views known and to make a difference is to get involved. Those who do not vote and still complain have little credibility. Joining a political party, communicating with your representative, helping to lobby members, or becoming an Internet activist are effective means of getting your voice heard.

Informed to Be Effective

Letters to an MP can be posted without a stamp. This is a long-standing tradition to encourage people to freely communicate with their MPs. All MPs also have email addresses. What message is the government trying to send, making it so easy to contact your MP?

coalition government: a government that is composed of members of different parties when a majority government is not elected. Members of different parties may be given Cabinet posts as members of the government.

constituents: citizens who live in electoral ridings across the nation

Figure 2-27 Cheryl Gallant is the MP for Renfrew-Nipissing-Pembroke. If you were to visit your Member of Parliament's office, what issue would you want to bring to the MP's attention?

CHECKPOINT

1. **How does a person become Prime Minister?**
2. **When can elections be called?**
3. **What is the difference between a majority and minority government?**

Putting Laws into Effect

Once the election is over, the government sets to work to govern the nation and implement its campaign promises through legislation. Although there are different levels of government in Canada, they all have one thing in common: they make laws. Making laws is not something that can be done quickly or without careful thought. Once laws are passed they are enforced with consequences. Bad laws can result in unforeseen situations and injustices. It is important to get laws right the first time. Just as you have to take all factors into account when making a major purchase or reaching an important decision, making laws requires careful thought.

CIVICS SKILLS POWER

Accessing Reliable Resources

Some people ask, "What has government ever done for me?" Because governments exist to serve the needs of people, they provide a lot of information through easily available sources. Here are some ways you can contact various levels of government to support your needs:

- The telephone book in every community has blue pages that provide contact numbers for federal, provincial, and municipal government departments and services.
- Most libraries have a reference section with resources such as yearbooks and almanacs that provide useful government information.
- The Internet provides information, downloadable forms, contact addresses, and telephone numbers for Members of Parliament and services at all levels of government:
  - ◆ You can look up your high school course and curriculum on a Ministry of Education website for your province. You can contact your MPP or MLA.

- ◆ You can download a passport application form from the Canadian government website. You can also find contact information for all government departments, information about the history and features of Canada, and news releases about recent government announcements and events.
- ◆ Type the name of your town and its province or territory into a search engine to discover community services, such as arenas or garbage pickup, courtesy of your municipal government.

You Try It

Choose a province other than your own. Find that province's website. Navigate the various buttons to discover the history of the province and the number of members in the provincial legislature. Who is the Premier of the province? Check the news releases to read about some recent government decisions.

Process for Making Laws	**Process for Completing a School Project**	
		Figure 2-28 Creating a law can be compared to the process you go through when working on a school project.

Process for Making Laws

- Prime Minister, Cabinet, or Member of Parliament generates an idea that requires a law.

- Civil servants research the arguments for the legislation as well as its legal impact.
- Legislation is drafted in a bill.

House of Commons
- **First Reading:** the bill is introduced in the House.
- **Second Reading:** arguments are presented in support of the bill.
- **Committee:** the bill is examined in detail by a committee of MPs; changes to the bill can be made.
- **Third Reading:** the final wording of the bill is debated and a final vote is taken.
- If the bill is passed, it is sent to the Senate.

Senate
- The same process is followed as that in the House, with three readings and a committee stage.

- If the bill is passed in the Senate, it is sent to the Governor General, who signs it into law.

Process for Completing a School Project

- You identify a topic by talking to your teacher.
- You select good focus questions.

- You conduct research into your topic based on your focus questions.

- You write the first draft of your project.
- You complete your research.
- You proofread your work.

- You complete the second draft.
- You ask an adult or a peer to proofread your work and offer suggestions.
- You write your final draft.

- You submit your final product to your teacher.

Government Services

Over the centuries governments have evolved in the services they provide citizens. Today, tax money collected by all levels of government is used to assist people in a variety of areas. The government provides information in the two official languages as well as in a multitude of languages reflecting the multicultural composition of the nation.

Some of the services provided for young Canadians by the federal government include:

- learning, educational activities, and school projects
- planning for post-secondary education
- employment programs for young people
- tax savings and benefits
- preparing for parenthood
- child safety
- child nutrition and health care
- services for Aboriginal families with children
- support for families with special needs
- services for immigrant families with children
- sports, recreation, and travel for families.

The federal government provides these services by deciding the best way to divide the tax money it raises.

For links to sites on youth services

Figure 2-29 Do you agree with the way the government is spending tax money? What changes might you suggest to better reflect your priorities?

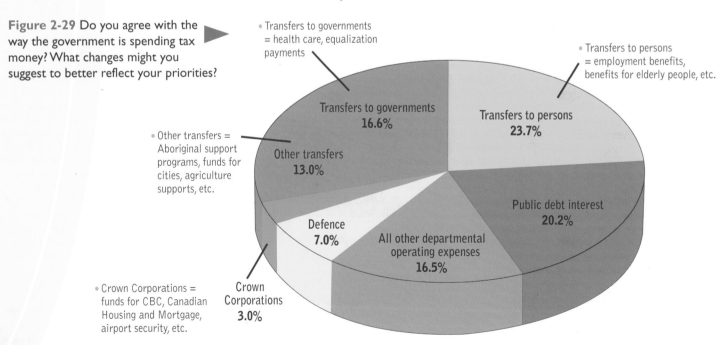

- Transfers to governments = health care, equalization payments
- Transfers to persons = employment benefits, benefits for elderly people, etc.
- Other transfers = Aboriginal support programs, funds for cities, agriculture supports, etc.
- Crown Corporations = funds for CBC, Canadian Housing and Mortgage, airport security, etc.

Transfers to governments 16.6%

Transfers to persons 23.7%

Other transfers 13.0%

Public debt interest 20.2%

Defence 7.0%

All other departmental operating expenses 16.5%

Crown Corporations 3.0%

Ministry	Services
Agriculture	Agriculture, Crops, Farm Tax Rebate Program, Foodland Ontario, Food Safety, Northern Development
Child and Youth Services	Children, Child Protection, Adoption, Child Care, Families
Community and Social Services	Unemployment, Welfare, Ontario Works, People with Disabilities, Seniors, Old Age Security, Domestic Violence, Homelessness
Community Safety and Correctional Services	Correctional Services, Public Safety and Policing, 9-1-1
Culture	Arts, Culture, History, Museums, Galleries, Historical Buildings and sites
Economic Development and Trade	Economic Overview, Economic Development
Education	Elementary/Secondary Curriculum, School Boards
Environment	Air, Water, Parks, Fishing/Hunting, Crown Land, Waste Disposal,
Finance	Business and Personal Taxes
Francophone Affairs	Services for French-speaking Citizens
Health	Health Card, Community Health, Family Health, Children's Health, Addictions, HIV and AIDS, Senior's Care, Telehealth Ontario, hospitals
Labour	Health and Safety in the Workplace
Tourism and Recreation	Travel Guides, Vacation Ideas, Festivals and Events, Tours and Excursion, Fishing/Hunting, Ontario Parks, Museums
Training, Colleges, Universities	Post-secondary, Financing, Training/Jobs
Transportation	Drivers and Vehicles, Disabled Person Parking Permit, Insurance, Ontario Road Map, Traffic Cameras, Road Safety

Figure 2-30 How many of these services have you and your family used?

The provinces and territories also offer a number of services to their citizens. Figure 2-30 shows some of the services the Ontario government offers through various Ministries. Taxes finance these services. People often complain about paying taxes, forgetting about the services they receive in return.

At first glance our government system can seem confusing. You just need to remember that the system is meant to best represent the needs of the residents of the country. The system can only work properly if citizens learn about the system and take on their responsibilites. Our freedoms can only be assured if citizens actively participate in the government process.

CHECKPOINT

1. How does an idea become a law?
2. Name five services that the government provides for young Canadians.
3. To what area does the largest amount of tax money go? Why?

CHAPTER REVIEW

Summing It Up

- Government has evolved over the centuries from a one-person rule to representative government.
- There are three levels of government in Canada: federal, provincial, and municipal.
- The federal level is divided into the executive branch with the Prime Minister, the Cabinet, and civil servants; the legislative branch with the House of Commons and Senate; and the judicial branch.
- The elected Prime Minister is the leader of the party that has the largest number of members voted into the House of Commons.
- Voting is an important responsibility of Canadian citizens.
- A law is made when an idea is drafted into a bill, presented to the House of Commons, and undergoes three readings and a committee stage, which is repeated in the Senate. If the bill is passed, it is signed into law by the Governor General.
- Governments provide services that impact many areas of our lives.

KEY TERMS

- popular will
- federal system
- federal government
- provincial government
- constitutional monarchy
- legislative branch
- bill
- speech from the throne
- riding
- executive branch
- judicial branch
- free vote
- opposition
- question period
- seat
- transfer payments
- vote of non-confidence
- mandate
- voters' list
- majority government
- minority government
- coalition government
- constituents

Thinking: To Be Informed

1. What do you think are the strengths and weaknesses of our system of government? Organize your answer in a plus/minus chart. With a partner make some suggestions for improvement.

2. Should there be more free votes in the House of Commons? Conduct research to support your position.

3. In the 2003 election, some advance polls used electronic voting machines. If citizens voted online, results would be known within minutes. Should technological options be pursued? Are there possible problems involved in using such technology?

Communicating: To Be Purposeful

4. Who are your elected provincial and federal members? What party does each member represent? What skills do your members have to make them successful? Write a letter or invite them to your class to find out about their skills and education.

5. What do you think is the most important issue that needs to be addressed by government in your community, the country, or globally? Design a visual representation of your issue and send it to the appropriate government department, explaining why you selected that level of government.

Applying: To Be Active

6. At one time the Bloc Québécois was the Official Opposition—the opposition party with the most seats. The intent of this political party is to break up Confederation. Is it appropriate to have a party whose main goal is to divide the nation as Her Majesty's Loyal Opposition? Defend your position.

7. You have been hired by the government to produce an information kit for first-time voters. What materials and information would you include in your kit? Your kit could include visuals, videos, CDs, etc. Provide a short rationale for each item you include.

3 CHAPTER

CANADA'S LEGAL SYSTEM

Rolling for Justice

Figure 3-1 Would you be willing to roll the dice to determine if you should be punished for a crime you may or may not have committed?

Let's play "Rolling for Justice." The directions are simple. For each scenario listed on the next page, roll the dice to determine a legal consequence. Record the outcomes for each of the six accused.

Possible Outcomes

- If you roll a one, no charge is laid.
- If you roll a two, a warning is issued.
- If you roll a three, the accused gets five years in prison.
- If you roll a four, the accused gets ten years in prison.
- If you roll a five, the accused is fined $1000.
- If you roll a six, the accused is fined $5000.

Literacy Hint

Activate Your Background Knowledge. What do you know about people who have been involved in a legal situation?

Scenarios

- Mehemed was crossing the street on a red light when he was spotted by a police officer. In other words, he was jay walking.
- Although she received a notice, Tabatha failed to appear in court for jury duty.
- Michelle was caught robbing a convenience store.
- Trouble had been brewing between two students at school and finally one decided to act. A fight broke out after school. One of the students was rushed to hospital with severe injuries. The other was arrested.
- Dana stole Shoba's MP3 player from the girls' locker room.
- The police were called to Doug's house because he was playing loud music after 11:00 p.m.

Discussion

Talk with a partner about your overall observations and conclusions.

1. How do you feel after going through this experience?

2. Did anyone get treated too harshly or too softly?

3. What could be done to avoid these random decisions?

4. Why does this not happen in reality in Canada?

KEY LEARNINGS

In this chapter you will explore the following topics:
- the rights and responsibilities of Canadian citizenship
- how the judicial system protects the rights of individuals and society
- how a citizen's rights and responsibilities can be either upheld or restricted
- the civic literacy skills of preparing a persuasive argument and making an effective presentation

What Are My Responsibilities and Rights?

Literacy Hint

Make a Connection. Think about your own situation first. What rights do you have in your home? What are your ongoing responsibilities as a member of a family? Which come first: rights or responsibilities?

Suppose a visitor to Canada asks you what it means to be a Canadian citizen. What would you say? You might mention that you have free health care, great sports—especially hockey and lacrosse—that you live in the second largest geographic nation in the world, and that it is a multicultural nation. If you thought further you also might say that you live in a democracy where you are guaranteed certain rights such as the right to vote, freedom of speech, and the right to a fair judicial system. All of these statements are accurate. That probably explains why the United Nations has at various times declared Canada to be the best country in the world to live in. However, with rights also come responsibilities.

When you join a sports team you are welcomed to a new community. You know that for the team to be a success, each member has both rights and responsibilities. You have the right to play on the team as an active member. You also have the responsibilities to obey the coach and participate in practices. Similarly, Canadian citizens have rights protected under the law and responsibilities to be good citizens. Is it possible to have rights without responsibilities? Your rights may be personal, but your responsibilities have an effect on others.

Figure 3-2 You have the right to eat your lunch in a clean, healthy cafeteria. What are your responsibilities in the cafeteria?

An example of a case involving student rights occurred in the Toronto District School Board in March 2005. Some students felt they should not be forced to participate in animal dissections in their Biology class. These dissections were done on preserved unborn pigs. Some students claimed religious objections. Other students, some who were vegetarians, felt sickened by the exercise.

A school trustee took up the case. He felt that if students were not given a choice between the actual dissections and using a computer program, their rights under the *Charter of Rights and Freedoms* were being violated. The students should have the right to refuse to take part in the dissection. However, they had the responsibility to learn the material in another manner. They could not use their objections as an excuse not to do the work or learn the content. Rights and responsibilities, in this case, went hand in hand.

What Are the Origins of Canadian Law?

Our system of laws has been influenced by three different judicial systems—Aboriginal, French, and British.

The Ojibwa, Pottowatomi, and Odawa made up the Anishinabe nation. These people lived primarily in the area around the Great Lakes. Their family and clan groups were led by a chief and an informal council of elders who oversaw the camps of their people. Decisions were made by consensus. The elders, chosen for their leadership abilities, used persuasion to gain acceptance for individual and group decisions. Men's societies were formed to enforce the rules when consensus could not be reached. Such intervention was rarely required. Early European writers were impressed by the lack of coercion employed by various Aboriginal governing systems like this one.

The French introduced their system of laws that included the *French Civil Code*. This Code was a series of laws that evolved from the Roman system of codified laws. It set out a list of crimes and penalties that were to be used in courts. The French influence would go through a number of changes from the laws of kings to the republican laws of the revolution to the codified laws of Napoleon. The *French Civil Code* formed the basis of the *Quebec Civil Code* used in Quebec today.

Britain had a parliamentary system with a House of Commons and a House of Lords. As the British established colonies around the world, they put their parliamentary and judicial systems in place. As a result, the fundamentals of British law apply to Canada. These fundamental rights include **habeas corpus,** which puts the burden of proof on the Crown and ensures certain legal rights.

Figure 3-3 The *French Civil Code* is still practised in some of France's former colonies, such as Louisiana, and in some countries controlled by France at the time of Napoleon, such as Belgium.

habeas corpus: the right of an accused to know the nature of the charge, the right to a fair and speedy trial, and the right to be presumed innocent until found guilty

common law: law developed in English courts that relies on case law and is common to all people

Common law forms the basis of British and Canadian law. Common law developed from the decisions made by the courts. Sometimes it is called case law. Judges look for previous cases that had similar circumstances to make their decisions. When there are no similar cases, the judge's decision sets a new example to be followed by others. Common law is not written in a formal code. It can adapt to the times. The rule of law is a fundamental principle of British common law. It seeks to make the law fair and accessible to all.

Canada also has codified some of its laws. This means that our laws have been arranged and recorded systematically. These records provide a description of a crime and the range of sentences that could be applied to a guilty party.

Criminal Law

As you saw in the opening activity, without a justice system, your fate could be determined by luck. Laws help maintain fair treatment for everyone in Canada. The law is divided into two parts: criminal law and civil law. Criminal cases reflect actions of an individual against society. Robbery, assault, and murder are examples of criminal offences. For instance, murder has an impact on all members of society who seek peace and order. In Canada, criminal law, or public law, is governed by the *Criminal Code of Canada*. The Code defines the various crimes and sets out the sentences for guilty parties. An example of a definition found in the *Criminal Code* deals with theft. Section 322 of the *Criminal Code* defines theft as:

(1) Every one commits theft who fraudulently [illegally] and without colour of right [belief that a person owns an item or property] takes, or fraudulently and without colour of right converts to his use or to the use of another person, anything, whether animate or inanimate, with intent

(*a*) to deprive, temporarily or absolutely, the owner of it, or a person who has a special property or interest in it, of the thing or of his property or interest in it;

(*b*) to pledge it or deposit it as security;

(*c*) to part with it under a condition with respect to its return that the person who parts with it may be unable to perform; or

(*d*) to deal with it in such a manner that it cannot be restored in the condition in which it was at the time it was taken or converted.

Literacy Hint

Think About It. A code is a set of rules that is written down for dealing with different situations. Your school's dress code and code of behaviour are examples. Reread the definition and description of *common law*. Talk to a partner about the ways that common law differs from a code.

Active Citizen

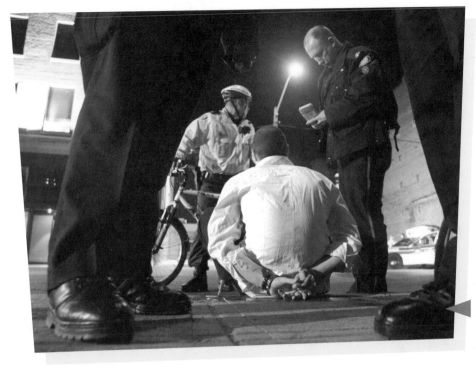

Figure 3-4 When a person is arrested, the accused is charged under the *Criminal Code*. What rights do you think the accused has?

The sentence for a guilty conviction is also specified in section 334 of the Code:

Except where otherwise provided by law, every one who commits theft

(*a*) is guilty of an indictable [serious] offence and liable to imprisonment for a term not exceeding ten years, where the property stolen is a testamentary [related to a will] instrument or the value of what is stolen exceeds five thousand dollars; or

(*b*) is guilty
    (i) of an indictable offence and is liable to imprisonment for a term not exceeding two years, or

    (ii) of an offence punishable on summary conviction (light penalty), where the value of what is stolen does not exceed five thousand dollars.

Can you see why people seek legal help to interpret our laws? The *Criminal Code* applies to all provinces and territories. It is meant to provide consistent definitions of criminal acts and sentences.

Civil Law

Civil law, or private law, deals with disputes between individuals and companies. It has many branches. Civil law deals with torts, contracts, family issues, wills and estates, property matters, and employment. A tort is harm or damage done to another person or that person's property. For example, let's say you teach snowboarding on the weekends. You have been invited to a party at a friend's house. As you leave, you slip on an icy patch in the driveway and break your leg in three places. You won't be able to teach snowboarding for the rest of the season. You could sue your friend for your lost wages because he neglected to salt the icy patch.

As attitudes and technology change, efforts are made to keep civil law contemporary. The Internet is one example. Is shopping online safe? When you give out personal information, who has access to it? To protect Canadians, the federal government passed the *Personal Information Protection and Electronic Documents Act*. This Act sets out guidelines for assuring individual privacy. It also indicates where information obtained electronically may legally be used. For example, if the information suggests that a crime has taken place or may take place, the information can be shared with the proper authorities. The Ontario government passed the *Municipal Freedom of Information and Protection of Privacy Act*. This Act provides the right of access to information. It also protects the privacy of citizens who provide personal information to the government or institutions. Nova Scotia and British Columbia have similar legislation.

Figure 3-5 What kind of information have you provided to others over the Internet?

In 2003, a Calgary resident received a credit card bill for over $20 000. He immediately knew that these were not his charges since his average bill was $500. He contacted his credit card company and learned that someone had stolen his credit card information. He didn't have to pay the bill and was issued a new card. This example of violation of privacy and theft is becoming more common. In extreme cases, people have had their identities stolen. Their personal information has been used to acquire passports, social insurance numbers, and credit cards. Such abuses can result in low credit rating, and it may take years to rebuild a financial reputation.

Both criminal and civil systems are meant to provide individuals and society with protection and justice.

CHECKPOINT

1. **Which three judicial systems influenced the development of Canada's legal system?**
2. **What is the difference between criminal and civil law?**
3. **What examples can you find to prove that the legal system needs to evolve if it is to address new crimes?**

Criminal System

Without a clear legal system that seeks justice, citizens are often at the mercy of the powerful. This was the case in Iraq under the government of Saddam Hussein. His legal system violated the rights of his people. The judges and lawyers of the legal system supported these violations, because they owed their positions to the government.

In August 2003, the United States and Britain toppled Hussein's government. The US government tried to establish a new legal system to restore order and prosecute criminals and political prisoners. However, before a new system could be put in place, the country was in chaos. People may have felt as you did when you rolled the dice at the beginning of this chapter. They had no idea what the punishment would be for any particular crime.

Canada's legal system is quite clear. The criminal system includes guidelines for the arrest and detention of the accused, trial procedures, and sentencing for those found guilty. All three elements work together to provide Canadians with a legal system that protects the innocent and punishes the guilty.

Figure 3-6 Criminal prisoners wait for their cases to be heard in Baghdad in August 2003. What challenges would lawmakers face in developing a new legal system in Iraq?

Charter of Rights and Freedoms

Canada's legal system is meant to protect society. People in Canada have rights guaranteed under the *Charter of Rights and Freedoms*. The Charter was established in 1982 and includes legal, language, and democratic rights to protect Canadians from abuses of power by governments.

Literacy Hint

Make a Prediction. What are some of the key rights and freedoms under the Charter? Check your predictions after reading the Going to the Source feature on page 71.

Figure 3-7 What Charter right does this photograph illustrate?

Below are excerpts from the *Charter of Rights and Freedoms*. Because the Charter is part of our Constitution, none of these rights can be taken away by the government.

Fundamental Freedoms

2. Everyone has the following fundamental freedoms:
   a) freedom of conscience and religion;
   b) freedom of thought, belief, opinion and expression, including freedom of the press and other media of communication;
   c) freedom of peaceful assembly; and
   d) freedom of association.

Democratic Rights

3. Every citizen of Canada has the right to vote in an election of members of the House of Commons or of a legislative assembly and to be qualified for membership therein.

Mobility Rights

6. (1) Every citizen of Canada has the right to enter, remain in and leave Canada.

Legal Rights

7. Everyone has the right to life, liberty and security of the person and the right not to be deprived thereof except in accordance with the principles of fundamental justice.
10. Everyone has the right on arrest or detention
    a) to be informed promptly of the reasons therefor;
    b) to retain [acquire] and instruct counsel without delay and to be informed of that right; and
    c) to have the validity of the detention determined by way of habeas corpus and to be released if the detention is not lawful.
11. Any person charged with an offence has the right
    a) to be informed without unreasonable delay of the specific offence;
    b) to be tried within a reasonable time;
    c) not to be compelled to be a witness in proceedings against that person in respect of the offence;
    d) to be presumed innocent until proven guilty according to law in a fair and public hearing by an independent and impartial [unbiased] tribunal;
    e) not to be denied reasonable bail without just cause;
    f) except in the case of an offence under military law tried before a military tribunal, to the benefit of trial by jury where the maximum punishment for the offence is imprisonment for five years or a more severe punishment;
    g) not to be found guilty on account of any act or omission unless, at the time of the act or omission, it constituted an offence under Canadian or international law or was criminal according to the general principles of law recognized by the community of nations [meaning the accused should not be found guilty unless an act is committed against Canadian or international law];
    h) if finally acquitted of the offence, not to be tried for it again and, if finally found guilty and punished for the offence, not to be tried or punished for it again; and
    i) if found guilty of the offence and if the punishment for the offence has been varied between the time of commission and the time of sentencing, to the benefit of the lesser punishment [meaning if found guilty and the law regarding sentencing has changed between the time of the crime and the sentencing, the lesser time is to be served].

1. Which of the above rights do you think are the most important for Canadians?

2. What rights would you add to these?

Just think, without the Charter:

- you could be arrested by police on your way to school, the mall, or a movie theatre without any reason
- you could be held by the police for an undefined time period and not be able to contact your parents/guardians
- you might not be able to protest against the government
- you might not be able to watch any television shows you like that are not approved by the government
- you might not be able to freely travel around the country.

These restrictions actually exist in some countries that do not guarantee citizen rights. Unlike other laws that can be struck down, your Charter rights cannot be taken away, because they are part of the Constitution.

Figure 3-8 How would you feel if the police detained you and your friends at the mall without having reasonable cause to do so?

Literacy Hint

Think Critically. What do you consider your most important rights under the Charter?

The Charter also states that the fundamental freedoms are only limited by what is considered reasonable in a democratic state. This means that your rights can be limited. You have the responsibility to respect the rights of others. For example, freedom of speech does not allow you to spread hate messages or threaten others. Consider the case of Ernst Zundel, a white supremacist. In 2005, he was deported to his native Germany after being convicted of spreading hate crimes against Jews and other groups. Zundel used the Charter to appeal his conviction. He claimed it protected his right of expression and opinion. The federal courts and the Supreme Court of Canada ruled that Zundel had stepped over the limits imposed in the Charter. His rights did not extend to the abuse of others.

Section 25 also limits the application of the Charter. It protects the existing rights of Aboriginal peoples, such as treaty rights.

Restricting Individual Rights:
The Arar Case

After the 9/11 attacks on the World Trade Center in New York City, many governments gave police more power to arrest and possibly deport suspected terrorists. On December 18, 2001, the Governor General signed into law Canada's own *Anti-Terrorism Act*. It includes the following:

- Police are allowed to set up electronic surveillance of suspected terrorists for up to one year.
- Police do not need to notify the person for up to three years.
- Police can require people to provide information on terrorist groups where they have reason to believe the person has information.
- Police can arrest suspects who they reasonably assume might try to leave the country.

This is a controversial issue. How much do you restrict individual rights to protect society? Societies must decide if fear of a threat by someone is a reasonable justification for limiting individual rights.

Figure 3-9 Maher Arar and his wife, Monia Mazigh.

In September 2002, Maher Arar, a Canadian citizen, was arrested in the John F. Kennedy airport in New York City. He was held in US custody under suspicion of having links to terrorist organizations. After two-weeks, he was deported to his native Syria. Critics suggest that since prisoners cannot be tortured legally in the United States, the government deported him to Syria, where torture is one interrogation procedure.

In 2003, Arar was released and returned to Canada. He started an investigation into why Canadian authorities had not been notified of his arrest and why he had not been deported to Canada. As a Canadian citizen he had the right to seek legal assistance from the Canadian consulate in New York. His investigation uncovered evidence that the US authorities had notified the RCMP of his arrest. The RCMP, however, had also suspected Arar of terrorist links. Based on this evidence, the government launched an inquiry into the circumstances of Arar's deportation and whether his rights had been compromised.

In June 2005, Arar received an apology from the Canadian government.

1. Why was Arar detained and deported to Syria?
2. Which of his rights as a Canadian citizen may have been violated?
3. Should governments have the authority to restrict individual rights where terrorism is suspected? Explain.

CHECKPOINT

1. Why was it felt necessary to include a list of guaranteed rights in the *Constitution Act, 1982*, under the *Charter of Rights and Freedoms*?

2. Select three rights guaranteed in the Charter and explain situations that might justify limiting them.

Legal Process

The *Criminal Code of Canada* identifies transgressions, or crimes, against society. A person who violates a section of the Code is charged. The *Criminal Code* has evolved over the years to include new types of crimes. For example, new laws deal with the Internet. These are also laws that target child pornographic sites and Internet bullying sites. Who could have foreseen such violations years ago? You can explore the issue of bullying on pages 76–77.

"You Are Under Arrest"

To better explore criminal procedures, let's look at a fictional case study. We'll follow two teens through various stages.

Mitchell and Silvana were both 18 years old and in Grade 12. They had known each other since Grade 9. They both lived at home but each experienced different lifestyles. Mitchell's father was unemployed and his mother worked to help pay the bills. Mitchell wanted to help but had difficulty finding a job because he had trouble with the law when he was 14. Silvana was doing well at school and had a part-time job. She didn't mind living at home but felt her parents were too strict. She wanted a little more independence.

One night Mitchell invited Silvana to go for a drive. While driving to Silvana's house, Mitchell realized he was short on money. Too embarrassed to borrow from Silvana, he decided to find it another way. He picked Silvana up and drove to the local convenience store. Once they were inside, Silvana noticed Mitchell was acting strange. He watched the owner, while pretending to look at some magazines.

All of a sudden Mitchell jumped over the counter and demanded that the owner open the cash register. Silvana could not believe her eyes! When the owner hesitated, Mitchell hit him in the face. The owner started to bleed and opened the cash register. Mitchell yelled at Silvana to help him collect the money. Silvana was not sure what to do, but when Mitchell yelled again she rushed over. She took the money and headed to the door. The owner's wife came out from behind a curtain and lunged at her. Silvana ran to the door and

Active Citizen
Website
For links to sites on dealing with bullying

Literacy Hint

Access Your Background Knowledge. Think of students or even friends you know who have had legal troubles. What faulty decisions led to an encounter with the law?

knocked over the owner's wife. The woman fell and hit her head on the floor. Both teens ran to the car and drove off. The owner made sure that his wife was all right and then called 911.

Figure 3-10 What kind of information does a video surveillance camera provide to police regarding the suspect?

What steps do you think the police would follow to capture Mitchell and Silvana?

Silvana and Mitchell drove around town trying to calm their nerves. Silvana was both shocked and excited about what had happened. Mitchell tried to explain how frustrating it was not to have any money. They pulled into a local fast-food restaurant and ordered some burgers. Suddenly, a patrol car pulled up behind them and two police officers approached Mitchell's car. One officer told Mitchell that the car had a missing brake light. She asked to see his licence and ownership. She returned to the cruiser to check on the ownership, while her partner remained by the car. Both Mitchell and Silvana were very nervous and scared but tried to remain calm. When the officer returned, she asked the two teens to exit the car. When Mitchell stood up, money fell from his pocket.

The officer told the teens that they resembled a description of two teens that had just robbed a convenience store.

What charges do you think Mitchell and Silvana would face? Turn to page 79 to find out more.

Figure 3-11 How would you feel if you were Mitchell or Silvana and the police arrested you?

Issue Analysis

Bullying can take many different forms. It can range from physical assaults to cyberspace bashing. You are being bullied if you are:

- being forced to surrender your cafeteria lunch money
- having your homework taken and copied
- getting email that makes negative comments about you
- finding a chat room where your appearance and personality are being ridiculed.

What is your definition of bullying? Whether it is about someone's body shape, hair colour, race, or clothing, bullying is pervasive.

How should bullies be treated to prevent further actions and to address immediate incidents? Determine which of these possible responses would best address the question.

"Bullying is harassment. It means making someone feel bad about who they are."
—Jasmin, Grade 12

"Bullies make people feel unworthy through verbal and physical harassment."
—Jacquie and Carolyn, Grade 12

Literacy Hint

Put Yourself in the Picture. If you witnessed or experienced bullying, where would you stand? Would you be part of the problem or part of the solution?

PERSON	SOLUTION
Parent #1	• All kids go through this bullying phase in their lives. • Kids always tease each other and learn to cope. • This issue is overblown in the media.
Parent #2	• The child needs to be spoken to and taught how harmful bullying can be to other children. • If another incident happens, the child should be punished, perhaps by restricting activities.
Teacher/Principal	• The student needs to be counselled about the impact that bullying actions have on others. • The student should be suspended for a second occurrence and the parents/guardians notified.
Police	• Bring in police officers to talk to the offender and explain the seriousness of the act. Issue a warning. • If bullying increases in frequency and severity, charge the student with harassment or assault and bring the offender to court.

Bullying primarily focuses on verbal and physical abuse. Sometimes, it leads to more tragic results. Read about Reena Virk and think about the kind of bullying that took place. How do you think these bullies should have been punished?

Date of Offence	• November 14, 1997
Victim's Name and Age	• Reena Virk (14 years old)
Sequence of Events	• Reena and several other youths gathered at a secondary school near Victoria, British Columbia.
	• An argument broke out between Reena and another girl.
	• Then, six girls physically assaulted Reena.
	• After the first assault, 16-year-old Warren Glowatski and Kelly Ellard, aged 15, severely beat Reena again.
	• Reena was dragged to a nearby gorge and held under water until she drowned.
	• One week later, Reena's body was found.
	• Warren was charged and convicted of second-degree murder. He received a life sentence with no chance of parole for seven years.
	• Kelly Ellard was convicted of second-degree murder, but appealed her conviction. Her second trial resulted in a hung jury (not all jurors could agree on a verdict).
Current Legal Situation	• In her third trial, Kelly Ellard was found guilty of second-degree murder in April 2005. She was sentenced to life imprisonment and will be eligible for parole in seven years.
	• She appealed the conviction and is seeking either an acquittal or a fourth trial.

Proactive approaches to bullying are being taken. Depending on the severity of the situation, these include:

• after-school programs with activities for young people

• anti-bullying campaigns that offer solutions to the problem

• programs that focus on productive activities for bullies and potential bullies

• arrests either under the *Criminal Code of Canada* or the *Youth Criminal Justice Act*, for those under 18 years of age.

1. Is bullying a problem in your school? What types of bullying occur?

2. How do you think bullying should be dealt with?

3. Find out if your school has an anti-bullying strategy. If it does, examine the program and assess its effectiveness. If it doesn't, as a class design an effective program.

Preparing a Persuasive Argument

Imagine yourself in trouble with the law. As you appear before the court, who do you want at your side to defend you?

- Your parents—who will say they love you and that you are a good person
- Your brother or sister—who will say that you're okay with them…at least most of the time
- A powerful lawyer or advocate—who will help the judge or jury understand the difficult situation you were in and the reasons you chose to act as you did (an advocate speaks on behalf of another person or persons, or in favour of a certain position).

Now, imagine you are the victim of bullying. You have to convey your fear, anxiety, and need for powerful intervention to school administrators. They believe that school is a place where you learn to survive no matter what the circumstance.

The ability to speak persuasively and powerfully is the skill you need in both these situations. There are three keys to being a powerful persuader whether you are writing or speaking:

- Have a clear purpose and feel the passion of your cause
- Know your audience and how to involve them in your topic
- Provide details or evidence that will convince the audience to think your way.

Purpose and Passion

Start by thinking, "What do I want to accomplish with this piece of writing, or this speech? What do I want my readers or audience to think, feel, and even more important, do when they finish reading my piece or hearing me speak?

For example: *I want the administrators to understand that the victims of bullying become less confident of dealing with their situation with each new incident. They are not capable of dealing with the problem alone, but require powerful and swift assistance.*

Know and Appeal to Your Audience

If you know and understand your audience, then you can find ways to involve them in your topic. You need some insight into how audience members may think. Speak straight to their frame of reference (See page 46 in Chapter 2 for "frame of reference.")

For example: *I know that school administrators have many jobs and may not consider bullying situations as top priorities. I need to give them insight into the victim and mob psychology so that they will realize the need to take action.*

Provide the Evidence

You might say that you have to put the PIE in persuasion — the Proofs, Illustrations, and Examples. If you want your reader or audience to understand what you think and feel, you have to give them a way to think and feel the same things. Powerful anecdotes, as already mentioned, are one way to get the message across. Here are some others:

- Statistics—Well-researched facts and figures are convincing. What statistics about bullying would make your case stronger?
- Draw a thumbnail sketch—Describe the appearance and emotional state of a bullying victim with a few sharp details that appeal to the senses.
- Quote an authority—Present an insight from an expert.

Note the quotations on page 76 about bullying and bullies. Which detail is most convincing to you?

- Give some history or background to the situation, mentioning especially the actions that can make a difference. Note the legal history of the Reena Virk case that shows how far bullying can go, and the legal consequences.

You Try It

Choose an issue that has been raised in your class, school, or community. Consider your own thoughts, feelings, and knowledge about this issue. Use some of the methods suggested to develop a persuasive argument that will convince your friends, parents, or classmates of the right course of action on this issue.

Preparing for the Trial

Mitchell and Silvana were taken to the police station where they both called their parents. They were worried about their parents' reactions. Mitchell's parents were angry but managed to keep their composure. Silvana's parents were very upset and kept asking her "Why?" The teens were fingerprinted and photographed while their parents tried to arrange **bail**. Silvana was granted bail since this was her first offence. Mitchell was detained because of his previous crime as a young offender. Both parents acquired legal help to prepare for the upcoming trial.

bail: temporary release of the accused granted in exchange for money or some form of security to ensure the accused will appear for trial

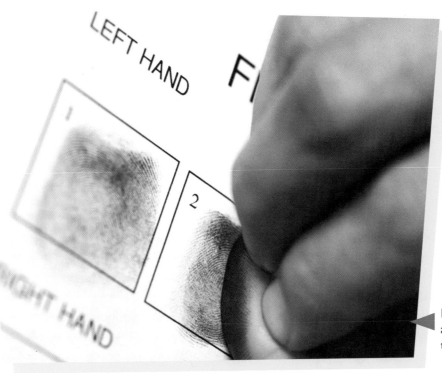

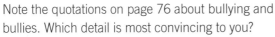

Figure 3-12 Why would having the accused's fingerprints on file be useful to police?

Crown: attorneys who represent the monarch and prosecute the accused on behalf of the community

conviction: the decision indicating that the accused is guilty of a criminal offence

The Charter requires that an accused be given a fair trial within a reasonable time period. However, gathering evidence and contacting witnesses also requires a lot of time. The purpose of a trial is for the accused to face representatives of the community or state. Since Canada is a constitutional monarchy, the community is represented by the monarch. The lawyers who represent the monarch are thus called the **Crown.** The Crown's purpose is to develop a case against an accused and seek a **conviction.**

Figure 3-13 Some schools put on mock trials for students to learn more about the judicial process. Larry Au took part in one of these trials at his school. He is considering a career as a police officer or a lawyer. He would like to try to simplify the legal language used so that all citizens can understand the procedures in trial cases.

acquittal: the decision indicating that the accused is not guilty of the charges brought against an accused

plea bargain: a deal between the Crown and a defendant, whereby the defendant pleads guilty in exchange for a lighter sentence

The role of defence counsel is to protect the rights of the accused, question the Crown's evidence, and seek an **acquittal.** Crown attorneys have to prove beyond a reasonable doubt that the accused is guilty of the crime. It is up to the Crown to prove its case; defence counsel merely has to establish reasonable doubt on the Crown's case to gain an acquittal. Defence counsel does not have to prove the innocence of the accused.

Prior to the trial, the Crown discovered that the owner and his wife were not totally certain that Mitchell and Silvana were the intruders because everything had happened so quickly. The Crown met with Silvana's defence counsel and proposed a **plea bargain.** The Crown would not demand jail time for Silvana if she testified against Mitchell. Silvana's parents convinced her to agree.

Your Day in Court

Mitchell and Silvana were brought into court on their appointed date. In some cases the suspect has a choice of trial by jury of one's peers or by a judge. Why might it be important to use a jury of one's peers?

All Canadian trials follow the same sequence as shown on the next page.

> **Literacy Hint**
>
> Think about what you already know about the court process. Write down the sequence of events based on your knowledge. Then, check to see which steps you may have omitted by reading the next section.

Active Citizen

Figure 3-14 The Canadian Trial Process

Crown ▶

Makes the opening statement
- Identifies the offence committed
- Summarizes the evidence that will be presented against the accused

Witnesses ▶

Examination of Witnesses
- Each witness takes an oath swearing to tell the truth, either by swearing on a Bible or making a formal statement.
- If the witness lies while on the stand, he or she can be charged with *perjury*.
- Answers questions from the Crown
- Is cross-examined by the defence

perjury: the criminal offence of knowingly making false statements in court while giving evidence under oath

Defence ▶

Follows the same procedure as the Crown
- If the suspect had an *alibi* for the crime, it would be presented.
- Crown cross-examines defence witnesses.

alibi: the defence that the accused was elsewhere when the offence was committed

Crown, then Defence ▶

Each side makes a final address to the judge and jury
- Summarizes their main points of the case

Judge ▶

Charges the jury
- Explains the charges as defined in the *Criminal Code*
- Indicates that all jury members must agree on the outcome: a unanimous decision

Figure 3-15 The judge plays an essential role in trials. What qualities do you think a judge should have? Pictured here is a mock trial where law students can test their skills.

People Power

Occupation: Chief Executive Officer of the National Aboriginal Achievement Foundation (NAAF)

Contribution: Roberta Jamieson demonstrated that women have provided and continue to provide effective leadership in First Nations communities

Fast Facts:
- First Aboriginal woman in Canada to earn a law degree, graduating from the University of Western Ontario in 1976
- One of the founders of the Native Law Students Association of Canada
- First non-parliamentarian appointed to a House of Commons committee
- First Aboriginal commissioner of the Indian Commission of Ontario
- First woman to be appointed Ombudsman for Ontario
- In 1994, appointed to the Order of Canada
- In 2001, first female elected Chief of the Six Nations of the Grand River

Her Story: Roberta Jamieson is a Mohawk from Six Nations of the Grand River Territory. She is a strong advocate of Aboriginal legal rights. Jamieson recognizes that her people have suffered due to lack of respect and acknowledgement from many levels of government. She herself experienced racism and sexism in her life. Yet, she continues to encourage First Nations peoples and governments in Canada to seek a dialogue based on mutual respect and the desire to deal fairly with one another.

Figure 3-16 In what ways does Roberta Jamieson continue the tradition of female leadership in First Nations communities?

Mediating disputes has been a constant theme in her public life. Jamieson believes she is following in the footsteps of Aboriginal women of the past who were what she calls "the conscience of the councils" and helped groups reach consensus. She believes that when consensus is reached, a long-lasting relationship is established.

Roberta Jamieson continues to inspire Aboriginal youth and women through speeches, international travel, and presentations to government committees. She symbolizes optimism and determination.

1. Which of her qualities would make Jamieson a good role model?
2. Why does Jamieson value reaching consensus?

Sentencing

The jury has a grave responsibility. The jury can either find an accused not guilty and release the person with no criminal record, or find the accused guilty and create a criminal record. If an accused is found guilty, the judge has some options in sentencing. The decision may depend on the seriousness of the crime.

Crime	Punishment
Murder	First degree: automatic 25 years
Theft	Under $5000: maximum 2 years Over $5000: maximum 10 years
Use of firearm in committing a crime	1–14 years
Spreading Hate Propaganda	Maximum 2 years

Figure 3-17 Range of sentences for sample crimes

Other than for first-degree murder (murder that is **premeditated**), the judge may impose a sentence ranging from the minimum to the maximum number of years. Except for first-degree murder offences, an inmate must be reviewed for **parole** after serving one-third of the sentence, or after seven years, whichever is less. When deciding on a sentence, a number of items are considered:

- rights of the victim to be protected from further crime
- rights of victims to present their concerns in the form of **impact statements** that explain how they have been affected by the crime
- rights of society to be protected from criminals
- right of the convicted to a sentence that matches the seriousness of the crime
- right of the convicted to participate in **rehabilitation** programs which provide the convicted person with counselling, skills, and advice to help the person re-enter society as a contributing member.

premeditated: planned ahead of time

parole: early release with conditions, such as reporting to a parole officer, not leaving a community, accepting a curfew

impact statement: a series of paragraphs written by either the victim or relatives of a victim outlining how the actions of the convicted affected their lives.

rehabilitation: the process of restoring to former standing, rights, privileges, reputation

Informed to Be Effective

A person called for jury duty must be 18 years old and a Canadian citizen. The list of potential jurors is generated randomly from the voters' list. Not all people called actually sit on a jury. Some are excused for various reasons. What reasons do you think a judge would accept to dismiss a potential juror? Would you like to serve on a jury if given the opportunity? Why do you think some people try to avoid jury duty?

Literacy Hint

Think Critically. What is your response to the sentences given to Silvana and Mitchell? Do you think that justice was served? Discuss with a partner.

Both Mitchell and Silvana were found guilty. Since Silvana did not have a prior criminal record and had agreed to testify against Mitchell, she was given a **suspended sentence.** She was placed on **probation** and ordered to perform community service that included talking to elementary school students about avoiding peer pressure. Mitchell was sentenced to a prison term.

Once the verdict is given both the Crown or the defence can **appeal** the decision, if either side feels there was an error in law. Appeals could be launched if defence counsel feels that the evidence provided was not properly handled or presented or that the judge acted in a manner that might have misled the jury. The Crown could appeal if the attorneys feel that the sentence was too lenient or that the judge prejudiced the jury. The Court of Appeal is the next level of courts. A decision by the Court of Appeal can also be appealed to the highest court—the Supreme Court of Canada.

Goals of Sentencing

The purpose of sentencing is to have the offender pay his or her debt to society and begin rehabilitation. The logic behind rehabilitation is to provide treatment and training to help offenders function in society. This reduces the chances that they will commit a new offence.

Figure 3-18 An artist's drawing shows Justice Catherine Wedge sentencing a man convicted of second-degree murder of his 17-year-old daughter. What do you think the judge needs to consider before deciding on a sentence?

Once Mitchell entered prison he found out about the various programs available to him. Mitchell had never been a strong student and always found reading difficult. He enrolled in a remedial reading program taught by teachers assigned to the prison. He also took an anger management course and learned how to deal with his frustration. The routine of prison also helped Mitchell develop his organizational skills since he worked part of the

Rights After Release

In July 2005 Karla Homolka was released from prison after serving her full 15-year sentence. She was convicted as an accessory to the murder of a number of teenage girls in the 1990s. Her husband at the time, Paul Bernardo, was sentenced to life in prison. As Homolka's release grew near, there was a strong public outcry for restrictions on her movements, where she could live, and what friends she could make.

There was a fear that she might reoffend. The courts had to balance society's fears with Homolka's rights. On one hand, she had served her full sentence. On the other hand, society had a right to be protected from possible future crimes. In the end, the courts set limitations. For a one-year period, she had to report to police on a regular basis and inform them of any change of address. After a year, another application would have to be made to the courts to have her re-evaluated as a potential threat.

1. Do offenders who have served their full sentences deserve the same rights as all citizens? Explain your view.

day in the prison kitchen. His good behaviour and work ethic convinced the parole board that Mitchell should be given day parole at a halfway house. This group home allows inmates more freedom during the day, but requires them to return to the home each night.

When inmates are released, organizations and programs are available to help them rehabilitate. The John Howard and Elizabeth Fry societies support

Figure 3-19 What help would individuals require after being released from prison to re-enter society?

Literacy Hint

Ask Yourself Questions. Which justice system would have a greater impact on an offender in your view? Are there some offenders who cannot be rehabilitated do you think?

sentencing circle: a justice system used in some Aboriginal communities that involves a process of healing for both the victim and the offender

Figure 3-20 Aboriginal Ganootamaage Justice Services of Winnipeg volunteers take part in a sentencing circle for a 20-year-old shoplifter, not shown in the photo, at the Aboriginal Centre. What impression does a sentencing circle give compared with a traditional courtroom?

male and female offenders and ensure their rights are protected. They also encourage and assist in rehabilitation. Both societies provide counselling and support groups for individuals while they are in prison and after their release. The societies also monitor the penal system to ensure the rights of the inmates are respected. They assist integration back into society by providing temporary housing, employment counselling, and educational opportunities. Both societies believe that the chances of individuals reoffending decrease if they are treated with respect and provided with the skills and support they need.

The Canadian legal system has recognized the cultural diversity of the nation and has allowed cultural values to be considered in sentencing. In parts of the country that have large Aboriginal populations, the courts have reintroduced Aboriginal forms of justice. These include community **sentencing circles** and penalties such as banishment from the community. The use of sentencing circles recognizes that some guilty parties with deep roots in a community can be reconciled with the victim and community. To be eligible for a sentencing circle:

- The convicted offender must be recommended.
- Respected elders must be willing to participate.
- The victim must be present or be represented.
- The court system must agree to suspend the usual sentence.

The offender is presented with the impact of the criminal act on the victim and community. A number of punishment options are available, such as:

- community service work
- compulsory school or work attendance
- participation in Aboriginal spiritual activities, such as sweats and forgiveness/sacrifice ceremonies
- participation in Aboriginal cultural activities, such as powwow security, elder assistant, and cleaning grounds
- curfew rules and regulations
- disassociation from the negative influence of peers
- speaking/teaching to students.

CHECKPOINT

1. How are the rights of the accused protected in a trial?
2. What purpose does sentencing someone found guilty hope to achieve?
3. What are some alternatives to prison for those who commit an offence?

Rights for All

Canada's system prides itself on protecting the rights of the accused and victims. The accused has the right to have an attorney and be presented with the Crown's case prior to the trial. Evidence that is submitted must be properly obtained. Otherwise, it may be rejected. Searching a residence without a warrant or stopping someone without just cause are examples of ways evidence is inappropriately obtained. Sometimes people feel that the accused have more rights than the victims. They feel that minor infractions should be allowed if the evidence proves the accused is guilty. Such an attitude has led to some wrongful convictions. Individuals and groups fought to have these cases reviewed. Two of these people—David Milgaard and Donald Marshall—were later released.

Figure 3-21 Some Canadians have argued that recognizing mistakes were made and dealing properly with them is an indication that our legal system works. Do you agree with this claim?

Suspect	Summary of Events	Concerns and Actions of Involved Citizens	Eventual Outcome
Steven Truscott	• 1959, 14 year old charged with the murder of 12-year-old Lynne Harper • convicted and sentenced to death • sentence is changed to life in prison • 1969, released and assumed another identity	• 1966, *The Trial of Steven Truscott* by Isabel LeBourdais questions the trial and verdict • 2000, Truscott seeks help from the Association in Defence of the Wrongfully Convicted, which files a motion asking the Minister of Justice to review the case • Mary Yanchus, a teacher from Truscott's home town organizes an email campaign asking the Justice Minister to conduct a review • students at Humberview Secondary School in Bolton, Ontario, post a petition online asking the public to support Truscott's appeal	• 2002, report presented to the Justice Minister indicating that there was good reason to believe that Truscott was innocent of the charge • Minister indicated that Truscott should take his case to the Ontario Court of Appeal
David Milgaard	• 1970, 20-year-old nurses' aide, Gail Miller, murdered • 16-year-old David Milgaard arrested and charged with Miller's murder based on testimony that placed Milgaard in the vicinity of the murder • Milgaard found guilty and sentenced to life in prison	• Milgaard's mother, Joyce, refused to believe her son had committed the crime • a report from the investigation located that raises doubt on the trial evidence • 1990, Mrs. Milgaard's request that the case be reopened was rejected • 1991, the Supreme Court of Canada ordered a new trial • 1992, Milgaard released • 2005, James Lockyer of the Association in Defence of the Wrongfully Convicted sought a commission to examine the process involved in the wrongful conviction of Milgaard	• 1999, Milgaard awarded $10 million in compensation • 2005, a commission opened hearings into the wrongful conviction

Suspect	Summary of Events	Concerns and Actions of Involved Citizens	Eventual Outcome
Donald Marshall	• 1971, Sandy Seale murdered in a Halifax park • 16-year-old Mi'kmaq, Donald Marshall, arrested and charged with murder • found guilty and sentenced to life • 1983, new evidence that some witnesses had provided false testimony • an inquiry found Marshall not guilty, but the Crown not blamed for the wrongful conviction • 1990, a Royal Commission reported Marshall was a victim of racism involving the police and legal profession	• Association in the Defence of the Wrongfully Convicted represented Marshall at the Royal Commission and submission to the Supreme Court of Canada	• 1990, declared not guilty of all charges • given $300 000 in compensation plus a monthly allowance

Figure 3-22 Susan Nelles leaves court in 1982, after she was freed on four counts of murdering infants at the Toronto Hospital for Sick Children. Nelles had suffered emotionally and professionally. Should she be compensated for her pain and suffering?

Even though there have been cases of injustice, the legal system can also provide examples where the system did work and set an innocent person free. The case of Susan Nelles demonstrates how the judicial system can function properly.

In 1989, a number of infants died at the Toronto Hospital for Sick Children. As the number of cases increased, suspicion fell on the nurses who were assigned to the ward. Police investigated and found that the infants had been given a lethal dose of a drug. It became a murder investigation. The police checked the records of the nurses who were on duty at the time of the deaths. Susan Nelles had been on duty. She was charged with murder. At the preliminary hearing, the defence noted that Nelles had not been on the ward for all the deaths and that another nurse had also been on duty at the time. This indicated reasonable doubt and Nelles was released.

As proud as Canadians are of their legal system, they know that mistakes can be made. Have you ever been in a situation where you were accused of doing something wrong, when you actually hadn't? Our system attempts to avoid such situations by providing an appeals process — either the Crown or defence attorneys can ask a higher court to review the decision and determine if it was just.

CIVICS SKILLS POWER

Making an Effective Presentation

An effective presentation informs and persuades an audience. To maintain audience interest, you need the skills and tools of persuasion outlined in the Civic Skills Power on page 78. To communicate clearly, appropriately, and dramatically to your audience, consider the use of voice, pace, organization, and audio-visual support.

Voice: Consider volume, tone, and pitch.

- *Volume*—Don't speak too loudly or too softly. Vary the volume for effect. A loud voice gets people's attention; a soft voice adds drama and evokes sympathy.
- *Tone*—Vary your tone to maintain interest and add drama. Your tone of voice conveys as much of a message as your words.
- *Pitch*—Try to keep your voice low, rich, and resonant. A high, squeaky voice can be unnerving or annoying.

Pace: Vary your pace or speed as you speak. Do not speak too quickly or too slowly. Quicken the pace to add suspense. Slow down the pace for a dramatic focus on a key example or anecdote.

Organization: Your presentation must have an introduction, content and illustrations to support your main argument, and a conclusion. The opening and concluding points of your presentation are key places to engage and impress your audience.

- Involve your audience immediately with a series of questions, or a thought-provoking statement. For example: *Have you ever met a person in a secluded area who was bigger, stronger, and a whole lot meaner than you? How would you feel if you had to face that person every day in your school?*

- The middle part of your presentation should present proof and examples that will make your case.
- The conclusion should indicate a direction for the audience to think or act. For example: *Ask yourself, "Can I know all this and not do anything about it?" There is something you can do. It is not easy, but you will have a more peaceful school with happier students.*

Audio-visual support: Help yourself and your audience understand your key message even better by using one of the following techniques:

- PowerPoint or other presentation software to capture key points in words and images
- digital photographs in a slide show or montage
- overheads of graphs, charts, or pictures
- posters or flow charts on Bristol board
- artifacts that convey a powerful message or arouse curiosity

Media Bites

You have likely seen news stories that capture a few words or a single key sentence from a political interview, a House of Commons speaker, or a media personality. These words or sentences are called *sound bites* if they are on the radio and *media bites* if they are on television.

You Try It

As you prepare your persuasive presentation, imagine which lines you might like to see in a media bite. Would it be your introductory statement or question, a key story or example from the middle of your presentation, or your final call to action? Imagining a media bite may help you to revise and refine what you say to give it more power.

For links to sites on the structure and function of the Supreme Court of Canada

Last Chance: The Supreme Court

The highest appeal court is the Supreme Court of Canada. This Court can refuse to hear a case if it feels the case is not a matter of national significance. The Court has nine justices. Not all of the justices hear each case, but all cases are heard by an odd number of justices. When a case is heard the justices listen to the lawyers from both sides and ask questions to determine the arguments for and against an appeal. Once the Court renders a decision, it is final.

The Supreme Court's role in our justice system has increased since the *Charter of Rights and Freedoms* came into being. When a case involves a Charter right, the justices must interpret the law in light of the Charter. If the law conflicts with the Charter, it may be struck down.

Some critics feel that this gives the Court too much power. After all, it is the role of the legislative assembly to make laws. Some of the Court's decisions may actually result in new laws. For example, in 2004, the federal government asked the Supreme Court of Canada to determine if the government could legally change the definition of marriage to include same-sex unions. The Court decision was that it could, but it also stated that religious officials could not be forced to participate in such marriages and that the House of Commons must still pass appropriate legislation.

Figure 3-23 LEAF is the Women's Legal Education and Action Fund. This non-profit organization works to ensure that the rights of females in Canada, as guaranteed in the Charter, are upheld in Canadian courts and by human rights commissions and government agencies. Here students in British Columbia participate in LEAF's No Means No peer-facilitated anti-violence program.

LANDMARK DECISIONS FROM THE SUPREME COURT

Case	Situation	Decision
"Rape Shield" Law upheld 2000 *R.* v. *Darrach*	The Court unanimously upheld provisions in the *Criminal Code* that limit the use of a woman's past sexual history as evidence.	This decision reaffirmed the importance of maintaining sensitivity to the equality rights of women when considering an accused's right to a fair trial.
Access to Legal Aid 1999 *New Brunswick (Minister of Health and Community Services)* v. *G. (J)*	The Court held that a poor, single mother had been unfairly denied legal assistance in a case where the mother sought custody of her children.	Access to a lawyer is a right guaranteed under the *Charter of Rights and Freedoms.*
Workplace Discrimination 1999 *British Columbia (Public Service Employees Relations Commission)* v. *British Columbia Government and Service Employees' Union*	The Court held that a female firefighter in British Columbia was unfairly dismissed because she had not passed one part of a physical examination.	If a workplace rule, in this case a test of running speed, systemically excludes women or other groups, it must be reviewed to ensure that it is truly required to properly perform the job.
No Means No 1999 *R.* v. *Ewanchuk*	The Court overturned a lower Alberta court ruling that had acquitted a man who had been charged with sexual assault. The Alberta court had ruled that the victim had given the attacker mixed messages regarding consent.	In a unanimous decision, the Court stated that a person's "no" means "no." No one has the right to sexually touch another person unless that person clearly communicates consent. Consent must be positively established: silence, inaction, or ambiguous conduct is never consent.
Mandatory Retirement 1992 *Dickason* v. *University of Alberta*	In the case of an Alberta professor who was forced to retire at age 65, the Court ruled that since she had signed a collective agreement with the university that indicated she was to retire at 65, the university was within its rights.	The case was not seen as one that required mandatory retirement for all professions. Various provinces are reviewing policies to determine if other professions may be violating employee Charter rights by forcing retirement at age 65.

Figure 3-24 What Supreme Court decisions have made the news lately?

CHECKPOINT

1. What are the rights of a person accused of a crime?
2. What is the role of the Supreme Court of Canada?
3. Why do you think the Court has an odd number of justices?

Youth Criminal Justice Act

Youths also commit crimes. Centuries ago, they were treated the same as adults in court. If convicted, they were sentenced to long prison terms in adult institutions. The government has since recognized that youths must be treated in a manner that reflects their maturity and moral development. The Canadian government has passed various Acts dealing with youth crime. These included the *Juvenile Delinquents Act* and the *Young Offenders Act*. The most recent was the *Youth Criminal Justice Act*.

The text earlier in this chapter on trials and sentencing applies to adults who are defined as citizens 18 years of age and over. The *Youth Criminal Justice Act* sets out the rights of an accused under the age of 18. It also addresses the arrest and trial process for the accused and the sentences for those found guilty.

The judicial system has attempted to protect the rights of young offenders, while recognizing that they need to be accountable for their actions. The following procedures from the *Youth Criminal Justice Act* demonstrate the balance.

- A young person must be informed (when arrested or detained) of the nature of the charge and that he or she has the right to counsel.
- If the young person cannot afford counsel and a legal aid program exists in the province or territory, the young person may apply for legal assistance.
- When a young person is arrested, the parents are to be notified or if no parent is available, a suitable adult who has a relationship to the young person must be notified.
- A psychological assessment may be ordered to determine if there are any extenuating [qualifying] circumstances that may influence the young person's actions.
- A youth justice committee may be established to give advice on any extrajudicial [outside the legal system] measures that may used; offer aid to the victim; ensure there is community assistance for the young person such as monitoring or supervision.

Young offenders also have the following rights:

- the right not to make any statements (except giving name, address, and age)
- the right to be told that anything they say to police may be later used in court
- the right to have a lawyer, a parent, or an adult present if the youth decides to make a statement.

When police arrest a youth, they are required by law to notify a parent.

Literacy Hint

Ask yourself questions. Should young offenders be treated the same way as adult offenders? What reasons might there be to treat them differently?

Active Citizen

Website

For links to sites on youth justice issues

Figure 3-25 Some youths are considering law enforcement as a career. Sarah Jane Riddell has been with the York Region Police for six years.

A judge experienced in dealing with young offenders presides over a young offender's trial. In serious cases, such as murder, the Crown may request that a young offender's case be heard in adult court. If the request is granted, the same rights and procedures for a criminal trial are followed. Should the age of majority be reviewed? Does this work against the chances for lowering the voting age?

Support for Adolescents

Our society is obligated to help and protect adolescents who are vulnerable and susceptible to abuse. Several organizations have been developed to provide aid and protection to young people.

Figure 3-26 A sample of organizations that provide support to youth.

Organizations	Purpose
Children's Aid Society	• protects adolescents in their home environment and removes any children suspected of abuse or neglect • ensures adolescents are provided the necessities of life
Legal Aid	• insures that adolescents appearing in court who do not have access to or cannot afford a lawyer are represented by a Legal Aid lawyer
Child Advocate	• represents children seeking or receiving help under the *Child and Family Services Act* • acts on complaints from children in provincial legal, health, and welfare systems
Ombudsperson	• investigates complaints against government agencies, such as complaints by young people of poor treatment or rights being abused, unusual delay in acquiring a driver's licence, or being denied a licence

People Power

As 12-year-old Kim Plewes began to dress for school, she noticed that most of her clothes were made in developing countries, such as Malawi and India. At school, Kim's teacher raised the issue of child labour. The label in her clothes immediately came to Kim's mind. This connection sparked Kim into action and she hasn't looked back.

In 1998, Kim took an active role in this issue by joining the organization Kids Can Free the Children as a volunteer and spokesperson.

Kim investigated situations of child labour around the world. She soon learned that many children in developing countries are forced to work in unsafe factories. Kim decided that such injustices had to be addressed. In 2002, she drew up a petition condemning child labour and took it to her friends and people in her community. Before long she had acquired over 6000 signatures from Canadians across the country. She went to Ottawa to present the petition to the government. She met with Peter Adams, Member of Parliament and then Chair of the Standing Committee on Procedures and House Affairs. He told her how to word the petition properly so it could be presented to the House of Commons. In May 2002, Kim's petition was read in the House. In response the government said that it had already signed a number of agreements supporting a ban on child labour as well as providing funds so that children could go to school instead of to work.

Kim then decided to work for justice whether it was to help fight child labour or to build

Figure 3-27 Kim Plewes volunteering in the Dominican Republic

homes for poor people in Nicaragua. She joined an organization called Leaders Today. As a youth speaker and facilitator for Leaders Today, her life has changed forever.

According to Kim, "One day I changed and decided to volunteer. One day I found my passion. Today I smile."

1. Why was organizing a petition a realistic way to address the issue of child labour?

2. What qualities does Kim exhibit that allow her to be a successful student leader?

Canada's legal system has evolved. Citizens now have guaranteed rights. Our system attempts to deal with the accused of all ages in a fair and just manner and to balance the rights of the individual with the security of society. Structures have been established to ensure a formal trial process and to provide a means to appeal court decisions. The system only works when citizens are aware of their rights and assume their responsibilities to obey laws and respect others.

CHECKPOINT

1. Why did the government feel that youths accused of crimes should be treated differently from adults?
2. What supports are provided to assist troubled youths?
3. What other supports might the government consider to help young people?

CHAPTER REVIEW

Summing It Up

- Canada's legal system is based on Aboriginal, French, and British systems.
- Canadians have guaranteed rights and responsibilities.
- There are two branches of law in Canada: criminal law, which deals with crimes against individuals and society, and civil law, which deals with person to person and property issues.
- The *Charter of Rights and Freedoms* sets out democratic, legal, language, and mobility rights.
- The court system involves local, federal, and provincial courts, the Courts of Appeal, and the Supreme Court of Canada.
- An accused person is guaranteed the right to a lawyer and a fair trial.
- A range of sentences exist, depending on the severity of the crime.
- The *Youth Criminal Justice Act* applies to youths under 18 years of age.
- Canada attempts to balance the rights of individuals with the protection of society.

- habeas corpus
- common law
- civil law
- bail

- Crown
- conviction
- acquittal
- plea bargain

- perjury
- alibi
- premeditated
- parole

- impact statement
- rehabilitation
- suspended sentence

- probation
- appeal
- sentencing circle

Thinking: To Be Informed

1. Have the rights of victims of crime been sacrificed to safeguard the rights of the accused? Discuss your answer to this question with a classmate. Keep short point-form notes of your opinions and be ready to share them with the class.

2. Our legal system stresses the need to protect individual rights. What responsibilities do you think people in Canada should have? Create a list including your reasons and share them with a classmate.

Communicating: To Be Purposeful

3. Is youth crime on the increase? Should the *Youth Criminal Justice Act* be made tougher? Research statistics on youth crime and respond to those who feel that young people are getting more violent and need to be dealt with in a more forceful manner. Write a letter to the editor of your local paper either supporting the case for tougher sentences or maintaining the current policy, debate the issue with your classmates, or create a montage of newspaper/Internet/magazine clippings that illustrate your opinion.

4. The legal profession is attractive to many young people. Yet, few students seem to realize that the profession includes more than just lawyers and judges. Research other occupations in the legal profession and develop a help wanted ad or recruitment poster for one of the positions. Include the educational requirements, a description of the job, and the salary.

Applying: To Be Active

5. Predict what issues related to the Internet or privacy or equality rights might have to be addressed by Canada's legal system. Compare your predictions with a partner.

6. Review the information from the *Youth Criminal Justice Act* and the purposes of sentencing to decide the following case. A 17 year old is tried and convicted of assaulting two 13-year-old students. The students were taken to hospital with severe injuries. The accused was abandoned as a baby and had spent most of his time in foster homes. The youth ran away from the last foster home and joined a gang. As the judge in this case, what rehabilitation programs would you recommend for this youth?

Culminating Performance Task: Making a Difference

You found out about the Culminating Performance Task (CPT) for this course in Chapter 1 so you should be thinking about what you want to tackle for your CPT.

At this stage, you should be looking for *one thing* that interests or concerns you—a need that you would like to address or a cause that you would like to support. Perhaps something at school or work will trigger your interest. Perhaps something that you come across while performing community service hours will interest you. Perhaps something that has suddenly happened (like a hurricane, tsunami, forest fire, or earthquake) in another community will concern you. Be aware of what's going on around you!

It's a good idea to find something soon, so that a good chunk of the work can be done before you get too busy toward the end of the course. Once you choose your topic, map out a series of steps to do something specific about your interest or concern. Pick something that you can get done with the time and resources available to you.

If you are stuck for ideas review the list of sample action plans on page 25. If you are still stuck, fast-forward to Figure 5-13 to review the extraordinary deeds of some ordinary young people, just like you.

Next Steps

In the next two weeks you should:

Active Citizenship	Process Steps
Be Informed	1. Discuss the CPT with teachers, classmates, and other advisors or role models. 2. Assess your learning skills to select an appropriate way to complete the task.
Be Purposeful	3. Select a topic that interests or concerns you enough to spend time on it. 4. Review the CPT assessment rubric to determine how much work you will need to do to earn the mark that you want.
Be Active	5. Make an action plan that outlines key steps and indicates when you will have the most time to complete them. 6. Network to determine who can help you with your task and where you can find useful information or support.

4
CHAPTER

MUNICIPAL GOVERNMENT AND YOU

Who Does What?

In previous chapters, you explored the responsibilities of the federal and provincial governments. But another level of government affects you daily. What responsibilities does your local municipal government have? Which departments are in charge of these activities?

The issues in the following scenarios could take place in your community. Can you figure out who you would go to in your municipal government to address each issue?

Figure 4-1 You and your friends play basketball whenever weather permits. Sometimes you want to play when it's dark but the court doesn't have lights. Who would you call to suggest lights be installed?

Figure 4-2 Your family lives in rural, northern Ontario. It has snowed heavily over the past several days. Your grandparents' road has not been plowed and they need to get out for a medical appointment. They have asked for your help. Who do you call? Which municipal department is responsible for snow removal?

Figure 4-3 You want to visit your cousin, who lives on the other side of town. It's too far to bike, and no one is available to drive you. You think you can get there by bus. Who would you contact to find out what route to take, what time the bus runs, and how much the fare is?

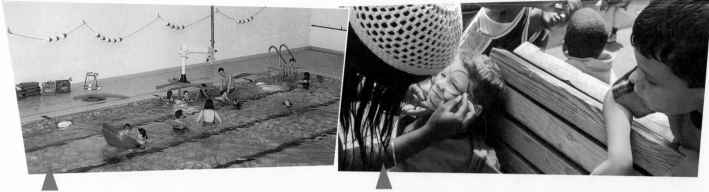

Figure 4-4 You have just moved to a new community. It is a hot summer day and you would like to go for a swim. You think there is a community pool, but you're not sure. Who would you phone to find out what facilities are available and their hours of operation?

Figure 4-5 You need a summer job. Since you enjoy working with younger children, you're interested in working at one of the municipality's day camps. Which municipal department would you contact for an application form for this job or any other job within the municipality?

Municipal governments provide a lot of important and necessary services for their residents. The situations described are only a few of the areas they cover. So how can you figure out all the responsibilities of your municipal government? A good place to start is the section called the Blue Pages in the telephone book. The Blue Pages list all the phone numbers for services that governments provide at the federal, provincial, and municipal levels.

Using your local Blue Pages, find your municipal government's listing. Create a chart that outlines the different departments in your municipal government and what each is responsible for. You will then have a practical directory that you can use when you need to get information from your local government.

1. What services were you surprised to find out were the responsibility of the municipal government?

2. Which municipal department do you think has the most impact on you personally? Why?

KEY LEARNINGS

In this chapter you will explore the following topics:
- the structure and function of Canada's municipal governments
- how laws and decisions are made at the municipal level
- the contributions residents can make at the local level
- the civic literacy skills of making responsible decisions and working collaboratively

What is Local Citizenship?

global citizenship: the responsibilities, rights, and privileges of being a member of the global community

local citizenship: the responsibilities, rights and privileges of being a member of your local community

In earlier chapters, you explored what it means to be a Canadian citizen. You also may have heard the term **global citizenship**. This term refers to the responsibilities we share with people around the world in taking care of the Earth. Have you heard the phrase, "Think globally, act locally"? What do you think that means? Your daily actions can have a huge impact, not only on your community, but around the world as well. You will explore global citizenship in a later chapter. Let's think about what **local citizenship** involves. It helps if first you can understand how your community works. Take the following quiz and see how much you know about your municipality:

1. Who is in charge of your municipal government?
2. Where is your town or city hall?
3. What does your Public Works department do?
4. Does your municipality have a town/city council? If so, how many members are on it and who represents you on the council?
5. When was the last municipal election held? What was one of the major issues in that election? What was the voter turnout?

Figure 4-6 Kingston's City Hall, seen here, was built in 1844. Would you recognize your municipal town hall? What do you think goes on there?

Active Citizen

How did you do on the quiz? Don't feel bad if you weren't able to come up with all of the answers. Many people don't know a lot about their **municipal government**. Many are also unable to define what local citizenship means. What holds us back when it comes to becoming more aware of our municipal government and our role as active citizens? Here are some possibilities:

municipal government: local government that includes a mayor and a council responsible for delivering services to its population as outlined in the provincial *Municipal Act*

- We don't really understand the role and responsibilities of local government.
- We have little knowledge of the local issues or their impact on us.
- We don't really think that local government is important to us.

Do any of these apply to you? To become active, you need to understand the role that municipal government plays in your daily life. Municipal governments provide services that improve your quality of life. They are responsible for things like clean drinking water, maintaining local roads, garbage disposal, and fire services. Do you use your municipality's arenas, baseball diamonds, or soccer fields? All of the parks and recreation facilities in your community are the municipal government's responsibility as well.

You may be starting to realize just how important your community is. As a local resident, you can play a decisive role in how your community looks and how it serves all residents. Consider the following questions:

1. What do you like best about your community?
2. What would you most like to see changed about your community?
3. If you left your community and returned 10 years later, what would you still want to find or see?

You have just identified a number of positive characteristics about your community. You probably also discovered a few areas where you can get involved to help improve what your community has to offer.

> ### Literacy Hint
> **Make a Connection.** What opportunities or facilities do you think are needed in your community for people your age?

Figure 4-7 As part of their 40 hours of community involvement activities, some students from Unionville High School volunteer at Information Markham. It is located at the Markham Civic Centre. The volunteers supply information by telephone and in person to people with questions about services available to the community. Pictured here is Kevin Kong.

One of Canada's largest youth centres and skateboard parks rolls into Newmarket

NEWMARKET, February 24, 2004

The Town of Newmarket ramps up for youth with the introduction of a state-of-the-art youth centre and indoor skateboard park at 56 Charles Street. Offering more than 23,000 square feet [7010 square metres] of space, this conjoined facility represents one of the best and largest of its kind in Canada, and launches a new era of recreation opportunities for youth in Newmarket.

"The Newmarket Youth Centre and Kinsmen Skateboard Park offers the winning combination of equipment, space and services combined with a safe and positive environment. Not only will youth have access to a huge skateboard park, but to a computer lab, gymnasium and support services as well. We're delighted to introduce such a remarkable facility to Newmarket," says Tom Taylor, Mayor of Newmarket.

From conception to completion, Newmarket youth—especially those who frequented the old youth centre on Main Street—were directly involved in the development of the facility. "From

Figure 4-8 The Newmarket Youth Centre and Kinsmen Skatepark is an example of different groups working together to fulfill an identified community need.

the development of a conceptual model to the planning of the opening event, the youth have been highly involved. It's truly a centre

for the youth, by the youth," says Brenda Farrell, Director of Parks, Recreation and Culture.

The 9000 square feet [2743 square metres] of skateboard park space provides skateboarders and rollerbladers with the opportunity to enjoy their sport year-round, while keeping them safe and their sports off the street. The facility also features a full-sized gymnasium and fitness centre, and offers volunteer services and employment and support resources.

"The journey that started ten years ago with an idea and desire to motivate and activate the youth in our community has come full circle with the launch of this exciting new facility. We now have the space and services to allow for an expanded focus on recreation programming and opportunities for youth in Newmarket," continues Farrell.

1. Identify the different community groups that participated in the development of the Newmarket Youth Centre and Kinsmen Skateboard Park.

2. List the opportunities and services the youth centre has to offer.

3. Many communities have local service organizations like the Kinsmen, Lion's Club, and Rotary Club. Name some local community projects in which organizations like these are involved in your community.

Municipal Governments— Making Communities Work

As you learned in an earlier chapter, provincial governments created municipalities. While federal and provincial powers are protected by the Constitution, municipal powers are not. A provincial government can give municipalities added responsibilities or take away their authority at will. Let's take a look at different kinds of municipalities.

Types of Municipalities

Ontario's municipalities are governed by the **Municipal Act**. The latest version was passed on January 1, 2003, by the Ontario provincial government. The *Municipal Act* is used as a blueprint for municipalities. It outlines the powers and duties of each community. It also describes how the local government is to be organized and structured.

Municipal Act

Upper-tier Municipal Government
- Provides a common set of services, such as fire and police services, to a group of municipalities
- An example is Oxford County, which contains a number of smaller cities and towns.

Lower-tier Municipal Government
- Responsible for local issues and concerns, such as operating budget and bylaws
- Ingersoll, Tilllsonburg, and a number of smaller townships are part of Oxford County.

Single-tier Municipal Government
- One level of government responsible for providing all services to its citizens
- An example is Ottawa.

Figure 4-9 What type of municipal government do you have?

Municipal Act: a set of guidelines that reflects the responsibilities and powers that a community has as well as how the local government is to be structured

upper-tier municipality: name given to the group of lower-tier municipalities that form the region or county

lower-tier municipality: a municipality in which the community is a part of a group of municipalities that form a region or county; a regional/county government provides certain services to the region as a whole.

single-tier municipality: a municipality in which only one level of government provides all services to its population

Amalgamation: When Municipalities Join Together

Did you know that as of January 1, 2005, Ontario had 445 municipalities? Since the mid-1990s, the provincial government of Ontario has organized the **amalgamation** of many municipalities across the province. In the amalgamation process, a group of communities around each other—each with its own municipal government—are joined together. The new community then has one common municipal government. Think of it this way. It would be like bringing together many different baseball leagues, each with its own set of rules, into one league under one common set of rules.

amalgamation: the process in which several smaller municipalities and their governments are merged into one large municipality with a single government

Making Responsible Decisions

Every day we make hundreds of decisions: What will I wear? What will I eat for breakfast? Will I do my homework now or later? What television program will I watch? Will I listen to the advice of my parents or my friends?

We make many of these daily decisions based on the way we feel at a certain moment—or on our needs. For example, if I am hungry, I probably need to eat. Often when we make these decisions, we only think of ourselves.

At a certain point, you realize that you are part of a community. This process may begin when your needs come into conflict with those of a brother, sister, or parent. You must recognize that other people have needs too.

When your desires, needs, and preferences are in conflict with the welfare of others, you must take responsibility for being a member of a larger community. Whose needs should you consider? For instance, consider that you have a large group of friends over for a party and you are playing music, talking, and laughing loudly late into the night.

- Do you think about waking the sleeping baby who lives next door?
- Do you consider the man suffering from cancer a few houses away? He needs peace and quiet.
- Do you consider the elderly couple across the street? They may be fearful of loud, boisterous teens.
- Do your friends throw pop cans and litter on the neighbours' lawns on their way home?

The circle of needs widens as your activities move beyond your own room and home.

How do you make responsible decisions about your behaviour in a community, or even about how you are going to vote? What's the process you need to go through? Once you have clarified your goals or your intention, consider using the following model.

Step 1

List the Goal and Alternatives. What are the different directions or courses of action you might choose to take to achieve your goal? For example, you could decide to have a party and invite many friends. Or you could ask only three or four of your best friends to come over for an evening of pizza, movies, and conversation. Maybe you'll choose to spend the evening by yourself.

Step 2

Identify the Pros and Cons of Each Alternative. What positive factors might make you choose one direction over another? What negative factors might influence your choice? List the factors in each column and then see how one list compares with the other. Even if the items in one column outnumber those in the other, you must still consider which items are more important and which might be trivial reasons. Read the items listed in the columns below and consider which are the more important conditions or outcomes.

Situation—Making a responsible decision to contribute to my community:

Alternatives:

1. Beautify the community with flowers and trees each spring
2. Organize a cleanup campaign once a month for parks and wildlife habitats
3. Volunteer once a week at the seniors' centre in town

MY CHOICE: ALTERNATIVE 2—ORGANIZE A CLEANUP CAMPAIGN FOR PARKS AND WILDLIFE HABITATS

Pros — Positive Conditions and Outcomes	Cons — Negative Conditions and Outcomes
Garbage will not create an eyesore.	This could be a very big job.
Parks will be clean and safe for small children with no smashed bottles.	I will have to give up some personal time.
Animals and birds will not be in danger from human litter, such as a duck getting its bill stuck in a pop can ring.	My studies may be affected.
Property values will rise because of the clean condition in the town.	I may not have as much time with my friends.
People in the community will appreciate our actions.	I may have to get down and dirty with garbage.
People will think teens are contributors.	I may think unkindly of people who litter.

Step 3

Assess the Pros and Cons. Weigh the importance of the items in each column. Your analysis may be similar to the following thoughts:

- I notice that I have the same number of items in each column.
- The "pro" items are important reasons to do the cleanup campaign, especially the second and third items.
- The word "I" is used often in the "cons" column. I am probably being somewhat selfish in my thinking here.
- The effect on my time to study and do assignments is something I need to think about very carefully.

Step 4

Make a Decision. Select the activity that presents the best balance of pros against cons. My friends and I could contribute in a positive and important way to the community by organizing a cleanup campaign, but we will have to limit our time so that we can keep up with our schoolwork.

Step 5

Review the Decision and Revise as Needed. We had planned for a team of five students to clean the area in three hours. It took five hours, and some people weren't very effective on their own. Next time we will try working in three pairs to complete the cleanup in three hours.

You Try It

Choose a problem or major decision in your life and list the alternative decisions or actions you could take. Use the process outlined here to analyse one of the alternatives and then make a decision.

With amalgamation, instead of each community being responsible for services to its residents, the newly amalgamated city brings these services together as one, removing any duplication. So instead of each community being responsible for police services, there would now only be one large police department to service the new municipality.

Figure 4-10 Some communities were not in favour of amalgamation. Some citizens voiced their opinions through posters and protests.

Active Citizen

Website

For sites on municipal government in Canada

A number of municipalities, such as the village of Erin and the township of Erin, voluntarily amalgamated in 1997. Others had no choice as the province exercised its authority and forced amalgamation. One example was Toronto. At the end of 1997, Ontario's capital had a population of 650 000. Its population changed to 2.4 million overnight when on January 1, 1998, five area municipalities—East York, Etobicoke, North York, Scarborough, and York—merged with Toronto.

Ontario's process of amalgamation between 1996 and 2001 reduced the number of municipalities from 815 to 447—a reduction of 40 percent.

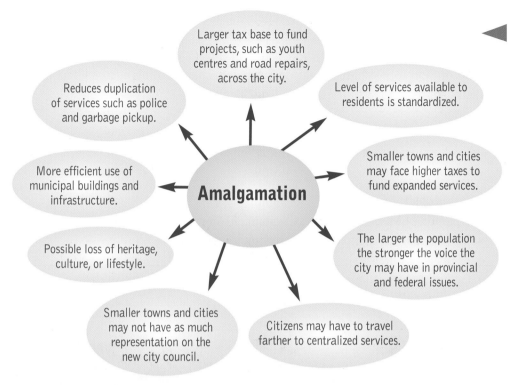

Reduces duplication of services such as police and garbage pickup.

Larger tax base to fund projects, such as youth centres and road repairs, across the city.

Level of services available to residents is standardized.

More efficient use of municipal buildings and infrastructure.

Amalgamation

Smaller towns and cities may face higher taxes to fund expanded services.

Possible loss of heritage, culture, or lifestyle.

The larger the population the stronger the voice the city may have in provincial and federal issues.

Smaller towns and cities may not have as much representation on the new city council.

Citizens may have to travel farther to centralized services.

Figure 4-11 Which of these outcomes of amalgamation would you consider to be positive? Which ones are negative? Based on what you have learned, would you support the amalgamation of more communities in Ontario?

What Is the Federal Role in Municipalities?

Until recently, federal involvement in municipal affairs was minimal. The Federation of Canadian Municipalities, which represents municipalities across Canada, has been lobbying the federal government for decades to take a more active role in the growth and development of Canadian cities. The organization felt that cities were key in the success of the Canadian economy. It demanded that the federal government begin investing financially in areas such as economic development, technology, and infrastructure. Updating and maintaining a municipality's **infrastructure** is an important job for all communities. Infrastructure includes the basic facilities and services needed for the functioning of the municipality. Many times municipal, provincial, and federal governments share the cost of infrastructure development in municipalities. Examples of infrastructure include

- transportation and communications systems
- water and power lines
- public institutions such as schools, post offices, and prisons.

In the 2004 election campaign, Prime Minister Paul Martin promised, under political pressure, to give cities a percentage of gasoline tax revenues and the General Sales Tax (GST). This was known as the "New Deal for

infrastructure: the networks of transportation, communication, education, and other public services required to sustain economic and societal activities

Figure 4-12 Why is maintaining infrastructure such as roads important to a municipality?

Cities." The 2005/2006 Liberal budget devoted 1.5 cents from every litre of gasoline sold to Canadian municipalities. How much do you think this was? If you guessed $600 million you would be correct! Combined with $700 million to be shared from GST rebates, communities across Canada would share in $1.3 billion of funding. The federal government also committed to increase this funding from gasoline tax to $2 billion by 2009/2010. Here is where some of this money has gone to develop local infrastructures across Canada. Think about why each of these improvements would be important to that community.

- Halifax Harbour cleanup: $60 million
- Upgrade of Montreal's subway system: $103 million
- Modernizing and expanding Toronto's transit system: $350 million
- Improving Canada–U.S. border crossings in British Columbia: $90 million
- Corridors for Canada highway infrastructure development in the Northwest Territories: $65 million.

Literacy Hint

Make a Judgment. From your perspective, which of these projects would be the most important one? Make your own list prioritizing the projects.

Figure 4-13 The Dempster Highway in the Northwest Territories will be one of the beneficiaries of the federal funding. Maintaining and improving roadways in the Arctic is a major cost for its territorial governments but a necessity for the movement of goods and people.

CHECKPOINT

1. Why is local citizenship important?
2. What is the difference between a single-tier municipality and a lower-tier municipality?
3. In your own words, describe the process of amalgamation.

Active Citizen

How Are Municipal Governments Organized?

Take a moment to think about your family. Do certain members have specific responsibilities? For example, is it your job to walk the dog or to take out the garbage? What about cooking? In some families, members take turns preparing dinner or getting the lunches ready for school. Families divide responsibilities to make sure that important chores are done and that the household runs smoothly. Municipal governments are organized much like families. Different departments take care of specific tasks to make sure the community runs smoothly.

Based on the *Municipal Act*, municipal governments have a number of responsibilities. Much like the federal and provincial governments, municipal governments have a variety of departments to meet the needs of residents and fulfill their role. The organization chart below reflects the important positions and departments in one municipal government.

Not every municipal government is organized the same way as shown in Figure 4-14. Smaller municipalities may have fewer departments or several

Literacy Hint

Respond to Reading a Chart. What was the most helpful way to read the chart below— from top to bottom or from left to right? What surprised you the most about the jobs and responsibilities of a city?

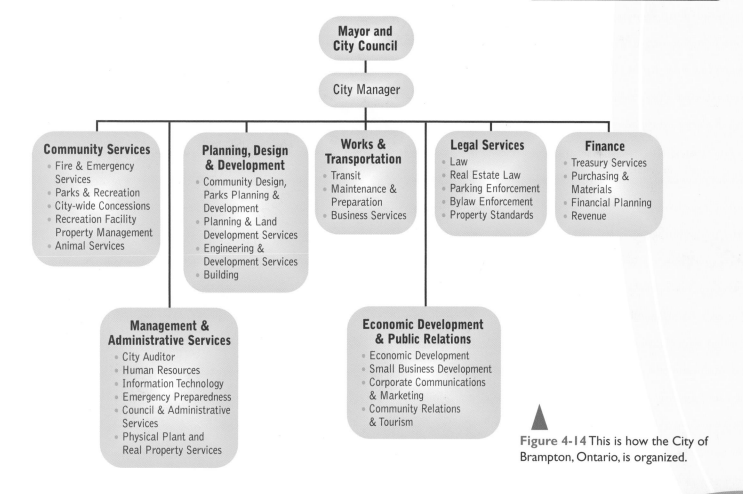

Figure 4-14 This is how the City of Brampton, Ontario, is organized.

that are grouped together. Take another look at the chart you developed of your local municipal government using the Blue Pages. Which of the departments are the same as Brampton's, and which are different?

Two important positions are at the top of the chart: the mayor and the city council. The mayor heads the city council and has the following responsibilities:

- ensures that the laws of the government are obeyed within the municipality
- oversees municipal employees and ensures that the various departments are fulfilling their job requirements
- ensures that council receives information regarding the finances, health, and security of the municipality.

Figure 4-15 Ottawa Mayor Bob Chiarelli (left) plays during the first Councillor's Hockey Cup game at the Winterlude Snowbowl. Why might Ottawa residents like to see their mayor involved in community activities?

councillors: people elected to represent the residents in different wards in a municipality

Municipal **councillors** are elected to represent different wards found within the municipality. Wards are much like provincial or federal ridings. Councillors make sure that any concerns of the residents of their ward are brought to the attention of the mayor and the rest of the council. The municipal council debates and votes on issues. For example, suppose a fast-food chain wanted to build an outlet on the vacant property next to your school. Many people, including you, may support this idea because of the convenience it would offer. Others may oppose it because it might increase traffic in the neighbourhood. Still others may feel that it will provide unhealthy meal options for students.

People on both sides of the issue would have the opportunity to voice their concerns at a municipal council meeting. This would give councillors the opportunity to hear a variety of opinions that would help them make an informed decision when it comes time to vote on the proposal.

Informed to Be Effective

In the 2003 Ontario municipal elections, only 40 percent of eligible voters bothered to vote. In 28 municipalities, entire councils were elected without opposition. Why do you think there appears to be so little interest in municipal government?

People Power

Hazel McCallion was born in Port Daniel on the Gaspé Coast of Quebec. After an education in Quebec City and Montreal, she joined the corporate world. She built a career over 19 years at Canadian Kellogg. In 1967 she decided to turn to the world of politics. It was only a few short years before she was elected Mayor of Streetsville. She served from 1970 until 1973.

Hazel McCallion is now the longest serving mayor in Mississauga's history. It began with her election as Mayor in 1978. At the age of 84, Mayor McCallion served her 10th consecutive term as mayor. During her many years as mayor, McCallion has shown a feisty and determined attitude to ensure that Mississauga becomes a community that offers, in her words, "a superior quality of life for residents, with great services at reasonable cost."

One of Mayor McCallion's major accomplishments during her time in office was to make Mississauga the only debt-free city in all of Canada. How did she accomplish this and why have other large urban areas across Canada been unable to achieve this lofty goal? Here are a few strategies that the mayor used to make Mississauga a model city in terms of economic growth:

- kept property tax increases to a minimum
- used a "pay as you go" philosophy in municipal spending (only made purchases if it had the money)

Figure 4-16 Mayor Hazel McCallion became involved in municipal politics in 1968.

- ran the city of Mississauga like a business, saving for large expenditures and setting aside a reserve fund for emergencies
- allowed residents to review budgets and provide input to city staff

It would be hard to argue that Mayor Hazel McCallion has not made a difference with her knowledgeable, purposeful, and active leadership in her community. Mayor Hazel McCallion has been truly dedicated to the residents of Mississauga.

1. How was Mayor McCallion able to make Mississauga a debt-free municipality?
2. Explain the "pay as you go" approach that Mayor McCallion used to run the city of Mississauga? Can you think of an example when this may not always work?

Literacy Hint

Make a Connection. Which services in the table has your family used?

We know what municipalities are and how they are organized, but what exactly do municipalities do for their residents? Municipal governments provide important social and health services, such as recreational centres and yearly flu shots through local health units. They are also responsible for delivering community development opportunities, such as recycling programs or ensuring that new housing projects meet the needs of the community. The *Municipal Act* outlines 10 areas of responsibilities:

Area	Examples
Public Utilities	electricity, water
Waste Management	garbage disposal, recycling
Public Roads	road repairs, snowplowing
Transportation Systems	buses, subways
Culture, Parks, Recreation, and Heritage	sports fields and facilities, community centres
Drainage and Flood Control	ditches, storm sewers, and other drainage systems
Parking	bylaw enforcement, public parking lots
Economic Development Services	marketing of municipality, zoning of commercial and industrial areas
Approval of Structures	fences, signs
Animal Licensing	animal control

Figure 4-17 Ten areas of responsibilities for municipalities

Municipalities have control over the areas noted in Figure 4-17 so that communities can develop laws and policies that reflect individual needs and circumstances. We can tell from the list that municipalities have a lot to do. Local bylaws are only enforced within the boundaries of the municipality. For example zoning bylaws are developed to control the types of buildings and activities in the municipality. This ensures that a school is not built next to a nuclear power plant or a hospital next to a noisy car factory. Many municipalities across Ontario have bylaws that don't allow smoking in indoor places. Does your municipality have a no smoking bylaw? Municipalities have bylaw officers to ensure that local laws are followed.

How do municipalities pay for all these services? Each municipality develops a yearly budget, allocating a certain amount of money for their

10 main responsibilities. Most of a municipality's operating budget or spending money comes from a process called the Municipal Property Tax Assessment. All property owners are assigned a yearly property tax based on the market value of their property. The higher the property value according to the province, the larger the property tax will be. This is an important tax because it allows the municipal government to deliver key programs and services to its population.

While the municipality collects these taxes from its residents, it does not get to keep it all. In Ottawa, for example, the municipal government keeps two-thirds of the property tax. The remaining third goes to the provincial government to help fund different programs in education, social welfare, or affordable housing.

Property taxes are not the only source of funding for municipalities. Revenue also comes from business taxes, sales taxes, and licensing and service fees. Federal government grants, such as the New Deal, and provincial grants, such as the SuperProject fund for local infrastructure projects, also provide revenue.

Literacy Hint

Respond to Reading a Chart. How does the pie chart help you understand where property tax dollars are spent?

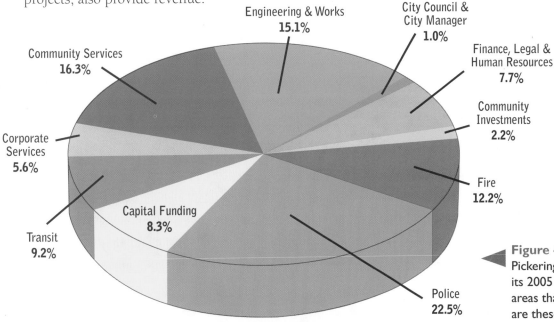

Engineering & Works
15.1%

City Council &
City Manager
1.0%

Community Services
16.3%

Finance, Legal &
Human Resources
7.7%

Corporate
Services
5.6%

Community
Investments
2.2%

Capital Funding
8.3%

Fire
12.2%

Transit
9.2%

Police
22.5%

Source: Pickering 2005 Budget, General Operating Budget Summary

Figure 4-18 Take a closer look at how Pickering, Ontario, spent its money in its 2005 budget. What are the top two areas that money was spent on? Why are these areas so expensive and important to the city?

CHECKPOINT

1. **Name five responsibilities of a municipality.**
2. **Explain in your own words how a municipality pays for the services it must provide for its residents.**

School Boards and Soft Drink Companies

Schools across Canada want to ensure that their students have a variety of learning materials and equipment that lead to a positive high school experience both in and out of the classroom. Schools also need to decide where best to spend their money based on the needs of their students. School boards are responsible for paying for part of these costs, but how do schools pay for the rest?

Take a look at the vending machines in your school cafeteria. Do you notice a trend? Are the same soft drink brands there every day? Coincidence? Think again! Many Canadian and US school boards have signed contracts with companies such as Coca-Cola and Pepsi, giving them exclusive distribution rights within their schools. Increases in funding for Ontario schools have not kept pace with increased costs. Schools looked for a new source of revenue. The soft drink companies stepped in and a relationship was born.

According to a report by the Toronto Star in 2003, fifty-nine percent of schools in Ontario use vending machines to raise money. School boards have received signing bonuses exceeding $1 million.

PROS

- Soft drink agreements help pay for program resources, such as audio-visual equipment, and provide funding for extracurricular programs, such as football equipment or team buses.

- Being a district-wide decision, there is opportunity for debate and discussions with many people, such as the school trustees, so that an informed decision can be made centrally.

- Soft drink companies are starting to offer more healthful choices, such as juice and water, in their vending machines.

- Vending machines offer a variety of choices for students at fair prices in convenient locations around the school.

CONS

- School boards are becoming dependent on this type of private funding, which may affect the public funding of education.

- Individual schools and their students have little or no voice in the decision to enter into these contracts with soft drink companies.

- Although provincial guidelines ask that carbonated drinks not be sold in elementary and middle schools, this does not apply to secondary schools.

- Students are a "captive market" and can only purchase items offered by the soft drink company that has the contract with the school board.

1. Describe how you would feel if all school boards ordered that only healthy choices should be available in vending machines.

2. Is it right for school boards to enter into exclusive contracts with a company that has a limited number of brands in return for using the profits to purchase items for your school? Discuss.

How Can You Make an Impact Locally?

Living in a democratic country like Canada brings a number of important benefits. Perhaps the most important is being able to influence government decisions. Have you ever actively participated in trying to bring about change? Being informed about issues that may affect you and participation in those issues are the key ingredients to making a difference. Municipal government is a good place to start, because it is involved in many issues that affect you daily.

You can participate in the decision-making process in both direct and indirect ways. Taking the time to vote or supporting a candidate in an election are ways you can get involved. The table below lists a few of the actions you could take.

For links to sites on youth and community activism

Figure 4-19 Think of counter-arguments for each of the obstacles standing in the way of taking action.

PURPOSEFUL ACTIONS FOR INFORMED CITIZENS

Action	Purpose	Obstacle
Exercise your right to vote.	Use your vote to approve or disapprove of those in power; change elected representatives to improve government, including your own student council.	Some citizens do not bother to vote; some citizens vote with limited knowledge.
Communicate your views and concerns about an issue you are passionate about.	Use emails, blogging, text messages, letters, and phone calls to express your concerns to your elected representatives, other political leaders, business leaders, and people with the same concerns.	Some people feel that communication does not change anything; others are not able to communicate effectively.
Influence public opinion.	Use letters to newspaper editors, press releases to media, posters, flyers, web pages, and illustrations to raise awareness and to gather support from other citizens.	Some people lack the time or dedication to produce an effective action; others are not able to communicate effectively.
Take direct action on an issue you are passionate about.	Join volunteer groups, **grassroots organizations**, service clubs, rights advocacy groups, or protest groups to work for a cause that you believe in.	Some people don't have the time or energy to get involved; others don't care enough to get involved.

When individuals work together to persuade others to join them in pursuing a common goal it is called grassroots organizing. Grassroots organizing usually starts at the local level. Some grassroots organizations have evolved into national and international organizations because of their

grassroots organizations: people working together at the local level to achieve a common purpose

People Power

Maren Beeston

Consider all the activities you are involved in in your community. Do you volunteer at the local animal shelter? Are you a member of a local choir? Maybe you take part in community cleanup days. Now let's meet Maren Beeston. When it comes to community involvement, Maren is one busy person! She lives in Hanna, Alberta. This small rural town has a lot going on thanks, in part, to Maren's active role in the community.

As a founding member of the Hanna Youth Council, Maren was able to bring youth issues to her local government and encourage greater youth involvement in municipal activities. The Hanna Youth Council has been able to complete a number of initiatives for the community. These include the organization of youth dances, various fundraisers, and decorating the local parks for holidays.

Next up for Maren was the Hanna Paper Recycling Project. Here's how she explained this youth-led project:

"The recycling project was born simply out of discussion with a friend. We just recognized that there was a need for better opportunity to recycle paper from business environments and we decided to make it happen. Like most projects we started small, we only do paper at the moment and we didn't take on any extremely high volume places such as the school. We thought that this was a great way to raise environmental awareness, help recycle, and raise money for our organizations without simply asking for handouts. The businesses pay a fee and we provide a service and

Figure 4-20
According to Maren Beeston, "It's surprising how much you can accomplish if you want it bad enough."

then that money goes to the separate organizations that supply workers to do pickups."

But perhaps Maren's biggest contribution and success in Hanna has been Summer Slam. Although Hanna is home to Canadian band Nickelback, Maren realized there were no musical instruction opportunities for youth. She successfully organized and led a committee of youth to budget, raise funds, and coordinate a summer rock music school. They brought music to the youth of their community. Now in its third year, Summer Slam has become more than just youth learning how to sing and play. It's about bringing people together to share their love of music and meeting people with similar interests.

1. Identify three ways that Maren has made a positive difference in her community.
2. If you had the choice, which of Maren's three projects would you like to get involved in? Why?

important contributions. Grassroots organizations give people an opportunity to join forces to affect political change or to contribute to a civil society by:

- educating the public
- fundraising for worthy causes
- providing services for people in need
- organizing public demonstrations
- networking with other grassroots organizations.

Grassroots organizations that receive no government funding are also known as **non-governmental organizations (NGOs)**. They are involved in a wide variety of areas. Each community has its own set of NGOs.

non-governmental organizations (NGOs): non-profit, independent organizations dedicated to making the world a better place

SAMPLE LOCAL NON-GOVERNMENT ORGANIZATIONS (NGOs)

Non-governmental Organization	Mission
Friends of the Ferguson Forest Centre — North Grenville County, ON	To prevent development of forested areas and protect them
Inuvik Community Garden — Inuvik, NT	To provide indoor garden plots for planting vegetables and plants in the Arctic
Daily Bread Food Bank — Toronto, ON	To eliminate hunger
Ottawa Arts Court — Ottawa, ON	To provide a permanent location for a variety of artistic endeavours
Windsor-Essex Non-Profit Support Network — Windsor, ON	To provide information and support to all NGOs in the area

Figure 4-21 Find out which NGOs work in your community.

More direct approaches to active participation in the decision-making process may include taking part in rallies on Parliament Hill or contacting a government official directly to express your concerns about an issue. Here are some other suggestions:

- attend public meetings
- sign petitions for causes important to you
- join your student council
- start a letter-writing campaign to newspapers and government officials
- educate yourself about issues by reading or watching the news
- organize a school action group or awareness campaign

Figure 4-22 NBA player Jamaal Magloire worked during McHappy Day in his hometown of Scarborough to raise funds to benefit local charities. Do you think that athletes have a responsibility to raise awareness and funds for important causes?

What Are Those White Ribbons All About?

So it is late fall and you are at the mall. You walk by a man wearing a white ribbon on his jacket. A few moments later, you see another white ribbon on the pocket of a shirt. Then you see one attached to a student's backpack. Do you know what the white ribbon stands for?

The White Ribbon Campaign (WRC) is an international organization that originated in Canada. It promotes men working together to end male violence against women. Started in 1991, the White Ribbon days run for one to two weeks and end on December 6. This date is recognized as Canada's National Day of Remembrance and Action on Violence Against Women. It marks the anniversary of the day in 1989 when Marc Lepine killed 14 female engineering students at a Quebec university. By wearing the white ribbon, men involved in the campaign are saying that they are making "a personal pledge never to commit, condone nor remain silent about violence against women."

Figure 4-23 Is this an effective poster to educate men and boys about the White Ribbon Campaign's message? Explain.

The White Ribbon Campaign is committed to raising awareness in local communities about male violence against women. Its goals include:

- educating boys and men about the issue in schools, at work, and at the community level
- working actively to support local women's groups
- raising funds to spread the White Ribbon Campaign's message throughout the world.

One of the more popular fundraisers for the White Ribbon Campaign is the White Ribbon Concert. It brings together a number of Canadian musicians under one roof. All the proceeds go directly to the WRC. In June of 2005, members of the Barenaked Ladies, Rush, Blue Rodeo, and Sarah Slean, just to name a few, performed a sold-out concert.

1. What does the white ribbon stand for?
2. How does the White Ribbon Campaign work at the community level?

Working Collaboratively—
Being an Effective Team Player

Anyone who has attempted a seemingly impossible task knows that getting help from others makes it easier to accomplish. There is always strength in numbers, especially when you wish to accomplish something important.

When you are truly part of a community, you need to know how to be an effective team player. Here are some tips about contributing effectively.

As a team leader:

- Know your strengths and talents and offer them humbly. You might say, "Here are some things I could do…"
- Recognize the strengths and talents of others and be appreciative of what they can offer.
- Get input from each member of the group about options. The more minds working on a problem, the more creative solutions will come forward.
- Encourage the group to prioritize options, but if no clear decision emerges, take the responsibility as leader to set a clear course of action.
- Lead by doing rather than telling. Model the behaviour you expect.
- Summarize the accomplishments of the group at the conclusion of your task.
- Make sure that everyone has a chance to shine by recognizing each person's contribution and by saying a sincere "Thank you."

As a team member:

- Share your strengths and talents so that others know what you can offer to the team efforts.
- Welcome the strengths and contributions of other team members.
- Honour all responsibilities and obligations to the team.
- Help appoint a leader and be supportive of the leader's decisions and directions. You may wish to volunteer your own leadership skills or clearly say, "I am happy to take direction from..."
- Partner with someone who lacks confidence or know-how and show by example what that person can do.
- Express appreciation for the efforts of the leader and other team members. Recognize that the accomplishments of the team were the result of many individual actions.

There is no room for egos on a team. A team is only strong when all members rely upon and appreciate the contributions of others. What you cannot do alone, you can almost always do with the help of others.

You Try It

Next time you have a group task in class, review the above suggestions and try following them. When you have completed the task, analyse how well your team worked together by cooperating with, supporting, and appreciating each other.

Literacy Hint

Think of a leader you know, perhaps the captain of a sports team or the president of the student council. What qualities does that person have that invite others to commit to his or her team?

Figure 4-24 Cleaning up a community site on Earth Day is a good example of thinking globally and acting locally. More than 6 million Canadians join 500 million people in over 180 countries in Earth Day events and projects to address local environmental issues.

Who would have thought that there is so much going on in your community? Communities are important. This is where we live, learn, and grow. Of the three levels of government, our local government is perhaps the most accessible. We can have a great impact on how our communities look and the services they offer. It is important to be active and have our voices heard so that local government can respond to our needs. Whatever avenue you choose, being informed about local issues and getting involved is an important step toward being a life-long active citizen.

CHECKPOINT

1. Identify three great opportunities your community has to offer you.
2. Name three things that could be improved in your community.
3. In what ways have you been an active member in your community?

CHAPTER REVIEW

Summing It Up

- Local citizenship involves rights and responsibilities. Local action can have a widespread impact.
- Municipalities can be structured as single-tier, upper-tier, or lower-tier municipalities.
- Ontario has amalgamated many municipalities. The process has positive and negative effects.
- A municipality's infrastructure includes the basic facilities and services needed to function.
- Mayors and councillors have important positions with key responsibilities in municipal governments.
- Municipal governments provide services for residents in 10 areas.
- A municipality pays for the services it offers mainly through property taxes.
- There are many ways to participate in the decision-making process of issues important to you.
- Grassroots organizations and non-governmental organizations (NGOs) provide opportunities to affect political change or contribute to a civil society.

KEY TERMS

- global citizenship
- local citizenship
- municipal government
- *Municipal Act*
- upper-tier municipality
- lower-tier municipality
- single-tier municipality
- amalgamation
- infrastructure
- councillors
- grassroots organizations
- non-governmental organizations (NGOs)

Thinking: To Be Informed

1. With a partner, brainstorm a list of ways to become active in your municipality or community. Start with actions that you have already taken. Share your list with the class.

2. Explain how the mayor of a municipality is in a key position to ensure that your community and services run smoothly. If you reside in a First Nations' community, explain how the Band Administrator or Services Coordinator serves this function.

Communicating: To Be Purposeful

3. How would you like people to remember your community as it is today? In groups of four, brainstorm ideas including mementos from your municipality that you would include in a time capsule.

4. Draw a diagram or chart of the organization of your local government. Then compare it with the Brampton model on page 109. What are the differences? What are the similarities?

Applying: To Be Active

5. Go back to the list you generated in the first question. Choose one action. For example, you may think that your community needs a strict bylaw to keep dogs on leash. What strategies could be used to generate action on this issue? Create an action plan for changing the situation.

6. Using a copy of a local newspaper, identify issues of interest to your community. Write to a local politician explaining your view on one issue. Then ask for his or her view or policies on the issue.

Hear My Voice:
Public Issues and Civil Action

Advocacy Anyone?

After years of patching and mending, the school can finally buy new uniforms for all teams. Of the four options in Figure 5-1, which uniforms should the school choose?

Uniform Colour	Advantages	Disadvantages
Blue	Sponsor will pay for professional quality uniforms.	Sponsor, Acme Candy Company, requires advertising space on the back of uniforms.
Red	Student fundraising over two years will pay for professional quality uniforms.	No other student council fundraising will be possible for two years, regardless of the cause or need.
Green	School board will pay for inexpensive quality uniforms for one team per year.	Uniforms will last about five years, but the school has ten teams. This will require constant funding that could have been used for other purposes.
Old and grey	As a tradition, these same uniforms have been worn for the past 20 years; fewer than 1 in 10 students participate in school teams today.	Old uniforms are badly worn, out-of-date, and uncomfortable. Parent volunteers will need to continue making necessary repairs.

Figure 5-1

The school has decided to involve four important groups or **stakeholders** in the decision-making process. They are students, parents and guardians, teachers, and administrators. Each group has elected a representative to participate in a decision-making meeting on its behalf. You will be assigned one of these four representative roles.

stakeholder: a person with an interest or concern in a particular issue or decision

- In the first 12 minutes, the members of each stakeholder group will meet to identify the option they prefer. For instance, all the students will meet together. Each stakeholder group will discuss how those in other groups might be persuaded to support their choice.
- During the next 12 minutes, you will participate in decision-making groups of four. Each new group will have one representative from each stakeholder group. In role, the representatives will attempt to persuade the others to vote for the specific colour that their group has chosen.
- Voting will take place by secret ballot in each group of four. In the case of a tie, the less popular colours will be dropped from the ballot. Then, another vote will take place.

The teacher will note the collective result on the board by tallying the colour selections of all groups.

1. What was the colour of choice for each stakeholder group? What motivated stakeholders to make their selections?
2. What was the colour of choice for the majority of decision-making groups? What most influenced decision-makers?
3. What were the most persuasive arguments? What were the least persuasive arguments?
4. What does this simulation reveal about collective decision making, persuading others, and about you?

Figure 5-2 How important are uniforms for creating a sense of community and team spirit?

KEY LEARNINGS

In this chapter you will explore the following topics:
- the resolution of contemporary public issues
- the diversity of beliefs and values of individuals and groups in Canada
- non-violent citizen participation
- the civic literacy skills of analysing public issues and using visual organizers to think critically

Public Issues and Compelling Arguments

On December 6, 1989, a bitter young man walked into the University of Montreal's École Polytechnique. He was armed with a semi-automatic rifle. The university had rejected Marc Lepine's application. He believed that the feminist movement was responsible for his rejection. He was convinced that women had been given places in school that rightfully belonged to him. He shot and killed 14 women in the university. He then killed himself. At the time, this was the worst mass murder in Canadian history. It became known as the Montreal Massacre.

News reports of this event were met with public outrage. This kind of thing was not supposed to happen in Canada. But it did. December 6 has been proclaimed as the National Day of Remembrance and Action on Violence Against Women. Each year, many Canadians participate in memorial services, wearing symbolic purple or white ribbons. Engineering schools have increased their efforts to attract women into the field.

Figure 5-3 Each year on December 6, Canadians from all walks of life remember the 14 women who were killed. They oppose all forms of violence against women and advocate stricter gun control. Here, an engineering student at the University of Victoria marks the anniversary.

Unrelenting public pressure on the federal government led to stricter gun control laws. Despite these laws and the gun registry program that was created, many Canadians remain dissatisfied. Some Canadians argue that there are still too many guns in circulation. Others argue that the gun registry violates their personal rights. Some Canadians argue that not enough is being done to protect women from acts of violence. How do you feel about these issues?

Literacy Hint

Respond to Text. What is your first reaction to the events in this account? What issues are raised in your mind as a result of this situation?

Active Citizen

Website

For links to sites on the Montreal Massacre and White Ribbon campaign

In this chapter we will focus on **public policy issues** and the actions that people can take to influence policy making. These issues spark discussion and debate about the need for government action. We have looked at sample public issues in each chapter. For example, in Chapter 1, you explored the issue of separate schools for Black students. In that issue, different viewpoints within the Black community were considered. In this chapter, we will investigate additional public policy issues at the local, provincial, and national levels. We will study what a public issue is and how dealing with issues can influence government action. Sample public issues are listed in Figure 5-4. What public policy issues are currently being reported by news media in your community?

public policy issue: a problem situation sparking public discussion and debate about the need for government action to address public concerns

Government Level	Sample Public Issues
Local	• Should pit bulls or other specific breeds be banned? • Should school boards make exclusive soft drink deals with suppliers? • Should curfews and dress codes be imposed on teenagers? • Should communities provide shelters for homeless people?
Provincial	• Should the province fund separate schools for Black students or any other single ethnic group? • Should students be required to stay in school until the age of 18? • Should hospitals and schools be privately owned? • Should the province and First Nations share resource revenues on treaty lands?
National	• Should euthanasia be legalized? • Should marijuana use be decriminalized? • Should smokers pay their own health care expenses? • Should Canadian soldiers be used as international peacekeepers?
Multi-Level	• Should the Kyoto Accord to reduce carbon dioxide emissions be scrapped? • Should the voting age be lowered? • Should tougher gun control legislation be enacted and enforced? • Should voting be made compulsory for all citizens?

Figure 5-4 What is your position on each of these sample issues?

When public opinion is united, governments often take quick and decisive action. This was the case after the horror of the Montreal Massacre. However, when opinions vary greatly or when large groups support opposite sides, political decision making can be complicated. This was the case with Canada's controversial same-sex union debate in 2004–2005. In situations like these, it becomes far more difficult to determine the common good—that is, the most good for the greatest number of people. In a diverse multicultural society, different values, beliefs, and customs are encouraged. That means that there can be many different points of view on matters of public concern.

For most public policy issues, strong arguments support both sides of the debate. In Canada's same-sex union debate, those in favour focused their arguments around equal rights. Those opposed focused their arguments around traditional morality. In the end, same-sex unions were officially recognized.

Figure 5-5 The legal recognition of same-sex unions was followed by a flurry of wedding ceremonies. What evidence of traditional values and what evidence of changing values are visible in this photograph?

Figure 5-6 How pubic policy can result from a social situation.

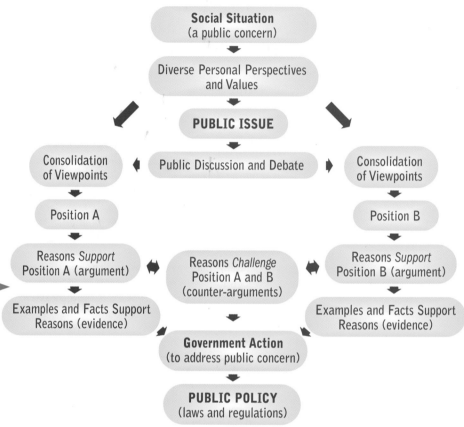

positive argument: view that uses evidence to support the position being taken

advocacy: arguing for a specific position to influence public decision making in a controversial situation

advocate: a person who argues for a specific position

counter-argument: view that challenges the conclusions or supporting information of adversaries

negative argument: view that exposes the weakness of the opposite position

adversary: one who takes an opposite position or presents an opposing argument

The strongest arguments in public policy issues are supported by factual evidence and professional opinion. **Positive arguments** that promote or support a particular position on a public issue are called **advocacy**. People who argue for a specific position are called **advocates**. Both **counter-arguments** and **negative arguments** are intended to weaken or damage a position made by an **adversary** or opposing group.

Troubling social situations are not always resolved through discussion, negotiation, and compromise. For example, frustrated animal rights extremists have spray-painted fur coats being worn by others. This is a violation of personal rights. This kind of action can lead to physical confrontation. In a civil society, remedies are needed to resolve serious conflicts without violence. We will explore conflict resolution strategies in the next chapter.

Figure 5-7 Protestors stage an anti-fur demonstration outside a fur show in Montreal. A steel leghold trap sits in a puddle of fake blood. Should the members of any group be able to force their values on others?

Personal Values and Public Policy

The main source of controversy in social situations is that different people may have different personal values. When public debate becomes heated and emotional, media coverage usually increases. Media coverage can both inform and influence public discussion and debate. The Robert Latimer case is one example. Robert Latimer was a Saskatchewan farmer. In 1993, he killed his 12-year-old daughter. Tracy Latimer suffered from a severe form of cerebral palsy. She was totally paralyzed and in severe, constant pain. Tracy functioned mentally at the level of a three-month-old infant. She had been operated on several times and needed even more surgery. According to doctors Tracy's quality of life would never improve.

Robert Latimer placed Tracy in the cabin of his pickup. He ran a hose from the exhaust to the cabin and started the truck. His daughter died of carbon monoxide poisoning. It is illegal in Canada to actively euthanize—or painlessly kill—another person. Canadian law permits only passive forms of euthanasia. This involves stopping medical treatments and allowing nature to take its course.

Latimer claimed that he was acting as a loving parent. In 1994, he was convicted of second-degree murder. He was sentenced to a minimum of 10 years in prison. Latimer was retried in 1997 after the Supreme Court of

Literacy Hint
What words or phrases in these paragraphs help you to understand the word "euthanasia"?

Canada ordered a new trial. He was convicted again. This time, the jury recommended a one-year jail term and the trial judge agreed. In 1998, the Saskatchewan Court of Appeal reinstated the minimum 10-year prison term.

In 2001, the Supreme Court of Canada upheld this decision. The Supreme Court refused to create a new category of compassionate homicide to give Latimer a lesser sentence. Groups advocating for the rights of those with disabilities argued that a lesser sentence would compromise their rights. According to Traci Walters of the Canadian Association of Independent Living Centres, the Supreme Court's final decision "sends a very strong message to society [about] people with disabilities, that our lives are just as important as anybody else."

Literacy Hint

Respond to Text. What are your feelings and thoughts after reading this account of Robert Latimer's actions? How do you feel about the sentence he received?

Active Citizen Website

For links to sites on the Robert Latimer case

Figure 5-8 Robert Latimer answers questions from the media on his farm on January 18, 2001, after the Supreme Court ruling. What are your views on this ruling?

The Sue Rodriguez case also focused on the issue of legalizing active euthanasia in Canada. She suffered from ALS (amyotrophic lateral sclerosis). This incurable disease attacks the central nervous system and eventually leads to total paralysis and death. Rodriguez was at an advanced stage of the disease. She wanted the legal right to die through doctor-assisted suicide. Rodriguez fought a lengthy court battle to earn the right to die with dignity. On September 30, 1993, the Supreme Court of Canada rejected her final

Active Citizen

plea. She committed suicide in February 1994, with the illegal assistance of an unknown doctor. Vancouver Member of Parliament Svend Robinson admitted being with her when she died. He was never charged.

The Rodriguez and Latimer cases raised important ethical questions about euthanasia. When should life be ended? Who should make the painful decision? Who should act to end another person's life? A substantial majority of Canadians would have to support active euthanasia before lawmakers would consider changing the law. Until the current law is changed, assisted suicide and compassionate homicide remain illegal in Canada. What is your personal view on this sensitive public issue? What values does your view reflect?

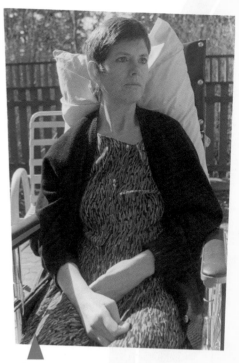

▲ **Figure 5-9** Sue Rodriguez chose to die through doctor-assisted suicide. If you were a doctor, how would you feel about being asked to perform such a task?

CHECKPOINT

1. **Why did the Montreal Massacre result in quick government action?**

2. **Explain the difference between an advocate and an adversary.**

3. **Give an example of a positive argument and a negative argument. Which is the stronger form of argument building? Explain.**

4. **How do personal values come into play with public policy issues?**

Citizens Taking Action

Have you ever faced a social situation that you wanted to change? Did it matter enough to motivate you to do something about it? Some students get involved in student government for this reason. Others get involved in the political process at some level. Many political parties have youth wings to recruit volunteers. As you explored in Chapter 4, some students prefer to get involved with non-government organizations (NGOs) and use their power to make a difference. Ideally, in a healthy democracy, everyone has power. However, informed, purposeful, and active citizens can use their power most effectively.

In Canada, governments generally act as a result of:
- promises made during elections
- changing circumstances
- court decisions
- changing public opinion.

This chapter focuses on changing public opinion.

▲ **Figure 5-10** Canada legalized the use of medical marijuana in 2001. How might changing public opinion have affected this issue?

CIVICS SKILLS POWER

Analysing a Public Policy Issue

When you look at an issue or a social concern, it may seem a simple matter to decide where you or others stand on that issue. As you look at the details for the issue in Figure 5-11, what questions come to your mind that might complicate your decision?

Issue	Who is involved?	What might they think?	Explanation
Should smokers be responsible for their own health care expenses?	Non-smokers	Yes, they should pay.	Smokers choose an unhealthy lifestyle practice. Others should not have to pay for the results of their bad habit.
	Smokers	No, we should not have to pay.	Everyone has freedom of choice. Non-smokers may also have bad habits that contribute to poor health.

 Figure 5-11

Ask Probing Questions About the Issue

Asking questions helps you to identify useful criteria to base your decision on.

- Do all non-smokers feel that smokers should pay for their health care?
- Do all smokers feel that they should not pay their health care expenses?
- What health care issues are being considered? Lung cancer and other diseases of the lungs affect smokers in greater proportion to the rest of the population. However, there are smokers who will never suffer these health problems.

- What lifestyle habits of non-smokers might cause them to have health problems? How do addictions to food or alcohol fit into this picture?
- What are the overall costs involved?
- In 2005, the British Columbia Supreme Court ruled that government can seek damages for smoke-related health care costs from tobacco companies. Where do tobacco companies fit into this issue now?

Even with these few questions, you can see that you must set a high standard when analysing public policy issues. On the next page you will find some steps to help you reach a decision on a policy issue.

Steps	Advocates	Adversaries
Know and remove your personal bias	My bias is that smoking is a dirty, dangerous habit. I am affected by second-hand smoke in some situations and it is not pleasant. I am worried I might get lung cancer.	My bias is that non-smokers are self-righteous. They think they are better than smokers. Non-smokers do not always make healthy choices about food or alcohol. They think I should not have freedom of choice.
Research and gather facts	According to Health Canada: • Less than 25 percent of the population are smokers. • Tobacco use was the cause of 30 percent of all fatal cancers in 2003. • Lung cancer accounts for 30 percent of the cancers in males and 25 percent in females. • Other cancers caused directly by smoking are lip, jaw, throat, bladder, and kidney cancer. • Second-hand smoke may cause non-smokers to suffer the same cancers as smokers.	According to Health Canada: • Heart disease resulting from poor lifestyle habits, such as overeating or inactivity, is the number one cause of death in Canada. • Heart disease is the most costly disease in Canada. • Twenty percent of cancers are caused by poor diet with a high proportion of dietary fat.
Analyse the information	• Heart disease is the number one killer of people in Canada. However, smoking is listed at the top of the lifestyle habits and choices that cause heart disease. • Tobacco use is a significant factor in cancer fatalities. • Heart disease is very costly. Society as a whole picks up the tab for treating victims of heart disease. • Can we make one group pay for its lifestyle habits and excuse another?	
Make a judgment	Asking smokers to pay their own health care expenses would be unfair, considering that we financially support the poor health that results from other bad lifestyle habits. However, we should do everything possible to persuade people not to smoke. We should also encourage a healthy lifestyle with proper eating habits and daily vigorous physical activity.	
Reach a decision	A fair policy would be to do everything possible to discourage young people from smoking, to prevent non-smokers from experiencing second-hand smoke, and to encourage healthy eating and living.	
Revisit the decision	As new information presents itself, review the decision to assess its appropriateness and how well it has been used.	

Figure 5-12 Steps to follow to reach a decision on a policy issue.

Reaching a decision on an issue of social concern and developing a public policy on that issue is rarely an easy process. Putting aside your personal biases, gathering the facts, and analysing the information will help you to reach a decision. Governments go through this same process when they make decisions about public policy.

You Try It

Choose one of the public issues listed in Figure 5-4 on page 125. Summarize the issue and the two sides according to Figure 5-11. Then, follow the steps in Figure 5-12 to reach a judgment and a policy position.

For links to sites on
youth achievement awards

The Power of One

In each chapter, you have explored examples of individuals who have used their personal power to make a significant difference. The changes that each individual has achieved benefit many others.

In all these cases, the individuals believed strongly enough in what they were trying to do to make the necessary personal sacrifices to succeed. These ordinary people cared enough to make a difference. They have achieved extraordinary results.

Name	Age	Community	Achievement
Mohamed Abdi	17	Ottawa, Ontario	Millennium Excellence Award Recipient Mohamed started a peer tutoring and student assistance program at his Somali community centre. He also started a stop smoking program at his high school.
Jessica Alber	17	Exeter, Ontario	Millennium Excellence Award Recipient Jessica organized the Panther Powerwalk, which raised over $20 000 for several charities. She also assisted with fundraising efforts to build a local youth centre.
William Chan	17	Calgary, Alberta	Millennium Excellence Award Recipient William organized Youth Helping Youth to raise money, food, and other necessary items for needy youth during the holiday season.
Matthew Ferguson	17	Pond Inlet, Nunavut	Millennium Excellence Award Recipient Matthew organized an Elders' Tea Party, launched a community cleanup, and organized a community softball program for the youth of Pond Inlet.
Sarah Gates	16	Lantzville, British Columbia	Terry Fox Humanitarian Award Recipient Sarah started a Vision for Sight program to fight blindness in developing nations. She also published a book of poetry on chronic pain, with all proceeds going to St. Paul's Hospital.
Lisa LeRoy	19	Pointe Claire, Quebec	Top 20 Under 20™ Award Recipient Lisa started a Free the Children Youth in Action group. She also raised funds to build a well in the Kono district of Sierra Leone.
Hannah Taylor	9	Winnipeg, Manitoba	Founder of the Ladybug Foundation Hannah raised more than $400 000 for the kind treatment of homeless persons.
Michael Thibodeau	17	Middleton, Nova Scotia	Top 20 Under 20™ Award Recipient Michael started Musicians for the Support of the Visually Impaired (MSVI). In this program the visually impaired are taught piano and theory free of charge.

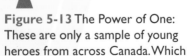

Figure 5-13 The Power of One: These are only a sample of young heroes from across Canada. Which civic achievements impressed you the most? Why?

Sometimes the dedication of a single person can be contagious. Other like-minded people quickly join the cause. Sometimes it only takes one person to start the ball rolling.

People Power

David and Rob Ellis

David Ellis was an 18-year-old honours student and school athlete of the year. He volunteered regularly to serve meals to single moms and young children from a mobile soup kitchen. On February 11, 1999, David was on the second day of his first job at a bakery in Oakville, Ontario. With minimal training, he was cleaning dough from an industrial mixer. The machinery accidentally started. David was drawn into the mixer by the rotating blades. Six days later, he died of massive head injuries. He never lived to see his first pay cheque.

On that day in February, Rob Ellis's life changed forever. Like many parents, he assumed that his son's workplace was safe. Rob Ellis believes that workplace safety should be a priority for all businesses. He also believes that his son David would still be alive today if the bakery had provided better training and installed an inexpensive safety switch on the outside of the mixer.

The bakery's supervisor was sentenced to a 21-day jail term. The bakery was fined $62 000. Rob Ellis and his daughter Marisa have become involved in Workplace Safety and Insurance Board campaigns to make every workplace safer.

During 2004, Rob Ellis spoke directly to over 100 000 parents, students, and business leaders about workplace safety. He reached millions more through positive media coverage. Young workers are eager to please their employers, but they need to ask basic questions to stay safe at work:

- What are the dangers in this workplace?
- What protective equipment and safety training are available?

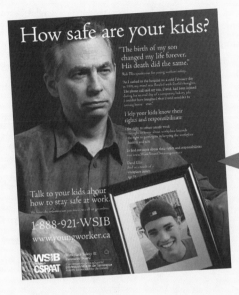

Figure 5-14 What motivates Rob Ellis to continue his workplace safety crusade?

- Who is the supervisor responsible to hear safety concerns?

Rob Ellis tells his audience "It takes guts to ask questions to a new boss. I know it does, I've been there…"

Thirteen workers between the ages of 15 and 24 were killed on the job in Ontario during 2000. In 2004, the number had been reduced to seven deaths. Rob Ellis is interested in further reductions. He does not want any other parents to be told that their child is never coming home from work.

1. Why do you think that young people are in a high-risk injury group?
2. What three things can you do to promote workplace safety at school and at work?

Strength in Numbers

"Many hands make light work" is an old proverb. It means that the workload is easier if the labour is shared. This is also true in the world of politics and public policy making. A determined advocate can achieve extraordinary results. By teaming with others to share the labour and to create a more sustained or broad-based effort, even more can be accomplished.

Our Charter right to freedom of association allows citizens to band together to pursue common goals. Many citizens organize to advocate policy change. Many **interest groups** are occupational or industry interest groups. These include the Canadian Medical Association, The Ontario Teacher's Federation, the Business Council on National Issues, and the Automotive Parts Manufacturers' Association. Teachers, students, parents, farmers, manufacturers, doctors, dentists, engineers, architects, consumers, and environmentalists have also organized interest groups. These groups attempt to influence policy making in their favour.

Interest groups are an effective use of people power to influence public opinion and policy making. Through organized groups, people can have a stronger and more focused voice in current issues. This can help shape public opinion and pressure governments into action. Public protests and demonstrations are sometimes used to bring attention to a troubling social situation and to promote a specific solution.

interest group: a group of individuals who join together to pursue common goals and to advocate for their cause

Figure 5-15 In March 2005, farmers descended on Queen's Park to protest the lack of government support for agriculture in Ontario. According to the cartoonist, what did they find when they got there? Why do you think that there is always a long line of groups advocating for government action?

Pressure Groups and Lobbying

Imagine you are an elected government official. A respected person in the community buys you dinner at a pricey restaurant. During dinner your host offers you an expensive Caribbean cruise. When dinner is over, you are given an information package. It outlines the benefits of nuclear energy as a clean power source. Then, you are asked to consider voting in favour of Bill C-88 to support the construction of a nuclear power plant in your community. The person explains that his clients will guarantee quality construction. They will build a sturdy power plant that will provide safe electricity for many generations. How would you react to this encounter? Would you change how you were originally going to vote?

You have just encountered a representative from a **pressure group** known as a **lobbyist**. Lobbyists are well-trained professionals. Pressure groups are interest groups organized to persuade policy-makers to make decisions that favour their interests. The Canadian Labour Congress (CLC), for example, attempts to persuade policy-makers to pass laws and regulations that support unions and working-class Canadians.

Pressure groups that are extremely well organized and effective are often called **lobby groups**. **Lobbying** is a much-used tactic by pressure groups. It is an organized effort to influence policy making through regular contact with government officials. Lobby groups use a variety of ways to influence public policy making:

- one-on-one meetings
- letter-writing campaigns
- public information campaigns
- position papers
- public opinion polls
- research findings
- information sheets.

Successful lobbying has persuaded governments to pass new laws and regulations, to reduce taxes, and to control pollution. It has also been used to increase social services, to protect certain industries, and to reverse earlier decisions. Some citizens and grassroots groups fear that this might give interest groups too much influence. How do you feel about the influence of interest groups?

Literacy Hint

Make a Connection. Has anyone ever given you a gift or an advantage and then expected something in return? How is this experience similar to the actions of some lobbyists?

pressure group: a group organized to persuade policy-makers to make decisions that favour their interests

lobbyist: a professional trained in the art of policy influence

lobby group: a well-organized group intended to influence policy making by engaging in regular dialogue with government officials

lobbying: trying to influence legislators

Figure 5-16 What is the purpose of this poster by MADD (Mothers Against Drunk Driving)?

Figure 5-17 Ontario Premier Dalton McGuinty is seen addressing the Automotive Parts Manufacturers' Association in 2005. Why would the premier prefer a meeting with this lobby group to meetings with individual manufacturers?

Case Study: Influencing Policy Making

Interest groups often pressure provincial governments into doing what they believe is the "right" thing. Often there are more needs to address than available resources. In the spring of 2005, for example, the Ontario government had $500 million to invest. Many interest groups attempted to influence its decision, as shown in Figure 5-18. In the end, the government used the money to support the provincial auto industry, one of the province's largest employers.

With this $500 million incentive and additional federal support, the province was able to secure a new Toyota assembly plant for Woodstock, Ontario. The auto manufacturer's contribution over 10 years is expected to be three times more than the amount the provincial government has provided. The plant will employ 1300 workers directly. It is estimated that another 3500 jobs may be created in supporting industries, such as parts

Proposed Use of Government Funds	Some Supporters/ Advocates	Advantages Proposed	Drawbacks
Pay off some of the provincial debt	bankers, accountants, business leaders	Governments that spend less on debt charges have more money to spend on other programs.	Proposed use does not create jobs or stimulate the economy.
Increase investment in health care	seniors, health care workers, social workers	As Ontario's population gets older, more health care services will be needed.	Health care is already a major source of spending; some of the money may not be spent effectively.
Reduce taxes for residents	taxpayer groups, retailers, manufacturers	Residents will have more money to spend to stimulate the economy.	There will be little lasting effect, unless tax reductions are repeated.
Invest in power plants to keep up with increased demand	environmentalists, industrialists, consumers	High polluting coal-fired plants can be replaced by cleaner technology.	Power plants are very expensive; $500 million may not be enough to build even one large plant.
Support farmers struggling to remain competitive	farmers, environmentalists, food bank operators	More of Ontario's food supply will safely come from Ontario farms.	Foreign food supplies may be less expensive for consumers.
Invest in the auto industry	parts manufacturers, business leaders, auto workers	More jobs will be created in one of the province's largest industries.	Ontario will become too dependent on one industry. When the auto industry has a bad year Ontario will suffer.

Figure 5-18 Spending Options for the Ontario Government. Which option do you prefer? Justify your decision.

manufacturers. Additional jobs will be created in town, supplying products and services to the families of autoworkers. For example, schools, hospitals, shops, and stores will be needed.

Protest Groups and Civil Disobedience

Some interest groups spend a large part of their time organizing public demonstrations to shape public opinion or to influence public policy. They are known as **protest groups**. Protest groups differ from lobby groups. Lobby groups attempt to influence policy by providing information to government representatives. Protest groups prefer more direct action to demonstrate their disapproval of government policies or practices and to influence public opinion. Protest groups use public demonstration strategies, such as rallies, parades, protest marches, sit-ins, roadblocks, and boycotts to achieve their goals. Examples include:

protest group: people who use public demonstrations to influence public opinion or to pressure governments and other organizations to act

- students and parents marching on district board offices to protest the planned closing of neighbourhood schools
- student **boycotts** of certain brands of athletic shoes and clothing until manufactures improve wages and working conditions for the people who make them
- students in schools with uniform dress codes protesting against the purchase of clothing manufactured in sweatshops in developing countries
- people of all ages participating in rallies to promote greater protection for women from violent acts.

boycott: refuse to buy or use a product as a form of protest

civil disobedience: the deliberate breaking of a law regarded as unjust to draw attention to the injustice and to pressure governments and other organizations to act

When traditional protest methods do not appear to be working, frustrated individuals or activist groups may resort to **civil disobedience**. Civil disobedience involves deliberately breaking a law regarded as unjust to draw attention to the injustice and put pressure on governments to act. Civil disobedience has three essential elements:

- The act must not involve violence.
- The act must be aimed at a significant law or practice.
- Protesters must assume responsibility for their illegal actions.

Those engaging in civil disobedience must be willing to face punishment when they break the law. This confirms the rule of law. This willingness to accept punishment also shows the strength of the protester's conviction.

Figure 5-19 What are these parents and students doing to draw attention to the planned closing of a school in their community?

One well-known example of civil disobedience led to India's gaining independence from the British Empire in 1947. Mohandas Gandhi used non-violent civil disobedience to protest the unjust treatment of the Indian people by the British. Setting an example, he urged his followers to boycott British goods, to ignore British laws, and to avoid paying British taxes. He led a successful campaign to gain independence for India by using dignified, non-violent protest and disobedience. This type of non-violent campaign is often called **passive resistance**.

passive resistance: a non-violent form of deliberate non-cooperation with government authority

Figure 5-20 Mohandas Gandhi, the father of passive resistance, is seen here (middle, head bowed) in 1930. He and supporters marched over 300 kilometres to the sea to collect salt in symbolic defiance of the British salt monopoly.

Active Citizen

Website

For links to sites on the work of Mohandas Gandhi and Martin Luther King

During the 1960s, American civil rights leader Martin Luther King, Jr. also used non-violent disobedience and protest marches to secure equal rights for Black Americans.

In Canada, First Nations have often felt forced to engage in civil disobedience to assert their rights to their treaty lands. For example, in 2004, the Grassy Narrows First Nation in northwestern Ontario blocked logging roads in their treaty territory. They were trying to prevent timber companies from cutting trees under a provincial harvesting licence. The First Nation believed that their land rights were being ignored. When they could not achieve satisfaction in initial negotiations, they resorted to civil disobedience. They disrupted logging activities and drew attention to their claims.

Oka: From Civil Disobedience to Armed Conflict

In 1990, the town of Oka, Quebec, decided to expand its golf course. The land in question was an ancient Mohawk burial ground. Frustrated by fruitless negotiations with town planners, a group of Mohawks decided to take more direct action. In July 1990, they set up barricades to block construction.

Mohawks from the neighbouring Kahnawake Reserve joined in the struggle by blockading the Mercier Bridge. This bridge was the main route connecting the island of Montreal to suburban communities on the south side of the St. Lawrence River. Angry residents threw rocks and insults at the Mohawks watching over the barricades.

The Quebec government responded by sending in heavily armed police officers to remove the barricades. Mohawk warriors defended their positions. In the gun fight that followed one police officer was killed. The police responded by sealing off all access to the reserve. The Canadian Armed Forces were finally called in as tensions among the Mohawk, residents, and police officers grew.

Women, children, and elderly Mohawks were allowed to leave the reserve. A small group of warriors refused to leave. Soldiers removed the barricades, and the bridge was reopened. The armed conflict lasted 78 days. Finally, on September 26, the Mohawk warriors came forward and 50 were arrested. However, construction of the golf course didn't resume. In 1997, the federal government purchased the disputed land from the town and gave it to the Mohawk Nation.

After the Oka conflict, more attention was given to Aboriginal land claims. Aboriginal peoples were included in important discussions with federal and provincial governments. From time to time, confrontations continued between police forces and Aboriginal protestors in different parts of Canada. For example, in 1995 a land claim dispute in Ontario's Ipperwash Provincial Park led to the shooting death of Dudley George, an unarmed protestor. It led to a major public inquiry.

Figure 5-21 A stuffed poncho holds a message for Canadian troops at Oka in September 1990. Do you consider the Mohawk actions at Oka to be an example of civil disobedience? Explain. Were the actions effective in your view?

Literacy Hint

Respond to Text. What do you think about the actions of the Mohawks, the police, and the residents?

CHECKPOINT

1. **List four things that motivate democratic governments to act.**

2. **Distinguish between interest groups, pressure groups, and protest groups.**

3. **What methods do lobby groups use to influence government policy making?**

4. **What are the three requirements of civil disobedience?**

Using Visual Organizers to Think Critically

Why is it important to think critically? We live in a time when the media bombard us with information and ideas. Many of us spend more time watching television or on the Internet than we spend in school, on work, or with our friends. How do we decide which information is important to our lives? How do we know what to believe?

Thinking critically is essentially deciding—using reason more than emotion—what and what not to believe. When thinking critically, we have a goal or purpose in mind: we want to make a decision, draw a conclusion, solve a problem, or project the likely outcome of a situation.

To engage in critical thinking, you must be:

- self-aware, knowing your own biases and emotions
- honest about your motives in any situation
- rational, weighing all the evidence on its merits

- open-minded enough to examine and evaluate all sides of an issue and to change your mind if offered new contradictory evidence
- disciplined enough to avoid making snap judgments and to resist outside pressures to think or decide a certain way or within a certain time frame.

Visual organizers, such as Venn diagrams and quadrants, can help you arrange information and ideas to make the path toward a decision clearer.

A Venn diagram uses one or more overlapping circles to help you compare and contrast information. In the overlap of the circles, you can note items or facts that are common to the issue you are considering. Look at the following example:

Figure 5-22 ▶

Issue: Should terminally ill patients be allowed to request assisted suicide?

Yes
- All people have freedom of choice.
- Only the ill person can say when suffering is too great.
- We do not allow animals to suffer, so why should we allow humans to suffer?
- Why prolong life without quality?

Common Ground
Terminally ill patients should not have to suffer.

No
- A higher power chooses our time to die.
- We have drugs to make people relatively comfortable to the end of life.
- Who makes the decision when the patient can't.
- There may be abuses such as terminating life for convenience rather than suffering.

Critical Analysis: This is a complicated issue. More information is needed about the numbers of people involved and the circumstances of the cases. Countries that allow assisted suicide may be helpful in clarifying how decisions are reached and whether there are abuses of the process.

A quadrant organizer allows you to examine what you know and feel, while looking at possible outcomes of a situation. Try using a SEED approach.

S = Self-awareness—your experience and biases

E = Examine all sides

E = Establish the facts

D = Decide where you stand and why

Figure 5-23 provides an example of a quadrant organizer using the SEED approach.

You Try It

Choose a current issue from your school or community. For instance, Should the school enforce a dress code? Should the community establish a curfew for young people to lessen violence? You might prefer to choose an issue of national concern, such as, Should the voting age be lowered? Use a Venn diagram or a quadrant organizer to think your way through the issues and then reach a decision.

Issue: Should pit bulls be banned?

Self-awareness:

What is my personal knowledge?
- My elderly aunt was attacked by a neighbour's pit bull and was hospitalized.
- I know of other dogs with bad temperaments that have attacked people.

What do I think and feel?
- I feel afraid when I see pit bulls or Rottweilers, because they were originally bred for certain tasks such as hunting or bear baiting.
- I think some owners are not responsible with their pets.

What are my biases?
- I don't like vicious dogs of any kind. I think owners should be held responsible for the behaviour of their pets.

Examine all sides:

What do other people think?
- Some people buy pit bulls or Rottweilers for protection and train them to be aggressive.
- Many people feel that pit bulls and similar breeds should not be banned.

Why do they have that point of view?
- They know that dogs respond to the treatment and training they receive. Socialization creates good dogs or bad dogs.

Is there anyone else to consider?
- Children, people with disabilities, and seniors may not realize that a dog may be dangerous or have the ability to protect themselves.

Establish the facts:
- Pit bulls are not always easy to identify because of crossbreeding.
- Pit bulls account for 50 percent of all dog attacks in the United States.
- Bans in two Ontario cities have reduced pit bull attacks by 95 percent.
- Strict measures against irresponsible owners have reduced all dog attacks by 70 percent in Calgary.

Decide:

I think that the responsibility for dog's behaviour lies with the owner. We should have stricter rules and penalties for owners. This could include people who train their dogs to be vicious, who do not contain powerful dogs properly, and whose dogs have a history of aggressive behaviour with people or other animals.

Figure 5-23

Thinking Critically About Public Policy Issues

Issues are everywhere. You have probably encountered policy issues at your school. For example, should late assignments be accepted without penalties? Debate on this issue seeks to strike a balance between accountability and compassion. How do you feel personally about this complicated issue?

- If a late assignment is evaluated as "A" quality work, should the mark be entered as a "B" or a "C" due to lateness? What exactly does "A" quality work mean? Do marks mean the same thing to all students?
- Are deadline extensions a student's right, or are they matters that need to be negotiated between teacher and student? What circumstances justify an extension? How would this play out in the world of work?
- Should students be able to hand in assignments at any time during the course — even well after other assignments have been marked and returned to the rest of the class?
- Does it matter how often a student hands in assignments late? Is it better to hand in work late rather than not at all?
- Is a no-penalty policy fair to students who work hard to meet deadlines? Could those students improve their marks by also taking extra time?
- When one student misses a deadline for a group assignment, should the whole group suffer?
- What is your teacher's policy regarding late assignments? Is it a personal decision, a decision by a department of teachers, a school decision, or a district-wide decision? Why would the source of this decision be important to consider?

You can now start to see how complicated issues can become. This one issue quickly produced 16 probing questions. Any position on this issue will require serious thinking. First, you'll have to strip the issue down to its core. Taking something apart to better understand its inner workings is called **analysis**. We have analysed or taken apart at least one issue in each chapter.

Next, you have to make sense of the bits and pieces of information that you have found. This requires organizing and relating. How does this new information connect with what you already know? How does it fit with your personal beliefs? What patterns or connections can you make? This generalizing, interpreting, and consolidating is called **synthesis**. Synthesis involves tying things together in a meaningful way. To arrive at a solid conclusion, you will have to assess the value of different bits of information. This kind of thinking is called making judgments or **evaluation**. Analysis,

Figure 5-24 Complications with assignments are often best dealt with through face-to-face dialogue. Are assignment extensions a student's right or are they matters that need to be negotiated between student and teacher?

analysis: taking a concept or idea apart to better understand it

synthesis: tying information together to build meaningful conclusions

evaluation: making a judgment about an idea's merit or value

Active Citizen

synthesis, and evaluation are key parts of **critical thinking**. Dealing with complex social issues requires critical thinking.

You have already encountered some public policy issues in this chapter. If you look through the local daily newspaper, you could probably find many more. In the first section of this chapter, you explored the issue of whether active euthanasia should be allowed for a terminally ill person in pain. To help prepare for the advocacy activity in this chapter and to support the culminating performance task, we'll explore one more public issue: the banning of pit bulls.

In Ontario, few issues have touched off emotional public debate like the decision to ban one specific crossbreed of dogs. On March 1, 2005, the Ontario Legislature approved Bill 132 (by a vote of 56 to 23), making Ontario the first province or territory to ban pit bulls.

This legislation bans the breeding of dogs defined as pit bulls by neutering them. Existing pit bulls must be muzzled and leashed in public. Owners of pit bulls and other dangerous dogs face fines of up to $10 000 and jail terms up to six months for any dogs that bite, attack, or pose a threat to public safety. This provincial law is intended to prevent a wide variety of local laws.

critical thinking: examining the thinking process to better understand its significance and the reason behind it

Informed to Be Effective

The purposeful examination of our thinking and the thinking of others to make better sense of our world is called critical thinking. Critical thinking involves:
- thinking actively and for yourself
- discussing ideas in an organized way
- being receptive to new ideas
- supporting viewpoints with evidence.

Are you a critical thinker?

Community	Date	Attack Details
Stouffville	April 1998	A bull mastiff attacked and killed an 8-year-old girl.
Chatham	June 2004	A letter carrier was attacked by two pit bulls. She lost her right ear and broke both wrists.
London	August 2004	A man walking the dog with his family was viciously attacked by two pit bulls attempting to kill the family pet.
Toronto	August 2004	A man walking two pit bulls for a friend was badly mauled by the dogs. Police needed 12 bullets to kill the dogs.
Ottawa	February 2005	Three pit bulls jumped a fence and attacked a two-year-old boy and his father as they were walking through a park. A month earlier, the same animals attacked two young boys.

Figure 5-25 Hershey is a pit bull that was abused by a previous owner. Hershey is now a therapy dog for St. John Ambulance. In 2005, Hershey was awarded a hero's medal for acts of bravery from the Toronto Humane Society. Should this dog be required to wear a muzzle and leash in public?

Figure 5-26 Sample pit bull attacks in Ontario

Public policy issues often become complex in our multicultural society. Conflicting views about social concerns and problem situations require critical thinking to deal with them.

Issue Analysis

Should Pit Bulls or any Other Specific Breed Be Banned?

YES

A variety of individuals and groups, including city officials, police chiefs, and hospital doctors, have presented the following arguments in support of the pit bull ban:

- Pit bulls were crossbred for fighting. Even though dog fighting was banned in the early 1900s, this criminal activity continues in some areas.

- According to a 2005 report from the Canadian Institute for Health Information, 10 883 Ontarians ended up in emergency departments for injuries related to dog bites in 2004. This represents a 38 percent increase over the previous year.

- Statistics presented by the American Veterinary Medical Association indicate that pit bulls, representing 1 percent of the dog population, account for 50 percent of all dog attacks in the United States.

- Police have encountered a number of dangerous situations involving pit bulls. Criminals and gang members use pit bulls to support their illegal activities.

- Bans in Kitchener and Winnipeg have reduced pit bull attacks from 20 per year to one per year.

NO

A variety of individuals and groups, including animal rights activists, veterinarians, and breeders, have presented the following arguments to challenge the pit bull ban:

- Pit bulls are crossbreeds that are difficult to identify and require the assessment of a veterinarian. Identification issues have led to several lawsuits in US courts.

- Human- and animal-directed aggression in pit bulls is a learned behaviour, not a genetic predisposition. Pit bulls are still used as rescue and service dogs.

- Dog attacks are the result of ownership problems that will not go away if a specific breed is banned. Irresponsible owners will simply switch to other breeds. The law must hold irresponsible owners accountable for their dogs.

- The Ontario Veterinary Medical Association (OVMA) does not advocate legislation naming specific breeds of dog as vicious. It encourages and supports responsible genetic selection and rearing, and training of dogs to control aggression.

- Calgary reduced the number of dog attacks by over 70 percent by targeting irresponsible owners and dangerous dogs, rather than banning specific breeds.

1. Identify the strongest two points made by each side on this emotional issue. What supporting evidence is provided?

2. With which position do you agree most? Explain why.

3. Survey public opinion to determine how your community currently feels about this public issue.

When conflicting positions on public issues are supported by strong arguments, critical thinking is required to assess the merits or value of each. When complex public issues, like the same-sex union debate, come down to value judgments (equality versus traditional morality), critical thinking is required to recognize the bias. The building blocks of logic and reason must be used to evaluate the potential of all arguments and counter-arguments to serve the common good.

CHECKPOINT

1. **What are the steps involved in analysing an issue?**
2. **Explain the difference between analysis and synthesis.**
3. **Complex social issues require critical thinking. Explain what critical thinking involves.**

CHAPTER REVIEW

Summing It Up

- A public policy issue is a public concern that sparks discussion and debate about the need for government action.

- Positive argumentation uses supporting evidence to build an argument. Negative argumentation attacks the supporting evidence of an opposing argument.

- Personal values are often involved in public policy issues.

- People who care enough can make a real difference.

- People join interest groups to work together toward common goals.

- Groups organized to persuade policy-makers to make decisions that favour their common interests are called pressure groups.

- Lobbying, a major pressure group activity, is an organized effort to influence government policy.

- Protest groups spend a large part of their time organizing public demonstrations to shape public opinion or to influence public policy.

- Civil disobedience involves the deliberate but non-violent breaking of a law considered unjust to draw attention to the injustice and put pressure on governments and other organizations to act.

- stakeholder
- public policy issue
- positive argument
- advocacy

- advocate
- counter-argument
- negative argument
- adversary
- interest group

- pressure group
- lobbyist
- lobby group
- lobbying
- protest group

- boycott
- civil disobedience
- passive resistance
- analysis

- synthesis
- evaluation
- critical thinking

Thinking: To Be Informed

1. What issues would you be willing to advocate for in your school or community? Who would you lobby? What strategies would you use?

2. Assess the strategies used by either Mohandas Gandhi or Martin Luther King, Jr. to achieve major changes in government policy. Make a web or chart for a class discussion.

3. Research one of the interest groups or organizations mentioned in this chapter to prepare a brief report on its membership, purpose, and accomplishments to date.

Communicating: To Be Purposeful

4. Write a letter to the editor or create a political cartoon to clearly state a position taken on one of the issues raised in this chapter.

5. Using the People Power feature as a model, create a profile outlining one Canadian's advocacy or activism. You may want to use one of the people mentioned in this chapter or you can use a person of your choice.

Applying: To Be Active

6. It's time for you to become an advocate. Choose an issue you are passionate about. Then choose the format your advocacy will take from the chart on the next page or after discussion with your teacher. Your teacher will help organize student groups according to issues and tasks of interest and provide a rubric outlining how your work on this performance task will be assessed.

Advocacy Task	Individual Contribution (the power of one)	Group Activity (strength in numbers)
A debate	Prepare, present, and defend a single persuasive argument to support a position on a public issue.	Teams of students advocate for a particular position by presenting their strongest argument.
A "speaker's corner" announcement	Prepare and present a logical and persuasive speech to support a position on the public issue of your choice.	Audience listens to speeches and offers constructive feedback and support for speakers.
A letter to an editor or a person of influence	Write a letter to advocate for a specific position on a public issue of your choice.	Read letters and offer constructive feedback and support for writers.
A one-minute public service announcement (PSA)	Create a script or storyboard for a one-minute message to advocate for a specific position on a public issue of your choice.	Review scripts and select the best one to produce as a group project.
A public demonstration	Prepare posters, signs, speeches, and slogans to promote a specific position on a public issue.	Coordinate individual efforts to simulate an actual public demonstration.

Figure 5-27 Advocacy task options

Culminating Performance Task: Making a Difference

In this chapter, you have been introduced to advocacy skills and challenged to put them to one of five suggested uses. The application that you select will provide an opportunity to practise some of the skills needed to successfully complete your Culminating Performance Task. With careful planning, you may be able to transform the advocacy task from this chapter into the course Culminating Performance Task.

Have you found a need that you would like to address or a cause that you would like to support? If yes, great! If not, try looking again at the list of young heroes in Figure 5-13. Or have you come across any leads while working on your compulsory community service hours?

Next Steps

Active Citizenship	Process Steps
Be Informed	Think critically about your concern.
Be Purposeful	Finalize an action plan to carry it out.
Be Active	Document the steps taken and the results. Obtain constructive feedback to improve your plan and execution.

THE GLOBAL CITIZEN TODAY

That's The Way the Cookie Crumbles— A Global Simulation

How would you like some cookies? This cookie break will simulate how Earth's wealth is distributed. Currently, about 80 percent of the world's people live in developing nations. They have access to no more than 20 percent of Earth's wealth. We'll use this **80/20 rule** to distribute the class's cookie wealth. Playing cards will be used to determine how many cookies each student will receive. You'll have the same number of cards as the number of students in your class. Figure 6-2 shows how the cards will be used. Your teacher will shuffle and deal the cards.

80/20 rule: approximately 80 percent of the world's people have access to no more than 20 percent of Earth's wealth

Figure 6-1 The United Nations' Human Development Index measures quality of life. It is based on life expectancy, knowledge, and standard of living. How does Canada compare to other countries on this map?

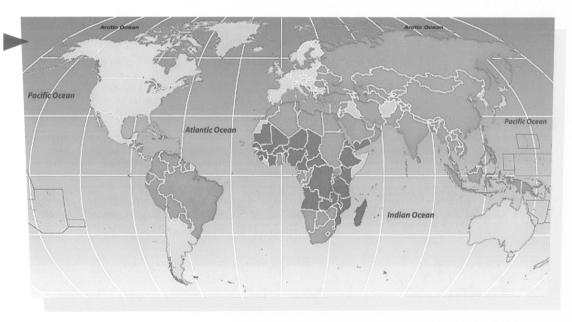

Human Development Index
- High
- Medium
- Low
- Not Available

SAMPLE COOKIE DISTRIBUTION FOR A CLASS OF 25 STUDENTS, USING 75 COOKIES

Category	Number of Students	Playing Cards	Cookie Distribution to Group	Cookies per Student
Developed Nations	5 (20%)	3 kings 2 queens	60 (80% of 75)	12 12
Developing Nations	20 (80%)	14 number cards	15 (20% of 75)	1
Most Poor Nations		4 aces 2 jokers		¼ crumbs only

Figure 6-2

Now that you have your cookies, how do you feel? You are probably excited if you are "wealthy" and not quite as thrilled if you are "poor." Now what will you do with your share of the cookies? If you have a lot of cookies, will you keep them all for yourself? Will you share with others? If so, who will you share with and why? If you are "poor" will you stick with what you've got, or try to get more cookies? How? Now enjoy those cookies!

1. What was your first instinct as a participant in this cookie game? What influenced you?

2. Did your strategy change when you talked to others with more or fewer cookies? How did your strategy change?

3. What did this activity reinforce about you and about the global community today? Do you see yourself as a member of this global community?

Literacy Hint

Make an Inference. Ask yourself why certain cards are associated with certain types of nations. Why do kings and queens represent the wealthiest nations? What conclusions can you draw from the way this deck has been dealt?

KEY LEARNINGS

In this chapter you will explore the following topics:
- what it means to be a "global citizen"
- the rights and responsibilities of citizenship within the global context
- how conflicts are resolved in matters of civic importance
- the civic literacy skills of developing a global perspective and resolving conflicts

Economic Justice, Power, and Wealth

As a student living in Ontario, you are likely part of the 20 percent of the world's people who have access to 80 percent of the world's wealth. You may live in Canada because you were born here. You may live in Canada because someone in your family decided to emigrate from another country. You may be from an Aborginal nation that has lived here since long before Canada existed. Or you may live in Canada because the living conditions in your birth country were unsafe in some way. Regardless of the reason, you have the opportunity to enjoy the many benefits of living in this country. Take a minute to reflect on some of those benefits.

Figure 6-4 lists some benefits in different categories. With a partner, brainstorm as many other benefits as possible. How many can you identify as a class?

Although you may enjoy many benefits because you live in Canada, 80 percent of the world's population doesn't. Moreover, many First Nations and Inuit people in Canada, particularly in northern isolated communities, don't have regular access to doctors or nurses. Clean drinking water is not available in all First Nations communities. Overcrowded housing is also an issue. As we explore problems that exist in developing nations, remember that these conditions sometimes exist in Canada, as well.

Figure 6-3 In the year 2003, the United Nations estimated that 1.2 billion people were without access to safe drinking water. Another 2.4 billion people lacked proper sanitation. As well, more than 3 million people die every year from diseases caused by unsafe water.

General Category	Situation in Most Areas in Canada	Situation in Some Least Developed Nations
Health care	• access to medical care regardless of income	• not enough doctors or nurses • people cannot afford to pay for drugs and vaccines
Standard of living	• access to clean drinking water	• water is scarce • people have to travel long distances to get clean water
Education	• public education available to all	• children cannot attend school without uniforms and paying for own books • parents often cannot afford to send all of their children to school
Human rights	• minimum wage laws protect workers from exploitation	• little wage or job protection • unsafe working conditions
Safety and security	• laws and police officers protect people from harm	• civil rights not always protected • police sometimes corrupt and violent

Figure 6-4

Sweatshops

Sweatshop is a term used for a workplace with poor conditions and where the workers are not treated properly. Sweatshop conditions do exist in some North American industries, such as textile manufacturing. However, the sweatshops that have generated the most attention from protest groups and the media are in developing nations such as Vietnam, Indonesia, and Cambodia.

To try to understand what it is like to work in a sweatshop, let's look at the experience of Carmencita (Chie) Abad. For six years she was a garment worker on the Pacific island of Saipan. During that time, she frequently worked 14-hour shifts, seven days a week, often without overtime pay. Other women who worked with Abad also claimed that they signed contracts waiving basic human rights. These rights included the freedom to join unions, attend religious services, quit, or marry.

sweatshop: a workplace where workers are poorly paid, have poor working conditions, and are often exposed to physical and psychological abuse

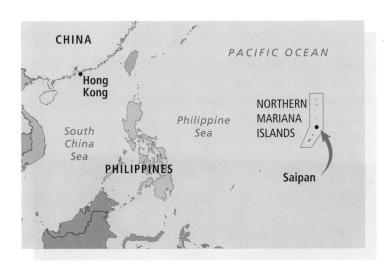

Figure 6-5 The map on the left shows the location of Saipan, where Carmencita (Chie) Abad worked.

On the right, Abad is at a press conference. How do the shifts that Abad worked compare with those of your parents, guardians or siblings?

Abad worked for the Sako Corporation, which made clothes for major US retailers. Fed up with the intolerable working conditions, Abad attempted to organize Saipan's first garment workers union. When factory managers learned that Abad was trying to organize a union, they began their own campaign against its formation. Their threats to close the plant frightened and intimidated the workers.

Because of her attempts to organize workers, the company refused to renew Abad's contract. Abad took her case to the US Equal Employment Opportunity Commission (EEOC). The EEOC stopped Sako from firing Abad, while it investigated the charges against the company. In September 2002, 26 major retailers settled a class action lawsuit targeting working conditions in Saipan. This landmark settlement provided back wages to workers and created a monitoring system to prevent further abuse.

In Canada, the Canadian Labour Congress and the Ethical Trading Action Group have developed a national "No Sweat" campaign. This campaign advocates ethical purchasing policies that promote humane labour practices. Students have picked up on the No Sweat campaign. As of late 2005, 13 Canadian universities have adopted No Sweat purchasing policies. These require university-licensed and bulk purchased clothing to be produced under fair working conditions. As well, 12 municipalities across Canada and six school boards in Ontario have adopted No Sweat policies of one form or another. The federal government has been asked to change the current *Textile Labelling Act*. Advocates want clothing labels to include names and addresses of factories where the clothes are made.

HIV/AIDS in Africa

How much do you know about HIV and AIDS? You have likely heard a lot about what this disease is, and you may have discussed it in classes. You may not know as much about the effects of HIV/AIDS in other parts of the world, like Africa. A 10-year-old African girl who is HIV-positive wrote the story on page 153. As you read her story, think about how she came to be infected, how she feels about her life, and what her future holds. Because this story appears as she wrote it, it contains a number of spelling and grammatical errors.

Active Citizen Website

For links to sites on HIV/AIDS in Africa

Figure 6-6 Almost 70 percent of the people living with HIV/AIDS in Africa between the ages of 15 and 24 are female. What steps could be taken to reduce the high number of African females with AIDS?

Going to the Source

Anna's Story

My name is Anna, I am 10 years old living in Namibia. I realized at my very young age that i am HIV positive. I develop lots of skin problem which never heal, and i heard my so called parent talking that i am HIV positive. I am not shock Because I did not look for it i don't know sex i only hear people talking about it. I know even if i die i am going to heaven.

My mother passed away in 2000, for HIV related illness, i saw her, when she was sick, She was very thin and i used to read in different books about this deadly illness. I don't know who my father is. But i know that both my parents are dead and i have no parent left. I only have my brother from a different father. My life is a disaster, i have my aunty who is looking after me but that is not enough....What i really want is love i want someone who will love me as i suppose to be loved and care for me and my brother. Please help or i should just die and go to where my parent are..........
Thank you.

Literacy Hint

Make a Connection. As you read the story about Anna, think of any 10-year-old children you know and compare their lives with hers.

1. How do you think Anna became HIV-positive?

2. What does the future hold for Anna? How does that differ from the likely future of a 10-year-old Canadian girl?

3. This story came from the website of AVERT, a British-based AIDS charity. Read some of the other stories on the AVERT website of children and teenagers who are HIV-positive. Compare their stories with Anna's.

The World Health Organization and the United Nations estimate that at the end of 2004 almost 40 million people were living with HIV/AIDS. The following is the situation in Africa:

- 26.6 million people between the ages of 15 and 49 are living with HIV/AIDS. Of that number, 15 million, or 58 percent, are women.
- 8.6 million people between the ages of 15 and 24 are living with HIV/AIDS. Of that number, 67 percent are women and girls.
- There are over 14 million orphans in sub-Saharan Africa alone.
- 2 million children under the age of 15 are living with AIDS.
- Only 8 percent of those who need treatment are receiving it.

Source: Statistics compiled from the World Health Organization, the United Nations, the Stephen Lewis Foundation and AVERT.

Literacy Hint

Get the Picture. Write all the numbers in the text —just the numbers—in a list on a piece of paper as you read. What picture is in your head as you look at these numbers?

Figure 6-7 Canadian Stephen Lewis is the United Nations' Special Envoy for HIV/AIDS in Africa. He is dedicated to bringing Africa's plight to the attention of Western nations and the world.

pandemic: a disease that thrives over a wide geographic area and affects a large proportion of the population

The spread of HIV/AIDS is now referred to as a **pandemic** because the disease has spread over a wide geographic area and affects a large proportion of the population. The statistics on page 153 focus on Africa because we will be exploring the HIV/AIDS situation of that continent. But the pandemic is not confined to Africa. There are growing numbers of cases in China and India. In those two countries, it is estimated there are three to five million victims. Russia is also seeing a rapid increase in the incidence of HIV/AIDS, which has spread to Ukraine and Belarus. Other areas of concern are Haiti, Jamaica, and Brazil. The San Francisco AIDS Foundation estimated that there were one million adults living with HIV/AIDS in North America at the end of 2004. How does that number compare with Africa's statistics?

So if HIV/AIDS is a problem throughout the world, why are we focusing on Africa? Africa is a special case for a few reasons.

- There are more people infected with HIV/AIDS in Africa than anywhere else in the world. This means that future transmission rates will remain high.

Active Citizen

- Because of the poverty of many African countries, there is no way for the sick to receive treatment. As a result, there are now millions of orphans in Africa.
- The situation in Africa is an emergency. Action must be taken now. If developed nations like Canada do not do more to help, a large part of Africa's population could be wiped out.

Most experts believe that the only way to stop the destruction caused by AIDS in Africa is to deal with the poverty that is afflicting the continent. And while most African countries are poor, most Western nations are very wealthy. This became evident on December 26, 2004, when tsunamis hit Indonesia and other parts of Southeast Asia. In a matter of weeks, the global community had donated more than $5 billion to tsunami disaster relief. Figure 6-9 compares the tsunami disaster with the AIDS disaster in Africa. You will explore the tsunami disaster later in this chapter.

Figure 6-8 Babies often get HIV/AIDS through the breast milk of infected mothers. Drugs can block this transmission, but they are too expensive for most Africans.

Tsunami Information	HIV/AIDS Information for Africa
• $5 billion (US) [$6.1 billion CAD] pledged by international donors in a matter of weeks following the disaster	• $3.6 billion (US) [$4.4 billion CAD] spent on global AIDS for the entire year in 2004
• tsunami death toll stands at about 150 000 (with about 50 000 missing and presumed dead)	• 6500 people die each day in Africa from AIDS
• around 50 000 children orphaned by the tsunamis	• 11 million African children orphaned by AIDS

Source: Nolen, Stephanie. (January 11, 2005). Federal tsunami aid hits $425-million…as cash woes hurt African AIDS fight. *The Globe and Mail*, A1.

Figure 6-9 Why do you think the world community responded more quickly to the tsunami disaster than they have to the AIDS pandemic?

In addition to raising money for African countries dealing with HIV/AIDS, many experts and high-profile artists are pressuring wealthy nations to provide debt relief to Africa. For example, in July 2005, musician Bob Geldof and other organizers coordinated the Live Aid 8 free concert series. These high profile concerts were staged to raise awareness for poverty-stricken African nations. They featured some of the top names in the music industry. Bono, the lead singer of the group U2, is another musician who has campaigned for debt relief. You can read his profile on page 156.

It appears that the work of people like Bono is paying off. In June 2005, the world's richest countries, including Canada, agreed to cancel $40 billion in debt owed by 18 nations (14 of them in Africa.) The nations receiving debt relief have to demonstrate that they are taking steps to combat government corruption. Consequently, not all poor nations are eligible for

People Power

Bono (Paul Hewson)

Occupation: Lead singer for U2

Contribution: Raising awareness about HIV/AIDS in Africa and the issue of debt relief.

His Story: In 1984, U2 performed at concerts called Band Aid and Live Aid to raise money for victims of Ethiopia's drought. Bono and his wife Alison Stewart travelled to Ethiopia shortly after the Live Aid performance to learn about the situation first-hand. They worked at an orphanage for six weeks. The visit changed their lives forever. Bono still remembers a father walking up to him and trying to give him his child. The father knew that if the child remained with his family, it would die.

Bono has been active in social justice issues ever since. Since the 1990s he has campaigned to bring about debt relief to the world's poorest countries. He believes that without debt relief, Africa will never be able to fight the progress of HIV/AIDS.

Fast Facts:
- Many countries in Africa spend more each year on debt than on health care or education.
- Many democratically elected governments are stuck with the debts racked up by the dictators who ruled before them.
- High interest rates and ineffective economic policies have multiplied these old debts over and over again.
- Between 1970 and 2002 Africa received $540 billion in loans. Despite the fact that,

Figure 6-10 Bono was rumoured to be a possible recipient of the Nobel Peace Prize in 2005.

over that same period, African countries repaid $550 billion—$10 billion more than the original loans—they still owe over $293 billion and it continues to grow.

Source: DATA website

Quotation: "When you sing, you make people vulnerable to change in their lives. ... But in the end, you've got to become the change you want to see in the world."

1. Why do you think Bono's experience in Africa made him an activist?

2. Review the Fast Facts in this feature. If African nations did not have to pay so much money for their debts, on what programs would they be able to spend money? How would that change the nature of life in these countries?

help at this point. But the countries that are receiving debt relief are planning improvements. Zambian officials have already said they will hire 7000 new teachers with the money. Tanzania is planning to build new hospitals and roads.

There are critics of the debt relief plan, though. Some people think the money being provided is simply not enough because Africa's total debt continues to grow. Another criticism is that the plan is too risky. It allows poor nations to apply for new loans, possibly creating a new cycle of dependency. As well, debt relief will not be given to countries with corrupt governments. Consequently, some of the countries in most need of assistance are being kept out of the reform process.

Informed to Be Effective

The World Bank estimates that Europeans spend $11 billion a year on ice cream. That same amount could fully fund the global fight against AIDS. If this fact amazes you and you want to do something to help, you could join the global campaign to "Make Poverty History." Check out their website.

Figure 6-11 In 2005, Canadian singer Sarah McLachlan took part in a Make Poverty History media campaign. Various celebrities snap their fingers every three seconds to represent the fact that a child dies of extreme poverty every three seconds. Do you think this is an effective way to build awareness?

CHECKPOINT

1. In what ways can wealthy nations use their power to bring justice for those in the developing world?
2. In what ways do the existence of sweatshops hurt those involved as well as Canadian workers?
3. How does the HIV/AIDS situation in Africa highlight some of the differences between wealthy and poor nations?

Globalization and National Governments

What Is Globalization?

globalization: a process accelerated by modern communications technology that multiplies and strengthens the economic, cultural, and financial interconnections among many regions of the world

When you read about wealthy nations providing debt relief for poor nations, you were actually exploring **globalization**. The nation-states of the world are now connected through economics, technology, and culture. As a result of our global "connectedness," an event in one country is quickly heard about in another. A problem in one country affects people living in other nation-states. Globalization has turned us all into global citizens rather than simply Canadian citizens. Simply stated, globalization means the closer integration of the countries and peoples of this world. This integration has been brought about by greatly reduced costs of transportation and communications, and the free flow of goods, services, resources, knowledge, and people across borders.

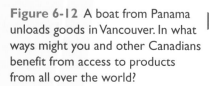

Literacy Hint

Make a Connection. Before you continue, stop and picture Canada and the globe. What are some ways we connect our nation to other parts of the globe?

Figure 6-12 A boat from Panama unloads goods in Vancouver. In what ways might you and other Canadians benefit from access to products from all over the world?

Globalization has resulted in the closer connection—both positive and negative—of peoples throughout the world. Think about the following examples of this closer connection.

- In Egypt, customers at a McDonald's restaurant buy a "McFalafel."
- In Canada, school children participate in holiday concerts rather than in Christmas concerts because of the diverse cultural backgrounds of the student population.

- Nepalese villagers watch MTV on television.
- Illegal immigrants from Mexico cross the US border every day, looking for jobs and opportunity.
- AIDS crosses international borders and strikes millions of people around the world.
- People burn coal, gasoline, and other fossil fuels that contribute to global warming. This can have catastrophic effects.

What other examples of globalization can you think of? Look around your classroom for ideas. Check out what people are wearing. Think about where you eat and what types of food you eat. What things do you have that are imported? What types of cars do you see on the street?

For links to sites on globalization

Figure 6-13 On the left, village children watch a program on a solar-powered television unit in Niger. What impact might television programs from around the world have on villagers like these?

On the right, Canadians take part in a yoga class. Many Canadians now practise tai chi, yoga, or other Eastern forms of mental or physical exercise to maintain their overall health.

The Link Between Technology and Globalization

Globalization is not new. It really began with the gradual spread of human beings around the planet thousands of years ago. Advances in technology, however, have dramatically accelerated the process. Consider this: in the past century alone we've moved from telegraph, railroads, telephones, and airplanes to satellites, space vehicles, computers, cell phones, and the Internet. These huge advances in technology have given people access to knowledge and links to other people that were never before possible.

Think about your own life. How do you learn about daily news—on the Internet, from the newspaper, or by watching television? Does anyone in your family have a cell phone or a pager, an electronic organizer or a handheld computer? How many televisions and computers are in your home? If you ask your parents or guardians about the technology that existed when they were teens, their answers would be very different from your own. Technology is moving at an extraordinary pace.

The answer to this question changes depending on whom you ask! Some people believe that globalization has had a positive impact on our society and our world. Others do not. What about you? What do you think might be some of the benefits of increased trade between nations? What might be some of the disadvantages of globalization? Below are some of the main arguments supporting and opposing globalization.

YES	NO
Consumers in wealthy countries can buy goods and services more cheaply because they are made in developing nations where labour and other costs are lower.	Only wealthy nations benefit from the increased flow of cheap goods because the profits made by multinational corporations are not passed on to the workers in developing nations.
Jobs are created in developing nations because they can make goods more cheaply than wealthy nations. They can do so because workers are paid less in developing nations.	Jobs are lost in developed nations when companies establish factories in developing nations that have large supplies of low-cost, low-skill workers.
Large corporations make higher profits because they receive the tax breaks from developing nations to build factories in those countries.	Profits made by large corporations stem from host countries that provide inadequate worker protection. Health and safety standards are lower than in developed nations. Benefits such as pensions and medical coverage often do not exist.
Increased flow of goods and services improves relationships between countries. When countries trade with each other, they need one another and are less likely to engage in conflicts or hostilities.	Countries lose their independence, or sovereignty, because they may feel they have to do what the wealthy nations want to keep the jobs in their own countries.

1. In what ways has globalization affected you or your family? Which of these are positive and which of these are negative? For example, has anyone you know lost a job because of globalization? Gained a job because of globalization?

2. Should there be a limit on how much profit a company can make? Should companies have to share a percentage of their profits with the workers that make their goods? Explain your answer.

Powerful Corporations

As globalization has increased, so have the profits of **multinational corporations**. A multinational corporation is one whose head office is in one country, with branch plants in others. Multinational corporations produce and sell their products internationally. Manufacturing goods cheaply in developing nations and selling them for a high price in developed nations generates huge profits for many multinational corporations. As a result, multinational corporations such as Wal-Mart, General Motors, Exxon Mobil, Ford, and Daimler Chrysler make more money than many countries! Look at Figure 6-14 to compare the **Gross Domestic Product (GDP)** of some countries with the sales of leading corporations.

multinational corporation: a company that operates in several countries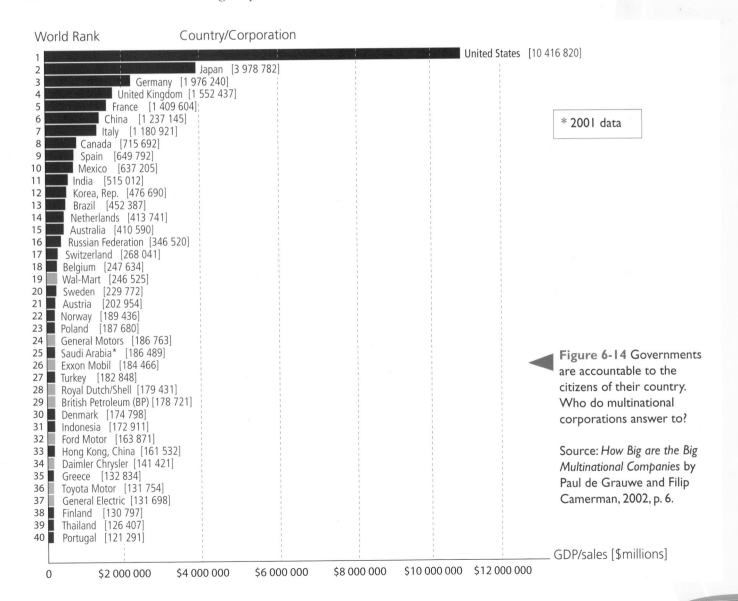

Gross Domestic Product (GDP): the annual total market value of all the goods and services, produced within the borders of a nation excluding trade with other countries

World Rank	Country/Corporation
1	United States [10 416 820]
2	Japan [3 978 782]
3	Germany [1 976 240]
4	United Kingdom [1 552 437]
5	France [1 409 604]
6	China [1 237 145]
7	Italy [1 180 921]
8	Canada [715 692]
9	Spain [649 792]
10	Mexico [637 205]
11	India [515 012]
12	Korea, Rep. [476 690]
13	Brazil [452 387]
14	Netherlands [413 741]
15	Australia [410 590]
16	Russian Federation [346 520]
17	Switzerland [268 041]
18	Belgium [247 634]
19	Wal-Mart [246 525]
20	Sweden [229 772]
21	Austria [202 954]
22	Norway [189 436]
23	Poland [187 680]
24	General Motors [186 763]
25	Saudi Arabia* [186 489]
26	Exxon Mobil [184 466]
27	Turkey [182 848]
28	Royal Dutch/Shell [179 431]
29	British Petroleum (BP) [178 721]
30	Denmark [174 798]
31	Indonesia [172 911]
32	Ford Motor [163 871]
33	Hong Kong, China [161 532]
34	Daimler Chrysler [141 421]
35	Greece [132 834]
36	Toyota Motor [131 754]
37	General Electric [131 698]
38	Finland [130 797]
39	Thailand [126 407]
40	Portugal [121 291]

* 2001 data

GDP/sales [$millions]

0    $2 000 000 $4 000 000 $6 000 000 $8 000 000 $10 000 000 $12 000 000

Figure 6-14 Governments are accountable to the citizens of their country. Who do multinational corporations answer to?

Source: *How Big are the Big Multinational Companies* by Paul de Grauwe and Filip Camerman, 2002, p. 6.

Globalization of world trade has resulted in a major shift of political and economic power from governments to corporations. At the same time, however, there is little evidence that these corporations are working to solve global problems. For example, let's say that a corporation made a $100-million profit by manufacturing its running shoes in a developing nation like Vietnam. Should that corporation have to pay workers a decent living, provide health benefits, and ensure a safe workplace? If that same corporation made its shoes in Canada, our labour laws would demand that the company do just that. Should workers not be entitled to equivalent pay and treatment no matter what country they live in? Suppose those corporations are polluting the air and water in developing nations. Should they not be held to the same level of accountability that they would be in their home country?

Figure 6-15 It has become common to name buildings after corporations. This is GM Place, home of the Vancouver Canucks. Would you be surprised to some day see cities named after powerful corporations?

How Does Globalization Affect You?

Sometimes it can be difficult to understand how globalization affects us as individuals. You may have heard about issues like rainforest deforestation, child labour in Asia, or poverty in Latin America. Do these problems sometimes feel so far away that they do not seem to be "real"? That happens for a lot of people. These problems may also seem to be too big for you to do anything about.

But, if these issues seem too difficult or distant to deal with, think again. We are more interconnected than ever because of improvements in transportation and communication technology like the Internet. Our world is becoming smaller and smaller all the time. What we do in Canada has a direct impact on the developing world. As well, the way that social, health, and economic problems are handled in the developing world has a direct impact on our lives here in Canada.

Not convinced? Think of the global impact of environmental damage. For example, US factories produce 50 percent of the air pollution in Southwestern Ontario. Consider the health and economic impact of the HIV/AIDS pandemic. As great numbers of young adults in Africa die of this disease, African countries become less and less productive. These countries then need additional aid from wealthy nations like Canada. Otherwise, the people are left to starve to death. As well, because travel is now so easy, diseases from one area of the world are easily transported to others. Sudden Acute Respiratory Syndrome (SARS), for example, was "brought" to Toronto from China in 2003.

Active Citizen

Figure 6-16 On the left, a group of administrative staff wear protective face masks at Scarborough Grace Hospital in Toronto where SARS first surfaced in this city in 2003. Hundreds of patients, staff, and visitors to the hospital were quarantined.

On the right, pollution we create in Canada contributes to global warming. Global warming affects every country in the world.

You have learned that economic injustice exists in the world. Because you live in a wealthy nation you may enjoy a number of advantages that others do not. This is certainly not "fair" for those who live elsewhere, but it *is* possible to make the world more just. You have explored the actions that others like Bono have taken to bring about change. You have also explored a number of techniques like letter writing that can be used to bring about change. There are times, however, when problems can best be solved by large, international organizations like the United Nations.

CHECKPOINT

1. **List two reasons why some people see globalization as a positive development. Then, list two reasons why some people see it as negative.**

2. **Explain how the power of multinational corporations has increased as a result of globalization.**

3. **Name two issues in other parts of the world that may affect you through globalization.**

Human Rights Around the World

The United Nations (UN) is an organization dedicated to the promotion of peace and human rights around the world. The United Nations was created in 1945 after the Second World War as an organization that would strive to maintain world peace. The UN now has 191 member countries that all agree on a number of global goals.

CIVICS SKILLS POWER

Developing a Global Perspective— Thinking Globally, Acting Locally

When you hear about difficult situations around the world, you want to do something to help, but often you feel powerless. What can you possibly do to make a difference for the millions who are suffering from HIV/AIDS in Africa? How can you help abused workers in another country?

You can find many examples in this textbook of people who have made a difference. Being aware of a global situation, they chose to act locally. They made their voices heard and extended a helping hand across the globe.

- Thinking globally means that you see yourself as a citizen of the world. When something happens on one side of the globe, you make every effort to find out the details and think about what you can do to provide assistance. You consider not just people, but all parts of Earth—the water, air, land, and all creatures that exist in those elements.
- Acting locally means finding a way to influence your country's leaders, appeal to international organizations, put pressure on corporations, or contribute to recognized charities that can make a difference.

Here are some key tools that a global citizen can use locally to influence world situations:

- *Raise awareness of the cause* by providing information to other citizens. You might use leaflets, brochures, posters, or paid advertising spots in the media.

- *Attract the media* by creating a newsworthy event such as a special concert, 24-hour fast, or a fundraising marathon. An event becomes even more high profile if you can persuade a celebrity or key politician to speak at it or even host the event.
- *Pump up the pressure* through letter writing, an email campaign, a protest march, sit-in, or petition. These tactics are particularly effective with politicians who depend on a positive public image to be re-elected.
- *Use your consumer power* by asking questions about the manufacture and testing of products. You might also refuse to buy products or boycott certain retail stores. Be sure to make your refusal or boycott obvious to the target.
- *Let your money speak for you* by contributing what you can to recognized charitable relief organizations that provide food, water, shelter, medical help, and education where it is most needed.
- *Use a combination of all of the above.*

You Try It

One person with motivation, energy, and determination can inspire many others. All it takes is one, and you can be that person. Figure 6-17 shows some significant global issues and a variety of options you might choose to act locally to assist the people or animals in these situations.

Active Citizen

Global Issue	Local Actions
Child labour and abuse of workers through dangerous working conditions, low pay, long hours	• Ask questions at retail stores about the origin and manufacturing processes for products. • Publicly refuse to buy products made using child labour.
Abuses of human rights such as imprisonment without charges or access to legal proceedings, torture, execution without trial or conviction	• Write letters to your Member of Parliament protesting these actions. Request that the Government of Canada raise the issue in International Tribunals or talks with other countries. • Organize a peaceful protest march on the embassy or consulate of any country involved in the abuses.
Millions of people suffering from HIV/AIDS in Africa	• Organize a letter-writing or email campaign to pharmaceutical companies. Ask them to make drugs to treat AIDS available to African countries at inexpensive prices. • Lobby the federal government to increase its foreign aid to African countries and tie this money to treatment of AIDS victims and support for their orphans.
Destruction of ancient rainforests in Clayoquot Sound, British Columbia, or the Amazon River valley	• Ask questions at local building supply and photocopying outlets about the source of their products. Indicate you will no longer be a consumer if products are made from old-growth wood. • Write letters to building supply companies and photocopying companies to discourage use of old-growth wood or pulp and paper from old-growth wood.
Natural disaster such as earthquakes, tsunamis, or hurricanes	• Contribute to the work of a relief agency such as the Red Cross or Doctors Without Borders. • Organize fundraising or a supply drive. Contribute funds or supplies to a relief agency.
Use of cruel animal testing practices for human hygiene (soap, shampoo) or cosmetic products	• Ask questions at point of purchase about how the product is developed. Ask if animal testing is involved. • Write to the company president and vice-president of product development explaining and requesting testing practices that do not use animals.

Figure 6-17 Global issues and some local actions you could take.

Goals of the UN include:

- the discouragement of war and the promotion of peace
- respect for international law
- working toward greater social progress and improved standards of living
- ensuring that all people are treated fairly and equally, recognizing the importance of human rights.

A Permanent Forum on Indigenous Issues was developed to ensure a relationship to Indigenous Nations who were not included as member states of the United Nations.

You have explored human rights in Canada and how these rights are a part of our Constitution. Democratic governments around the world try to ensure that their citizens are treated fairly and equally. But do all the citizens of the world receive the same treatment from their governments with their human rights being respected? In 1946, a Canadian named John Peters Humphrey was asked by the UN to prepare a report on global human rights. The 400-page document was called the *Universal Declaration of Human Rights*. Here are a few of the rights included in the Declaration:

- All human beings are born free and equal in dignity and rights.
- No one shall be subjected to torture or cruel, inhuman, or degrading treatment or punishment.
- Everyone has the right to an education.
- Everyone has the right to a standard of living that ensures the health of the parents and family.
- Everyone is entitled to these rights no matter their race, colour, sex, religion, or political preference.

Do many of these rights sound familiar? The majority of Canadians already enjoy these rights as well as other rights found in the Declaration. So can we assume that all 191 countries of the United Nations ensure that their citizens have these human rights? Unfortunately, the answer is "no." The *Universal Declaration of Human Rights* is not seen as international law and the UN does not have the power to force its members to follow it. Instead, the UN tries to persuade and use public opinion to have all countries around the world adopt these rights for its citizens.

The world has changed since 1946. One of the growing concerns for the UN was the treatment of children around the world. So in 1990, the UN and its member countries adopted the *Convention on the Rights of the Child*. This document is a charter of rights and freedoms for all youth under the age of 18.

Figure 6-18 The United Nations brings together state governments from around the world to work toward the common goal of world peace.

Active Citizen Website

For links to sites on the United Nations

Active Citizen

UNITED NATIONS CONVENTION ON THE RIGHTS OF THE CHILD

Basic Rights for Children	How Are These Rights Enforced?
<ul><li>Right to survival and to develop to the fullest</li><li>Protection from harmful influences, abuse, and exploitation</li><li>Participate fully in family, cultural, and social life</li></ul>	The UN has developed a set of standards or guidelines. They show countries what they need to offer to their children in three different areas:<ul><li>health care</li><li>education</li><li>legal/civil and social services</li></ul>

All countries must be moving toward these standards. By having established a set of goals for countries to achieve, the UN can assess or grade each country's progress in meeting the needs of their children.

Figure 6-19 Which of these rights do you enjoy?

Why don't all countries offer basic human rights to their citizens? It is important to remember the diversity of the world around us. Let's take a closer look at some examples of the ideas and beliefs that influence how countries respond to human rights issues.

Type of Government: Political systems and organization of governments can be found across the spectrum from oppressive authoritarian governments to democratic governments. Countries with governments elected by the people tend to pay more attention to human rights. China's communist government has regularly ignored human rights issues for its people. For example, in 1989, students protesting for democratic elections were fired upon in Tianamen Square by the Chinese military. More recently, China has been trying to ensure that Chinese language websites are censored if they use words like human rights and democracy.

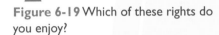

Informed to Be Effective

According to a UN report, Canada would be ranked 48th out of 174 countries if it were judged solely on the economic and social well-being of its Aboriginal peoples. Consider the following facts from that report:
- Poverty affects 60 percent of Aboriginal children.
- Twenty percent of Aboriginal people have inadequate water and sewer systems.
- Life expectancy among the Inuit is 10 years lower than for other people in Canada.

Figure 6-20 Throughout history, the struggle for democracy has faced many challenges. A peaceful push for democracy by Chinese students in 1989 led the Chinese government to use military force to stop the protests. Thousands of people were killed.

Literacy Hint

Respond to text. How do you react to these human rights issues? How do they help you to value your rights as a Canadian citizen?

Social Structures: In many countries, a social hierarchy exists. This system ranks a person's importance in that society. For example, India had what was known as the Caste System. People were born into four categories or castes. The category dictated whom a person could interact with and the types of jobs he or she could perform. Modern-day India is trying to abolish this system. It has introduced a charter of rights that bans discrimination based on gender, caste, race, or religion.

Religion: Around the world, many religions do not recognize the same rights of women that we value in Canada. A girl from a lower class of society in the Hindu faith is not independent. She is considered to be the property of her father or husband. Another example occurred in Afghanistan between 1996 and 2001. The Taliban (religious students) were in power during that period. They had a very strict interpretation of Islamic law and imposed a number of conditions upon females. These included:

- Girls could attend school only until the age of eight.
- Women were not allowed to hold a job.
- Females had limited access to medical care.
- Females had to follow a very strict dress code.
- Women were not allowed to move freely around the country.
- Women were not permitted to leave their homes without a male relative.

Figure 6-21 Student Sarah Rose Black (right), with help from her friends, organized a Vow of Silence march to raise awareness of child exploitation in Southeast Asia. What is a government's responsibility to protect its most vulnerable citizens from abuses?

Can the United Nations Be Fair, Impartial, and Effective?

The branch of the United Nations called the Security Council strives to maintain world peace. The Security Council is made up of five permanent members—China, France, Britain, Russia, and the United States. It also has 10 elected members from the UN. These elected members serve two-year terms. Canada has been on the Security Council three times since its creation, including from 1998–2000.

All members of the United Nations agree to abide by and support the decisions made by the Security Council. Here are a few of its responsibilities:

- maintain international peace and security
- help solve global disputes
- watch for threats to peace or acts of aggression and decide what action should be taken
- take military action against aggressive countries, if necessary.

Figure 6-22 The United Nations asks all member countries to contribute troops to help maintain peace around the world. Here, Canadian UN peacekeepers offer food and water to Haitians in the village of Nan Ciroil. Earlier, the Canadian peacekeepers had built a school in the village.

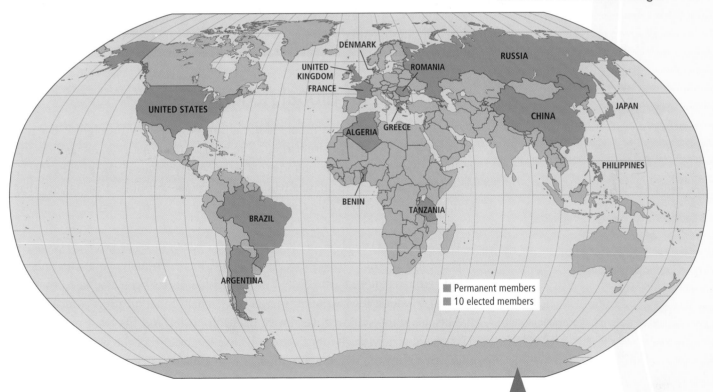

Figure 6-23 Looking at the members of the Security Council above, do you think that the world is equally represented? If not, what problems could this cause?

veto power: the ability to reject a resolution

resolution: when individuals or groups decide on a predetermined course of action

It is important to note that each of the five permanent members has **veto power**. This means that if any of the permanent members disagrees with a **resolution** put in front of the Security Council, the Security Council will not go forward with the outlined plan of action. The power of the veto is used regularly and sometimes reflects the bias of the countries using it. For example, suppose the Security Council is presented with a resolution to impose economic sanctions against a country that is accused of human rights violations against its citizens. If one of the permanent members is a major trading partner with this country, it would not want to see economic sanctions against it. That permanent member would probably veto or vote against the resolution and it would not be passed.

CHECKPOINT

1. **Name three rights from the *Universal Declaration of Human Rights*.**
2. **People in some countries are not able to enjoy basic human rights. Name two reasons for this.**
3. **Describe in your own words what veto power is.**

Importance of Global Action

Why is it important to get involved in helping solve global problems? The idea of strength in numbers is important. The more voices that pressure politicians to listen, or the more active hands that help with a solution, the greater the possibility that positive change will occur. Let's take a look at a case study that shows positive results when the global community got involved.

Case Study: The Holocaust and the Lessons Learned

The Second World War was a devastating war in which many countries and ethnic groups suffered, especially European Jews. It has been estimated that close to 6 million Jews were murdered in German concentration camps by the **fascist** authoritarian government of Adolf Hitler and his Nazi party. Only 10 percent of Jewish children were still alive by the end of the war. Arguably, this was one of the worst **genocides** in world history. The world has learned many valuable lessons from this event.

fascist: a system of government that is not elected, and in which property is privately owned, but in which all industry and business is regulated by a strong national government

genocide: the systematic and planned extermination of an entire national, racial, political, or ethnic group

- Countries around the world are no longer as tolerant of crimes committed by other countries or the violation of human rights. International intervention has been successful in stopping human rights crimes from being committed in some countries, such as Kosovo and East Timor.

- The development of international laws has established a common set of rules for all countries to follow. The establishment of the UN International Court of Justice (1945) and the UN International Criminal Court (2002) now make both states and individuals liable for crimes they may commit against other groups.
- A global understanding of morality and the importance of not looking the other way when such crimes are being committed emerged after the Holocaust. The events of the Holocaust and its impact are taught to all levels of students in countries around the world. It enables students to see the connection between past events and their impact on today's society.

For links to sites on Holocaust education

Figure 6-24 Prime Minister Paul Martin and Holocaust survivor Louis Danto and his wife Rachama prepare to lay a wreath at the Centennial Flame on Parliament Hill in Ottawa. Why are Holocaust Awareness Day activities so important?

Canada has played an active part in international justice, and our legal system has been considered a model for other countries to follow. Canada participated in the Nuremberg Trials that prosecuted German war criminals after the Second World War. Canada was also instrumental in establishing the International Court of Justice in 1946. Global recognition of Canada's involvement in the area of international justice is also found in two more recent examples.

Figure 6-25 Louise Arbour arrives at the first day of the 61st session of the Commission on Human Rights at the United Nations in Geneva, Switzerland. Arbour is the UN High Commissioner for Human Rights.

negotiation: the process of resolving disputes through direct communication between the disputing parties to reach a mutually agreeable solution

mediation: a method of conflict resolution in which a neutral third-party helps two disputing parties arrive at a mutually agreeable resolution

arbitration: the settlement of a dispute by the decision of an impartial third party, such as a judge or arbitrator

In 1996, the United Nations established a special tribunal, or court, called the International Tribunal for Rwanda and Yugoslavia. The purpose of this tribunal was to take action against the governments accused of genocide in both Rwanda and the former country of Yugoslavia. Louise Arbour, a Canadian and former Supreme Court Justice, was named the lead prosecutor for these tribunals.

The International Criminal Court (ICC), based in The Hague, Netherlands, ensures that the greatest of international crimes do not go unpunished. The ICC is made up of 18 judges. Their first elected president was another Canadian, Philippe Karsch, who is now in charge of the world's highest court.

Conflict Resolution

Peaceful conflict resolution should always be the preference in disputes. This strategy works at all levels of society, probably even right in your school. Does your school have peer mediators that work with students to help solve ongoing problems? Many times disagreements just need an impartial voice to help the disputing groups come to a solution. While some disputes are relatively simple to solve, others are more complex and need a different strategy for finding a solution. There are three main approaches to conflict resolution:

- **Negotiation** occurs when two parties or groups in dispute meet face to face to discuss the issue, exchange viewpoints, and work out a compromise agreeable to both sides.
- **Mediation** occurs if direct negotiations do not work. The two parties agree to work with a neutral person called a mediator to come up with a solution or compromise.
- **Arbitration** is usually the last approach when negotiations and mediation have failed. Both parties submit their positions and arguments to an impartial arbitrator, who has the power to make a decision after hearing both sides of the dispute. Both parties must accept and abide by the final decision of the arbitrator.

Conflict resolution can be a time-consuming process when the issues are complex. The Civic Skills Power on pages 174–175 develops this skill.

CHECKPOINT

1. **What lessons were learned from the Holocaust?**
2. **Describe the difference between mediation and arbitration.**

Responsibilities of the Global Community

Have you ever heard the saying, "History repeats itself"? If this is true, then we should be able to learn from the mistakes of the past. However, these lessons are often forgotten. Sometimes international law is not followed or enforced. Sometimes a country may see no benefit for its people to intervene on behalf of another country. Explore the following case studies of global inaction to determine what the consequences are when countries look the other way.

Nuclear Armament

Nuclear weapons have existed since the end of the Second World War. The United States used these weapons of mass destruction on Japan. Since then, other countries have felt it important to create their own nuclear weapons. They see that having nuclear weapons sends a clear signal to their neighbours and other countries that they are a powerful force to be left alone. India and Pakistan are two countries that have been building up their store of nuclear weapons.

Pakistan and India have had an ongoing dispute over a piece of land called Kashmir. Four wars have been fought over this region that contains no significant natural resources. India has claimed victory each time. As a result of the tension that has developed because of these ongoing disputes, both India and Pakistan have built up their supplies of nuclear arms to protect themselves. Within weeks of each other in 1998, both Pakistan and India tested these weapons close to the border of Kashmir to intimidate one another.

> **Literacy Hint**
>
> Add to your background knowledge by looking up "nuclear weapons" on the Internet. What makes these weapons so frightening?

Figure 6-26 Pakistan tests a short-range nuclear-capable missile in 2004. Do you think that the UN has a responsibility to convince Pakistan and other countries to stop the development of nuclear weapons?

CIVICS SKILLS POWER

Resolving Conflicts:
Peacemaker or Peace Breaker?

Whenever you have two people, even if they are closely related or friends, you will have two frames of reference and two points of view (see pages 46–47). There is potential for conflict in almost every situation:

- You want to go to an action movie, but your sister wants to see a comedy.
- You like to keep your bedroom neat, but you have to share it with your brother, who is sloppier.

Are you a *peacebreaker*? Is conflict an aggravating feature of your daily life? How does conflict affect you and others? How do you think it affects countries that are always at war and the people in those countries? You may know from personal experience that fighting or disagreement of any kind often leaves emotional scars that are slow to heal. These experiences can lead to lasting anger, bitterness, and lack of trust.

Are you a *peacemaker*? Do you try to resolve differences between people? You may realize that conflict is not always a bad thing and can actually have a positive result. Conflict may force us to see things differently, or to be thoughtful in a way we had not considered before a disagreement. As a peacemaker, you can act as a mediator.

In any situation of conflict, whether it is between individuals, groups, or countries, it is crucial for the mediator to follow a series of steps aimed at bringing about a resolution. One warning: These steps do not ensure success. Each side in the conflict must be willing to give a little to get a little, but if one side is not willing to give anything, negotiations may break down.

Step 1

Work co-operatively to arrive at a set of ground rules and a time frame.

- Ground rules ensure that each party has a certain number of opportunities and minutes to present a case or position, provide evidence, and even rebut the other party's presentation.
- A time frame sets a reasonable deadline for reaching a resolution to the situation. With individuals, a reasonable time frame might be an hour or two. With countries, a week may not be sufficient time.

Step 2

Ensure that each party to the conflict has an opportunity to speak and be heard.

- Individuals or countries in conflict have strong reasons for the positions they take based on their unique frame of reference. Often, when a group shares background stories and facts, the opposing group realizes and understands that group's position.
- Each party involved in the conflict deserves a good hearing by the other. Are you a good listener? You give another person true respect when you make the attempt to listen carefully, when you do not interrupt, and when you ask questions to clarify what the person is saying.
- The mediator should take notes of key points from each side to assist with Step 3. These are details that may point toward a solution.

Step 3

Summarize and clarify the key messages of each party.

- The mediator has an important role in determining the issues in the conflict. The two individuals or groups involved may be highly emotional and lack distance or objectivity. The mediator, relying on notes taken during Step 2, should repeat some key points to ensure that everyone understands.
- The purpose of this step is to arrive at a list of key problems or issues that must be solved together.

Step 4

Take issues one by one and discuss alternatives for solutions.

- The mediator's role is crucial in providing reasonable alternatives for each party involved in the conflict. You may have heard of a "win-win" situation. In other words, each individual or group must have a stake or a sense of success in the chosen solution. The mediator must often put the win-win solution together from bits and pieces of information and various suggestions to create a compromise or synthesis position.

Step 5

Formalize the agreement and get each party to sign the document.

- To ensure a common understanding, the final agreement must be stated in writing. Each side should be given an opportunity (perhaps in private) to read a draft copy of the agreement and suggest amendments (changes).
- Each party signs the final document as an indication of good faith to keep the terms of the compromise solution.

Step 6

Establish a process for checking on the success of the agreement.

- Involve both sides in choosing an acceptable monitor— a person who will check to see that each group is living up to the agreement.
- Set checkpoints—dates in the future—when the agreement will be formally monitored. You may also wish to include opportunities for unscheduled monitoring of the agreement.
- Establish a "safety valve" clause. This provides an opportunity for either party to request a meeting to discuss their concerns that the other side is not living up to the agreement.
- Step 6 should be written into the agreement itself.

You Try It

Think of a conflict situation that arose recently in your family or with your friends. How might you have followed Steps 1 to 6 to be a peacemaker in this situation? What issues would you have noted in Step 2 and clarified in Step 3? What alternative solutions could you have explored and written into an agreement in Steps 4 and 5?

Why have the UN and other countries not intervened to stop the development of nuclear weapons in Pakistan and India or other countries around the world? Countries can claim nuclear weapons are a source of self-defence. As a result the United Nations and the Security Council have no real reason to intervene based on international law. How many countries around the world do you think have nuclear arms? Under the Nuclear Non-Proliferation Treaty of 1968, five countries were identified as having

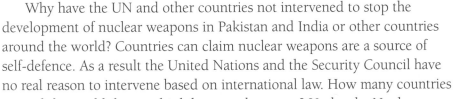

nuclear weapons. They included: United States of America, Union of Soviet Socialist Republics (now Russia), United Kingdom, France, and China.

Since then, Pakistan, India, and North Korea have declared they have developed nuclear weapons. It is also believed, but not confirmed, that Israel and Iran have nuclear weapons, as well.

The global community must be concerned as more and more countries look to arm themselves with nuclear weapons. The potential for the use of these weapons increases as more and more countries acquire them. We only need to look to the devastating impact that nuclear weapons had on Japan to realize the seriousness of this issue. Should nuclear weapons be banned worldwide or do countries have the right to arm themselves?

Literacy Hint

Make a Connection. How would you feel if Canada had nuclear weapons?

Genocide

Earlier in the chapter you explored the idea of genocide in relation to the Holocaust. Examples of genocide continue to be found in recent history. Both the African country of Rwanda and the former Eastern European country of Yugoslavia experienced an unimaginable number of deaths as one ethnic group dominated another.

Rwanda was the location of the world's largest genocide since the Holocaust. Rwanda contains two main ethnic groups—the majority Hutus and the minority Tutsis. On April 6, 1994, the President of Rwanda, Juvenal Habyarimana, a Hutu, was killed when his plane was shot down. His death caused outrage among the Hutus in the country as many assumed Tutsis committed the act. In a three-month period in 1994, Hutus killed 800 000 Tutsis and Hutus who were sympathetic to the Tutsis. It is believed that up to 30 000 Hutus participated in the genocide.

Figure 6-27 Thousands of victims of the 1994 genocide are buried in this cemetery outside Kigali, Rwanda. Put yourself in the place of this young Rwandan girl as she walks through it. What might your thoughts be?

The situation in Yugoslavia was similar to that in Rwanda, except that religion combined with ethnicity played a role in the genocide there. Yugoslavia had three main ethnic groups—the Serbs (Orthodox Christians), Croats (Catholics), and Albanians (Muslims). Conflict among these three groups resulted in genocide committed by the Serbs against the Muslims in the newly created country of Bosnia.

Due to ethnic tensions, Yugoslavia separated into a number of smaller countries in the early 1990s. Bosnia was made up of mostly Muslims, but over 30 percent of its population was Serbian. The former president of Serbia, Slobodan Milosevic, sent troops into Bosnia to reclaim the newly independent country as part of Serbia. Through **ethnic cleansing**, the Serbian army systematically murdered well over 200 000 Muslims, with 20 000 people still missing. Over two million Muslims were left as refugees, forced to leave their homes and country.

ethnic cleansing: the systematic elimination of an ethnic group or groups from a region or society, either through deportation, forced emigration, or genocide

Figure 6-28 Bosnian Muslim Hajra Catic stands next to dozens of photographs of missing Srebrenica citizens. Catic was a survivor of a 1995 Srebrenica massacre by Bosnian Serbs.

Canada's Place in the Global Community

As the world becomes more globalized in the 21st century, what will Canada's role be? What should we as a country focus on? How do you think other countries see Canada? At one time, Canada had the fourth largest military in the world. We then developed a reputation as peacekeepers under Prime Minister Lester B. Pearson in the 1960s. What about our continued efforts to help the developing world by providing foreign aid? Should this define our country in the 21st century? Or should we focus on our abundance of natural resources and the important role we play in supplying these goods to countries around the world? Many might believe that our multiculturalism and immigration policies best reflect Canada's role.

Figure 6-29 What do think Canada's role is in the age of globalization?

The role Canada plays in global issues will continue to evolve. We now better understand the impact globalization can have on Canada's land and people. From an economic perspective, the North American Free Trade Agreement (NAFTA) in 1994 with the United States and Mexico had a major impact on how we deal with imports and exports from these countries. Culturally, think about the music you listen to and the television shows you watch. Are they mostly made-in-Canada products or do they come from the United States? For many of us the answer would be the United States. Globalization impacts our lives every day.

From a political point of view, Canada can be described as a **middle power** among the countries of the world. While we are widely respected, we may not have as much influence on global issues as we once did. Many Canadians believe that we still play a major role in providing troops for peacekeeping efforts around the world. This is no longer a role that Canada fulfills on a large scale. Canada has reduced its military, and now ranks 33 in the list of countries that provide peacekeeping services for the United Nations.

Canadian Issues and Globalization

As the process of globalization continues, Canada has a number of issues it should consider:

- Do we want to return to our former military glory and have our federal government begin to invest our tax dollars in this direction?
- Can we afford to have powerful multinational corporations outside of Canada make decisions that affect Canada? Foreign ownership means profits leave Canada. Many companies that we associate as being Canadian, like CN Rail, Tim Hortons, Air Canada, and Petro-Canada are now over 50 percent owned by foreign companies.
- Should Canada move from NAFTA toward more integration with the countries of the Western Hemisphere and the Free Trade Area of the Americas (FTAA)? This would mean that 34 countries from North America, Central America, the Caribbean, and South America would trade a variety of goods without any import tariffs or taxes.
- Does Canada have a responsibility to increase the amount of money dedicated to foreign aid? Many developed countries, including Canada, agreed to set aside 0.7 percent of their **Gross National Product (GNP)** for foreign aid. Countries such as Denmark, the Netherlands, Luxembourg, Norway, and Sweden are all meeting or exceeding the established goal. Unfortunately, none of the G8 countries, the eight countries with the largest economies, has met this target. Canada currently provides 0.25 percent of our GNP.

middle power: countries that are not considered superpowers but still have some influence internationally

Figure 6-30 Canada has a large abundance of natural resources, including oil and gas reserves. Would it surprise you that over 50 percent of all the oil and gas companies in Canada are foreign owned?

Gross National Product (GNP): the annual total market value of all the goods and services produced within the borders of a nation

Active Citizen

Canada has a number of important issues to consider as it shapes its role in the global community. Which of the above issues should the government be most concerned about in your opinion?

Canadian Actions in Tsunami Relief Efforts

On December 26, 2004, a massive earthquake struck off the Indonesian island of Sumatra. The resulting tsunami sent a number of huge waves that crashed onto the coastlines of Indonesia, Malaysia, Myanmar, Thailand, Bangladesh, Sri Lanka, India, as well as Somalia in Africa. Close to 180 000 people died. Close to 50 000 people were still unaccounted for as of May 2005. The economic impact was felt immediately as tourist resorts and fishing villages were destroyed.

The global response was immediate. Donations of food, water, clothes, medicine, expert help, and money came from countries around the world. The chart you looked at on page 155 shows countries that donated billions of dollars to help those areas affected. Sometimes though, money needs to be combined with human expertise to provide an effective solution.

The Canadian Forces Disaster Assistance Response Team (DART) set up Operation STRUCTURE to help in the tsunami relief effort. The DART is made up of a number of skilled people for this type of situation. Doctors, nurses, engineers from a variety of backgrounds, as well as soldiers went to Sri Lanka to begin the rebuilding process. The team began its preparations to go to the

> ### Literacy Hint
>
> **Make a Connection.** Do you recall what you were doing on December 26, 2004? Compare your day with what happened to people in Indonesia and the other countries hit by the tsunami.

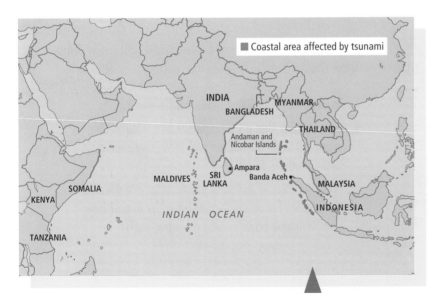

■ Coastal area affected by tsunami

Figure 6-31 Natural disasters can happen at any time in any part of the world. The powerful tsunami that hit Indonesia and Southeast Asia on December 26, 2004, was devastating. It caused destruction as far away as Somalia in Africa.

On the right, Banda Aceh was one location that was devastated by the 2004 tsunami.

People Power

Bilaal Rajan

Occupation: Eight-year-old student, child spokesperson for UNICEF Canada

Contribution: Raising money for victims of a 2001 earthquake in India, the victims of a 2004 Haitian hurricane, and the victims of the December 2004 tsunamis

His Story:

- In 2001, when Bilaal was just four years old, he heard about an earthquake in India. He decided he wanted to do something to help and began selling oranges door-to-door with his grandfather to raise money for the relief effort.
- In 2004, Bilaal learned about children affected by tropical storms in Haiti and other Caribbean countries. He again wanted to do something to help. His parents suggested he donate his allowance. Instead, he decided to sell cookies donated by his father's company. He raised over $6000 and donated the money to UNICEF.
- As a result of his fundraising efforts, he was named UNICEF's Child Ambassador for Canada in 2004.
- In his new role, he has even more power to make a difference. The day after the December 26, 2004, tsunami disaster, Bilaal launched UNICEF's Canada Kids Earthquake Challenge. He spoke at schools and encouraged every child in Canada to raise $100 to help children in the affected areas. As of March 2005, his efforts had brought in $2.5 million.

Figure 6-32 Bilaal Rajan, left, meets Thai school children whose families suffered from the December 26, 2004, tsunami.

Quotation: "You have not lived until you have done something for which someone cannot repay you."

1. In what ways has Bilaal made a difference?
2. Do you think that a young person like Bilaal is able to reach out to other children and youth more successfully than an adult? Why?
3. What qualities of character are necessary to develop the concern for others demonstrated by Bilaal? How does someone acquire these character traits?

Figure 6-33 The DART coordinates its humanitarian efforts with the government of Sri Lanka and the other agencies involved in the relief effort. Why is this important to do?

affected areas within hours of the tsunamis' impact. Surveying the situation, determining the goals for the team, testing equipment, and gathering the necessary supplies for an extended mission were all part of the preparations. Travel was delayed though for a number of reasons, including the fact that the Canadian military did not have suitable aircraft to transport the team and their equipment to Sri Lanka. This was solved by renting planes from the US military to get the DART into Sri Lanka to begin their relief efforts.

The DART arrived in the Sri Lankan region of Ampara on January 10, 2005. It surveyed the situation and began its humanitarian relief efforts. The United States was critical of Canada's response because the DART arrived 15 days after the tsunamis hit. Despite the criticism, the DART was able to achieve many important goals during its 40-day mission. The medical staff treated 5500 patients while engineers assisted in the rebuilding of schools and bridges. The DART also moved 50 000 people who were stranded in isolated areas to safety and shelters. Perhaps the biggest achievement was providing three million litres of purified water to those in the Ampara region of Sri Lanka.

So are you up to the challenge of being a global citizen? The first step is being informed about the issues happening around you. The world is a much larger place than the community we live in or even our country. It is important to remember that events that take place in one part of the world may have implications or consequences in other parts of the world. As you read through the different issues presented in this chapter and how they relate to globalization, what opinions did you form? Is globalization a good thing? What are some of the concerns you have about the creation of a global economy and your role in it?

CHECKPOINT

1. Why do some countries feel that they need nuclear weapons?

2. Explain in your own words what genocide is.

3 Which do you think are the two most important issues to do with globalization that Canada should focus on? Why did you select these two?

4. Do you think developed countries like Canada have a greater responsibility to provide relief aid than developing countries when global tragedies like the tsunami occur? Why or why not?

CHAPTER REVIEW

Summing It Up

- Wealthy countries can take significant steps to bring about greater economic justice for countries whose people are living with poverty.

- The closer integration of countries through globalization has brought about both positive and negative change.

- The United Nations is dedicated to promoting human rights and peace around the world.

- The global community can affect positive change when it chooses to act.

- Peaceful conflict resolution can take the form of negotiation, mediation, or arbitration.

- Global inaction can have severe consequences.

- Canada has issues to face in the 21st century as it considers its emerging global role.

KEY TERMS

- 80/20 rule
- sweatshop
- pandemic
- globalization

- multinational corporation
- Gross Domestic Product (GDP)

- veto power
- resolution
- fascist
- genocide

- negotiation
- mediation
- arbitration
- ethnic cleansing

- middle power
- Gross National Product (GNP)

Considering the Issues

Each of us has a different picture of the perfect world. Others will share some parts of your picture. Some of your ideas may generate disagreement. However, there may be a core set of ideas that can form the basis of our perfect world. How many of the following points would be part of your perfect world? What other points did you include when you visualized your perfect world?

- love and happiness in my life
- food, clean water, shelter, and medicine for all
- equality between women and men
- no wars
- no gun violence
- democratic governments
- no more poverty, closing the gap between rich and poor
- free education
- protection of Earth's resources
- no death penalty
- no use of torture, including within prisons
- protection of human rights for all people.

You may have been able to make a decision on some of these points fairly quickly. This is probably because you already have a strong opinion about the issue; for example, gun violence or the death penalty. Other points may have taken you longer because they aren't as clear-cut to you, or maybe you do not feel you know enough about the issue. What other factors may have influenced your perspective on each of the above issues?

Strategies for Bringing About Change

Whichever issues are important to you, there are many strategies you can use to bring about change. For each of the strategies shown in the photographs on page 188, use a T-chart to consider the advantages and disadvantages of the strategy. Then determine whether the strategy reflects The Power of One (an individual strategy) or Strength in Numbers (a group strategy).

Literacy Hint

Stop and consider the elements of your own picture of a perfect world before reading ahead. Then compare it with the list below.

Active Citizen Website

For links to sites on youth action

Figure 7-4 Elizabeth May of the Sierra Club, in wheelchair, is on her 13th day of a hunger strike on Parliament Hill. Her goal is to have the federal government help move about 100 families out of a toxin-ridden neighbourhood in Sydney, Nova Scotia.

Figure 7-5 Greenpeace is an environmental activist group concerned with climate change and saving the ancient rain forests. Here they use Niagara Falls to showcase their concerns.

Figure 7-6 Poppies are dropped alongside a child's note at the National War Memorial during a Remembrance Day service. Each year on November 11 services are held to honour the veterans who fought for democratic beliefs.

Figure 7-7 Members of the Advisory Committee on Accessible Transportation (ACAT) volunteer their time to help ensure that the Toronto Transit Commission is accessible to all people. ACAT Vice-Chair Mazin Aribi, in wheelchair, helps cut the ribbon at a newly accessible subway station.

Figure 7-8 In 2004 Wangari Maathai was the first woman from Africa to be awarded the Nobel Peace Prize. Over the past 30 years, it is estimated that her organization, the Green Belt Movement, has planted over 30 million trees to fight the effects of deforestation.

People Power

David Suzuki's Perfect World

Name: David Takayoshi Suzuki

Occupation: scientist, environmentalist, author of more than 30 books, long-running host of CBC's *The Nature of Things*

Contribution:
- He is Canada's leading spokesperson for sustainable development and a persuasive grassroots activist.
- Through over 40 years of public broadcasting, he has raised awareness of such issues as medical marijuana, the growth of big business farming, and the future of the Arctic.
- In 1990, he founded the David Suzuki Foundation, a non-profit organization dedicated to the conservation of the natural world.

His Story: Suzuki was born in Vancouver in 1936. His father helped to shape his interest in the natural world while taking him camping and fishing. Suzuki earned his PhD in Zoology from the University of Chicago. After returning to Canada, he began teaching at the University of British Columbia, in Vancouver. In 1971, Suzuki became the host of *Suzuki on Science*, a weekly CBC television show. Four years later, he began the CBC radio broadcast *Quirks and Quarks*. In 1979, *The Nature of Things* began, a popular and respected television program.

Suzuki has received great recognition for his work. He has received a number of awards from the United Nations. He is an Officer of the Order of Canada. He has 15 honorary doctorates from universities in Canada, the United States, and

Figure 7-9 In April 2004, the CBC challenged Canadians to answer the provocative question: Who is Canada's greatest Canadian? David Suzuki ended up in fifth spot.

Australia. Both the Heiltsuk and the Haida people of British Columbia have formally adopted him.

Quotation: "What do you do with waste? Why, you throw it away, of course. But think about the term, 'throw it away.' Where exactly is this 'away' place and what happens to things when they get there?

1. Based on the information above, how do you think David Suzuki would describe a "perfect world"?

2. What tools has Suzuki been able to use to convey his message? Why are these tools effective?

3. Where does the garbage go in your community? Do you picture this spot when you throw things away? Does your family recycle? If so, where are the materials sent for recycling?

How Can *I* Make a Difference?

One way you can learn how to make a difference is to find out how others have made a difference. When you read the information on the following pages, you may be surprised to see that people who make a difference are "just" regular people like you. By taking action, however, they have been able to make a significant contribution to their local and global communities. They all began with the power of their own convictions.

Terry Fox: Marathon of Hope

In 1977, at the age of 18, Terry Fox was diagnosed with bone cancer. His right leg was amputated to prevent the disease from spreading. While in hospital, Terry was moved by the suffering of cancer patients, many of them young children. He decided to run across Canada to raise money for cancer research. After 15 months of training with his artificial leg, Fox persuaded the Canadian Cancer Society to help sponsor a cross-Canada run.

His Marathon of Hope was intended to raise both money and awareness for cancer research. His dream was to raise one dollar for every Canadian. Canadians witnessed both his discomfort and determination as they followed his progress on nightly newscasts. Fox could average only about 40 kilometres per day on his artificial leg. After 143 days, just outside of Thunder Bay, Ontario, he was forced to stop running because of sharp chest pains. The cancer had spread to his lungs. Fox returned to Vancouver for more treatments but the cancer continued to advance. He died on June 28, 1981, at age 22.

Although Fox did not finish the Marathon of Hope, he had reached his goal. He had raised $24.2 million dollars. He became an inspiration to millions of people. They were touched by his strong desire to make a difference for others, even at the cost of tremendous personal sacrifice. The Terry Fox Run is now held annually in many communities around the world. The Terry Fox Foundation has raised over $360 million for cancer research. In 2005, Terry Fox became the first Canadian to appear on a coin. He was commemorated on the $1 coin.

Craig Kielburger: Founder of Free the Children

Craig Kielburger didn't start off thinking he would become an activist at the age of 12. It just happened that way after he read a news report that upset him. The story was about another 12-year-old who had been murdered in Pakistan. The boy, Iqbal Masih, came from a very poor family. When he was four years old, his parents sold him into slavery for about $15. For the next six years, he was chained to a carpet-weaving loom. There he was forced to

Figure 7-10 Terry Fox cared enough to do something about cancer research. Can you name a local hero who has made a difference in your community?

tie tiny knots for hours at a time. Severe malnutrition and years of cramped immobility stunted his growth.

In 1992, Iqbal and some other children stole away from their carpet factory to attend a freedom day celebration held by the Bonded Labour Liberation Front (BLLF). Iqbal chose to stand up and give a speech about his sufferings. The speech was printed in the local papers. Iqbal then refused to return to his owner. He contacted a BLLF lawyer and obtained a letter of freedom, which he presented to his former master. He began to attend a school for children freed from slave labour. He also travelled the country speaking out against the use of child labour. One day he was shot dead, while out riding his bike with his friends.

Craig photocopied the article and took it to school where he made a short presentation to his classmates. He told them he wanted to find out more about child labour and try to do something about it. He asked if anyone else would like to do the same. That night a group of students met at Craig's home and began planning. They created a name for their group after they read about a demonstration in India where people were chanting, "We want freedom! Free the children!"

Figure 7-11 Iqbal Masih was 12 years old when he was murdered. Many suspect he was killed by angry members of the carpet industry who disliked the young activist.

Figure 7-12 Craig Kielburger was also 12 years old when he read about Iqbal's murder. His concern resulted in the creation of an organization called Free the Children.

Free the Children became an international organization, with over 100 000 members in 35 countries. Over one million people have participated in the projects and campaigns of the organization.

Free the Children's many accomplishments include:

- building more than 400 primary schools in developing countries in Latin America, Asia, and Africa
- shipping more than 200 000 school and health kits, worth more than $8 million (US), around the world
- leading campaigns against sweatshops and child labour
- creating alternative sources of income—by providing milking animals, small machines, and arable land—for poor families in countries in Latin America, Asia, and Africa.

Although Free the Children has accomplished a great deal, it began by taking small steps. Its goal was to raise awareness about child labour and exploitation. It used the following strategies:

- started petitions
- wrote letters (to newspapers, the Prime Minister of Canada, and other world leaders)
- made flyers, posted information on bulletin boards, and set up displays in public places to raise awareness
- gave speeches to students in various classes and schools and to community groups
- organized fundraising events like garage sales, car washes, bake sales, and walk-a-thons.

Free the Children has created a website with information about the group and their actions. Visit the site to learn more about them and their work around the world.

Literacy Hint

Evaluate What You Have Read. Which one of these Free the Children's strategies do you feel you could or would do?

Informed to Be Effective

Did you know that the Canadian International Development Agency (CIDA) offers many overseas volunteer positions for youth? CIDA can also hook you up with over 200 volunteer agencies in Canada. This is one way for you to gain valuable experience and to make a difference in the world. Visit CIDA's website for more information.

CHECKPOINT

1. Review the list of issues related to the perfect world on page 187. For which issues would you be willing to get involved in civic action? In your opinion, what other issues in society require action?

2. Create a list of strategies for bringing about change from this section of the textbook. Don't forget to include strategies that were depicted in photographs.

People Power

Have you ever learned about an issue or problem and thought, "What can I do to help?" Ryan Hreljac had one of those moments in 1998 when he was in Grade 1. The Kemptville, Ontario, student was listening to his teacher explain a school-wide campaign to help African children who were living in poverty. When Ryan learned that hundreds of thousands of African children died every year from drinking unsafe and contaminated water, Ryan wanted to do something about it.

Armed with the information that $70 could pay for a well in Africa, Ryan set out to raise this money. He reached his goal through performing various chores. But when he went to WaterCan, a small not-for-profit agency that helps build wells in developing countries, Ryan was told that the real cost of drilling the wells was $2000. The $70 only covered the cost of the pump.

Ryan was determined to raise enough money for a well. He went back to doing more chores. Since the Canadian International Development Agency matches WaterCan's donated funds two for one, Ryan only had to raise half of the $2000. With help of articles in local newspapers about Ryan's fundraising efforts, the donations began to arrive. Within two months, Ryan had received over $7000 in donations and Ryan's first wells were built in the African country of Uganda. An NGO called Ryan's Well was born.

In July 2000, Ryan and his family had the opportunity to travel to Uganda to see the results of Ryan's hard work. Over 5000 children lined the

Figure 7-13 Every eight seconds one more person dies because they don't have access to clean water. Ryan's efforts in Africa have given people a renewed hope.

road leading to the community of Angolo, clapping as the truck arrived carrying Ryan.

Ryan's Well is more active than ever in building wells and bringing fresh water to those in need. As of June 2005, Ryan's Well had built 168 wells in nine countries. These include Malawi, Uganda, Nigeria, Tanzania, Guyana, and Guatemala.

A recipient of the Order of Ontario, Ryan Hreljac proves one person can make a difference.

1. List the ways that Ryan used to accomplish his goals.

2. Many people in developed countries take their fresh water supply for granted. Brainstorm with a partner ways that you could help preserve our fresh water.

Taking Responsible Civic Action

Throughout the chapters in this book, you have read many examples of individuals and groups that have made a difference.

- David Suzuki, a powerful advocate for the environment, has reached thousands of people through his writing and television programs. He continues to raise environmental awareness.
- Craig Kielburger, a powerful young voice, brought the issue of enforced child labour to international attention. His work continues today with many supporters through Free The Children.
- Ryan Hreljac had a young child's simple desire to save other children from drinking unsafe and contaminated water. His persistent efforts grew into an organization that continues to provide clean drinking water.

You can make a difference as a single voice or as an inspiration to others. Figure 7-14 shows what you can do as an individual, and how you might draw others together in the same cause.

There is a saying, "If you want melons, plant melons." In essence, those words mean that you must model what you wish to see in others. The power of one is the ability to demonstrate thinking and actions based on a view of the world that says, "We are all in this together and we must help and support each other." The strength of many is to influence significant change with one powerful voice.

Strategy	The Power of One	Strength in Numbers
Elections and the Political Process	Work for the candidate of your choice distributing literature, canvassing voters, and getting out the vote on election day. Be sure to vote when you are 18.	Join with friends or join the youth organization of a political party to lobby for issues important to you and to support the political process.
Letters and Email	Write a letter or email to the mayor, your Member of Provincial Parliament, the Premier of your province, your Member of Parliament in Ottawa, a Cabinet minister, or the Prime Minister. Express your concerns and indicate appropriate directions.	Organize a campaign with your class or friends to bombard a company or government representative with letters or emails all sent on the same day or within the same hour.
Petitions	Gather signatures to support an issue or to object to a course of action by a company or government.	Email your petition to friends and relatives in other parts of the province or country. Ask each one to gather at least 50 signatures. Provide an address for each person to forward the petition.

Strategy	The Power of One	Strength in Numbers
Fund, Food, or Supplies Drive	You have read that individual fundraising efforts can gather national and international support. Start by asking your relatives, neighbours, and friends to donate money or clothing to support disaster relief or food to a food bank.	Involve many others in your cause through your school, place of worship, teams, clubs, or by advocating for your relief effort at town council. Your sincerity and passion for a cause will inspire others to help and contribute.
Candlelight Vigil or Walk for Peace	Choose one night a week or every night for one week and stand in front of an embassy, place of worship, community centre, or club with a candle and a simple message. Your silent vigil will attract the interest and questions of others and you will have a chance to spread your message.	Organize an evening candlelight vigil or walk for peace. Sing a song that encourages peace or thoughtfulness of others.
Boycott	You may decide not to buy clothing or shoes from certain countries or companies that use child labour, have unsafe working conditions, pay unfair wages, or use cruel animal testing for their products.	Spread the word and organize friends or relatives who think as you do. Use email, posters, or leaflets to raise awareness with others and encourage them not to buy certain products.
Volunteering	Dedicate one or two hours per week to helping others. Volunteer at a seniors' home, help at a food bank or soup kitchen, or do yard work for elderly people who are sick. Your generosity can make a difference.	Organize a volunteers' club at school to provide assistance to seniors, beautify the community by cleaning up parks and wildlife areas, start food drives for the local food bank, or support a charity or foundation.
Random Acts of Kindness	In a small but persistent way, you can surprise others with your generosity or helpfulness. Do something thoughtful or kind when it is least expected. Have lunch with a student that others avoid. Help a senior cross the road, or hold the door for a mother with children.	Start a "random acts of kindness" campaign at your school or in your community, encouraging others to express their thoughtfulness in unexpected ways every day.

Figure 7-14

You Try It

As part of your culminating activity, choose one or more of the strategies above and explain or illustrate how you would use them to further the cause or issue you have chosen.

How Can *We* Make a Difference?

In the previous section you explored how individuals can make a difference in their local communities and the world by taking responsible civil action. These individuals all had a strong desire to help others, a willingness to work very hard, and an ability to persevere to achieve their goals. But it can be hard to work alone. While individuals may get the ball rolling, it can be helpful to enlist the help and support of others to achieve their goals. They can help lobby politicians to bring about changes to laws and regulations, get involved in fundraising, or raise awareness of important issues. They might help put together an online petition or a mass email campaign to bring attention to a particular social problem. In this section of the text, you will explore two issues where people are working together in groups to bring about change. Their strength is in their numbers.

The Anti-Tobacco Movement

If you smoke, when did you start and why? If you don't smoke, what prevented you from starting? Perhaps you didn't start smoking because you were concerned about the health risks. After all, we all know that smoking can kill us, right? Even smokers admit that. So, why do some people smoke? The simplest answer is because cigarettes are addictive. Once people start smoking it can be very difficult for them to stop.

We know smoking-related diseases end up costing our society millions of dollars in health care costs. We know that cigarettes are addictive. So why doesn't the government just make cigarettes illegal and stop companies selling them?

Basically, cigarettes are a legal product because there is a strong pro-tobacco lobby that wants to keep tobacco farmers and processors in business. You came across the term lobby group in Chapter 5. It is a group of people engaged in trying to influence legislators or other public officials to favour

Literacy Hint

As you read this section, create a Venn diagram to compare the Power of One strategies with the Strength in Numbers strategies. Then find the common elements.

Active Citizen
Website

For links to sites on organizations working for change

Figure 7-15 Do you think labels like this one influence the behaviour of smokers? If not, then why do you think the government requires companies to include the warnings on cigarette packages?

WARNING
CIGARETTES CAUSE LUNG CANCER

85% of lung cancers are caused by smoking. 80% of lung cancer victims die within 3 years.

lung cancer   Health Canada

a specific cause. Two of the largest pro-tobacco lobby groups are the Tobacco Growers' Marketing Board and the Canadian Tobacco Manufacturers' Council. Another reason tobacco remains a legal substance is that the government makes millions of dollars in tax revenue from the sale of cigarettes. It does not want to lose that revenue.

There is also a powerful anti-tobacco lobby in Canada. The Canadian Coalition for Action on Tobacco represents a number of anti-tobacco and anti-smoking groups in Canada. The Coalition is working to restrict the impact of tobacco on our society.

Considering Both Sides

Both groups want to influence the government and the general public to agree with their own opinion. Depending on which of the two groups is most successful, the way we view smoking in Canada may change.

As you read in the Issue Analysis on pages 197–198, second-hand smoke poses a real health threat to non-smokers. That is why the anti-tobacco lobby has pushed to have public places smoke-free. You may think this is a reasonable request, or you may feel that this infringes on the rights of smokers. But what if you actually knew someone who had died from the effects of second-hand smoke? Would that change your feelings on this matter? The feature on page 199 focuses on a woman who is dying of lung cancer although she has never smoked a cigarette in her life. Consider her story.

Should Smoking Be Further Restricted?

There was a time when people smoked freely in public places. Even as recently as the 1990s, smokers enjoyed the right to smoke in elevators, restaurants, bars, offices, and even hospitals. Slowly, the right to smoke in public places is being removed. The province of British Columbia banned smoking in all restaurants, bars, and pubs in 2000. In 2001, the city of Edmonton banned smoking in all public places where children are served. Similar bylaws were passed in Winnipeg, Manitoba, and in St. John's, Newfoundland, in 2002. More and more communities are passing their own anti-smoking bylaws.

Literacy Hint

Assess your own biases before you read the chart on page 198. How do you feel about smoking and smokers? What is your own experience of smoking? Your biases will influence your final response to the question above.

WHY SMOKING *SHOULD* BE RESTRICTED

- Smoking remains Canada's largest preventable cause of death, responsible for 45 000 premature Canadian deaths each year.

- Smoking puts non-smokers at risk, too. Health Canada indicates that exposure to second-hand smoke increases the risk of lung cancer by 25 percent and of heart disease by 10 percent.

- The younger people are when they start smoking daily, the sooner serious smoking-related illnesses like heart disease will develop.

- The World Health Organization estimates that if current smoking patterns continue, by the year 2030, 10–11 million people will die annually from tobacco.

WHY SMOKING *SHOULD NOT* BE RESTRICTED

- A full smoking ban would cause hundreds of bars to go out of business and reduce the profits of many others.

- Tobacco is a legal crop grown by taxpaying citizens, and it creates jobs.

- Higher tobacco taxes or a ban on smoking will only increase smuggling of cigarettes.

- Banning smoking will force smokers to smoke "secretly," making it even more difficult for them to quit their addiction.

There is a third dimension to the argument over tobacco. Tobacco is a plant that was grown in North America prior to European contact. Different varieties of the tobacco plant were and are used for ceremonial purposes. Some First Nations communities produce and sell manufactured tobacco products at lower prices than products that can be bought in stores. The sale of tobacco at a lower cost is making some First Nations a destination of choice for tobacco consumers. Many First Nations have unemployment rates exceeding 50 percent and perhaps very few economic development prospects.

BOTTOM LINE

Tobacco continues to be a legal product in Canada. In September 2005 the British Columbia Supreme Court ruled that the government can seek damages for smoking-related health care costs from tobacco companies.

Figure 7-16 Are people allowed to smoke in public places like restaurants in your community?

1. Do you think enough is being done to restrict smoking in Canada? Do you think there is already too much legislation? Explain your answer.

2. Should First Nations be concerned about the growth of the tobacco economy in their communities where this is occurring? Explain.

3. Write a letter to the health minister of your province or the country to express your views on this issue.

Healthy Living

Health Canada

Home > Healthy Living > Tobacco > Second-hand Smoke > What You Can Do > Wear a Blue Ribbon > Second-hand smoke is a real threat

Second-hand smoke is a real threat

Heather Crowe is dying of lung cancer. She's never smoked a cigarette. She got lung cancer from breathing in second-hand smoke while working in a restaurant.

Profile: Heather Crowe

Heather Crowe never smoked. But she worked in a restaurant with a smoking section. Now Heather has lung cancer.

Years ago, when Heather began working as a waitress, she didn't know second-hand smoke could damage her health. As little as 15 years ago, the tobacco industry said second-hand smoke did no harm, and she felt secure in her workplace. Today, Heather can no longer work. Her livelihood is compromised, her health is affected, her future is gone.

What is second-hand smoke and why is it so dangerous?

- It's the smoke that's released from the end of a burning cigarette.
- It's the smoke that's exhaled by a smoker.
- It contains more than 4,000 chemicals, including carbon monoxide, formaldehyde, benzene and hydrogen cyanide.
- It contains the same toxic chemicals as the smoke inhaled by the smoker.
- Even after a cigarette is out, second-hand smoke remains in the environment (furniture, carpets, blinds ...) and is still toxic.

- Ventilation systems, air purifiers and designated smoking areas are not enough to provide protection from second-hand smoke.
- More than 1,000 nonsmokers will die this year in Canada due to tobacco use; over 300 lung cancer deaths and at least 700 deaths from coronary heart disease will be caused by second-hand smoke.

You can make a difference.

- Let people know how bad second-hand smoke is.
- Discuss your concerns with coworkers and employers.
- Support municipal bylaws that restrict smoking in public places.

Source: Health Canada website

1. Why is second-hand smoke so dangerous?
2. Why do you think Heather Crowe allowed her story to be used in this way?
3. What actions could you take to help stop people from smoking?

Figure 7-17 Zoocheck Canada is the only Canadian organization with a specific focus on captive wild animals. What are some of the reasons that captive wild animals need protection?

Literacy Hint

As you read through the ten points on influencing the government, imagine an issue that you feel strongly about. Consider how you and a group of other youths could use the information provided by Zoocheck to create a campaign to make a difference.

How Do Groups Lobby the Government?

When a group wants to lobby the government for a change in law or policy, it uses a number of tactics. Each tactic is meant to persuade people that its cause is important. The following overview shows you the steps that Zoocheck Canada follows when it attempts to influence the government. Zoocheck is a national animal protection charity. Established in 1984, the organization attempts to promote and protect the interests and well-being of wild animals.

1. Pick Your Battles Carefully
Make sure you select a campaign that you feel passionate about, but one that will be able to generate public support. Some important battles have to be delayed until the public is ready for them.

2. Know the Political System
Correctly identify the level of government responsible for your issue and then do your research to understand how it operates.

3. Get To Know Politicians and Their Staff
Develop friendly relations with politicians and their staff members before you need to ask for something. Make sure they know who you are and what cause or organization you represent.

4. Map Out Your Strategy
Do not try to "wing it." Good campaigns look easy because of the many hours spent in preparation.

5. Get Your Facts Straight
Know your facts and statistics inside out. You will not have a second chance to make your case.

6. Develop an Extensive Resource Base
Collect information from a variety of sources. Consider videos, photographs, inspection reports, newspaper clippings, articles, books, eyewitness accounts, and expert testimony.

7. Put Together a Strong Team
Identify and train one or more people in your group to be spokespersons. See if you can get an expert to donate his or her time.

8. Network
Try to hook up with other groups or organizations that have similar concerns. See if students and teachers will become involved in your campaign. Get the word out over the Internet and through the phone, fax, mail, text messaging and/or blogging.

9. *Get the Media to Work for You*

Prepare a dramatic media event to receive media coverage. Send an information kit to the editor of your local newspaper requesting a review. Respond promptly to news items that concern your group with your own press releases and you may be called for a quote.

10. *Now Get to Work Lobbying*

Identify sympathetic politicians. Ask them to sponsor proposed legislation and see it through the political process. Identify a staff member that you will be able to keep in close touch with. Request meetings with the politicians you want to influence. Begin a petition or letter-writing campaign.

Once you have taken these steps, don't forget to assess the effectiveness of your actions. Make adjustments as necessary for your next set of actions.

Tackling Auto Insurance Rates

Imagine you want to raise some money for a charity. You decide to sell 100 chocolate bars door-to-door in your neighbourhood. What kind of a profit would you want to make for the charity to feel good about your efforts? Would you be happy with a $50 profit? A $100 profit? More?

What about a profit of $4.2 billion? That's the profit that insurance companies in Canada made in 2004. You may have heard people complain about high insurance premiums. A premium is the fee that people pay to an insurance company for insurance coverage of their homes, businesses, vehicles, and even their lives. If you have a car accident, the insurance company pays for repairing damages to your car and any others involved in the accident. It is illegal to drive in Canada without auto insurance.

> ### Literacy Hint
> **Make a Connection.** What do you know about auto insurance rates? How much will you have to pay for insurance when you drive?

Figure 7-18 The insurance industry has stated that the September 11, 2001, attacks on the World Trade Center in New York City almost brought the industry to financial ruin. What individuals, groups, and/or businesses do you think might have made insurance claims after this incident?

When Canadians learned that insurance companies made billions of dollars in profit in 2004, they were outraged. Most Canadians have watched the premiums they pay increase by a significant percentage each year. Insurance companies had argued that the increases in auto insurance were necessary. They stated that the industry was facing financial ruin following the terrorist attacks on the World Trade Center in New York City on September 11, 2001. The industry raised rates to help make up for the huge claims that had to be paid after the attacks. So when the news of the huge profits came out, Canadians were shocked.

In the News

Ontarians expect lower rates

by Canadian Press
posted February 23, 2005

Ontario drivers should expect dramatically lower auto insurance premiums, given the record $4.2 billion profit posted by the industry, Finance Minister Greg Sorbara said Tuesday.

"There is capacity, given these very handsome profits, for insurance companies to bring down much further auto insurance rates," Sorbara told the legislature. "That's what we should be expecting from the auto insurance industry in this great province."

Friday's announcement of yet another year of record profits for Canada's home and auto insurance industry has been dubbed obscene by critics.

For a second day in the provincial legislature, the New Democrats demanded the government introduce legislation to force insurers to give some of the money back to the public.

"People know that those big insurance company profits came out of drivers' pockets," NDP Leader Howard Hampton told the legislature. "Are you going to force insurance companies, big insurance, to give the drivers who have been ripped off an auto insurance rebate?"

Sorbara said there's an expectation the industry will bring down rates and repeated, once again, the Liberal mantra [a commonly repeated word or phrase] that premiums have come down 10.6 percent since they've taken office.

"I'm confident... that if we continue down this road, we're going to see further significant reductions in automobile insurance rates in this province," he said.

After posting the profits, The Insurance Bureau of Canada predicted that improved finances would translate into savings for drivers to the tune of $1.4 billion in 2005.

At least one consumers' group isn't convinced.

The Consumers' Association of Canada has said that money will likely end up going to shareholders and not the insured public....

1. *Who* is involved in this story?
2. *What* are the main events?
3. *When* did the events take place?
4. *Where* did the events take place?
5. *Why* did it happen?
6. *How* did it happen?

One of the largest groups working to have auto insurance premiums reduced is the Consumers' Association of Canada (CAC). This group lobbies politicians to change insurance laws. It also raises public awareness of the high costs of insurance. The CAC has asked the government to launch a **Royal Commission** to review the rising costs of insurance.

Mainly because of the work of lobby groups like the Consumers' Association of Canada, the government is now putting pressure on the insurance industry to lower premiums on all insurance rates.

The largest group on the other side of this issue is the Insurance Bureau of Canada (IBC). This organization represents the insurance companies that provide about 90 percent of the home, auto, and business insurance sold in Canada. The IBC argues that insurance company profits of over $4 billion in 2004 are not outrageous. In fact, they argue that if we consider the earnings made by insurance companies from the years 2000–2004, these profits actually only represent six cents of every dollar collected by insurers. Figure 7-19 demonstrates how incoming premiums were spent.

Royal Commission: a government inquiry into an issue that includes extensive research, consultation with experts, public hearings, and a final report released to the public. The government is not compelled to act on the report.

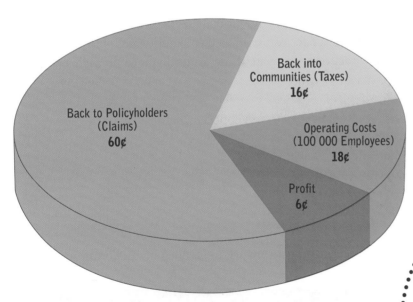

Source: Insurance Bureau of Canada. (2005, February). Property and Casual Insurance Financial Results 2004.

Figure 7-19 What do you think is fair to consumers and to the insurance industry? Do you agree with the way the insurance industry represents its profits?

The graph in Figure 7-19 makes the profits earned by these companies seem less outrageous. But why do you think the profits were calculated over a four-year period? The answer is that the insurance industry didn't make nearly as much money in the years 2001 and 2002. When you average those two years in with the high profits of 2003 and 2004, the overall profit margin looks lower.

Informed to Be Effective

Insurance and Young Drivers

Not everyone pays the same auto insurance premiums. Rates are based on a number of factors, including

• *Gender:* male drivers pay more for insurance because they are more likely to be involved in an accident.

• *Type of car:* "sports" car premiums are much higher than "family" car premiums.

• *Years of driving experience:* new drivers usually pay higher premiums

Which, if any, of these factors do you think are reasonable?

Figure 7-20 Do you think it is fair that young male drivers have to pay more whether or not they have been in an accident?

The IBC also argues that the insurance industry is good for Canada. It employs about 100 000 people across the country and pays close to $20 billion in claims. As well, the IBC argues that the $4.2 billion in profits the industry made in 2004 is far less than the estimated $6 billion in taxes the industry paid to the federal and provincial governments.

Informed, Purposeful, and Active Citizenship

So, you have reached the end of this course in civics. You have been armed with tools to assume the responsibilities of democratic citizenship—informed, purposeful, and active citizenship. In return, you will receive certain rights and freedoms. You have probably figured out that in any democracy rights and freedoms cannot exist without responsibilities.

Any society or group is as strong as its weakest members. You have the knowledge and skills to be a strong member. The question is, "Do you have the inclination to be a strong member?" You and your classmates will be the politicians and decision makers of the future. You can make a difference locally, regionally, nationally, and globally by acting responsibly.

To make a difference, you will need to be informed, purposeful, and active. By your actions, motivate those around you to do their part. You have some steps ahead of you:

Figure 7-21 What kind of action will you take to make a difference?

- Choose your challenges/issues/concerns/battles.
- Set your goals.
- Put your plans into action.
- Assess your effectiveness.
- Refocus your efforts.
- Celebrate your successes.

Roll up your sleeves and get to work to create a better community or society.

CHECKPOINT

1. Create a list of examples of democratic citizenship from this chapter.
2. In what ways do large organizations like the Canadian Coalition for Action on Tobacco and the Consumers' Association of Canada act as responsible citizens?
3. In what ways do businesses like insurance companies and tobacco farmers and processors act as responsible citizens?

Active Citizen

CHAPTER REVIEW

Summing It Up

- We are members of our local and global community and have the right to take action to make these communities better reflect our own values.

- Both individuals and groups can work to bring about change.

- There are a great many strategies for affecting change, including: raising public awareness, raising money, protesting, writing letters, and lobbying.

- David Suzuki, Craig Kielburger, and Ryan Hreljac are three Canadians who have achieved extraordinary results through their civic action.

- Powerful lobby groups are able to change public policy through their actions.

- Democratic citizenship involves becoming informed, purposeful, and active about issues that affect you and your society.

KEY TERM

- Royal Commission

Thinking: To Be Informed

1. Research the term "altruism" (or concern for others). Identify the characteristics of people who seem to be driven to help others.

2. If you decided to raise money to support Ryan's Well, how would you go about doing it? Create a list of the different ways that you could raise money either on your own or with others.

Communicating: To Be Purposeful

3. Create a timeline that documents some of the changes that have been made in public smoking policy within your community or across the country since the year 2000. Include visuals within your timeline.

4. With a partner, role-play a discussion between a new young car driver and an insurance agent. Discuss why rates are higher for males than females.

Applying: To Be Active

5. Create a pamphlet, poster, or comic book on how to treat the environment well. The information and images you include should target children in elementary school.

6. Create a public awareness pamphlet or short speech on an issue or topic of your choice. You may want to consider topics you have explored in earlier chapters. The pamphlet or speech should provide information on the issue or topic and make suggestions on how others can support your cause.

Culminating Performance Task: Making a Difference

At this late stage in the process, you should have found a topic for your culminating performance task. Hopefully, you have not changed your mind about its importance to you. If you have, be sure to keep all your rough work. Even though the topic changes, sometimes the process steps are quite similar. If you are only now getting around to this major responsibility, quickly identify the essential elements reflected by the summary chart. Be realistic about what can be accomplished with the time and resources available to you. Even at this late stage, take the time to be informed. Do your homework so that you clearly know what you are talking about.

If you are stuck for ideas, review the Culminating Performance Task information boxes at the end of Chapters 1, 3, and 5. If you are still stuck, conference with your teacher to identify a workable task.

Next Steps

If you have been working on this task throughout the course, you should now be in cleanup mode. You should be making final revisions and improvements. In the remaining time, you should focus your efforts on:

Active Citizenship	Process Steps
Be Informed	• Review the assessment rubric to self-assess the degree to which you have completed the assigned task.
Be Purposeful	• Discuss your action plan with teachers, classmates, and other "advisors." • Select the contents of your project portfolio to include in your final product.
Be Active	• Execute the final stages of your action plan, making revisions as required. • Prepare the final product that will be handed in for marking (edit contents for clarity and flow; check spelling and grammar). • Assess the effectiveness of your action plan (the extent to which you have actually made a difference).

GLOSSARY

80/20 rule approximately 80 percent of the world's people have access to no more than 20 percent of Earth's wealth

acquittal the decision indicating that the accused is not guilty of the charges brought against an accused

adversary one who takes an opposite position or presents an opposing argument

advocate a person who argues for a specific position

advocacy arguing for a specific position to influence public decision making in a controversial situation

alibi the defence that the accused was elsewhere when the offence was committed

amalgamation the process in which several smaller municipalities and their governments are merged into one large municipality with a single government

analysis taking a concept or idea apart to better understand it

appeal an application to a higher court to review the decision of the lower court

arbitration the settlement of a dispute by the decision of an impartial third party, such as a judge or arbitrator

artifacts material evidence of a distinct community and its shared values and culture

autocracy a system in which a single person or authority has the power to make decisions

bail temporary release of the accused granted in exchange for money or some form of security to ensure the accused will appear for trial

bill proposed legislation

boycott refuse to buy or use a product as a form of protest

bylaw a law or rule passed by a municipal council and applicable only to that municipality

citizen a member of a state or nation, with certain rights and responsibilities

citizenship the responsibilities, duties, and rights of a member of a state or nation

civics the study of the duties and rights of citizenship

civic literacy skills skills in the areas of research and inquiry, critical and creative thinking, communication, decision making, conflict resolution and teamwork used for community building

civil disobedience the deliberate breaking of a law regarded as unjust to draw attention to the injustice and to pressure governments and other organizations to act

civil law the area of law that deals with legal relationships between individuals and between individuals and organizations

civil society a caring, peaceful, and supportive society where human dignity is respected

coalition government a government that is composed of members of different parties when a majority government is not elected. Members of different parties may be given Cabinet posts as members of the government.

common good what is best for the community and all its members because it best promotes dignity, security, and prosperity

common law law developed in English courts that relies on case law and is common to all people

community a group of people who have joined together to pursue common needs and goals

consensus a system of decision making based on one common agreement supported by all members

constituents citizens who live in electoral ridings across the nation

constitutional monarchy a nation under a monarch whose powers are restricted to those granted under the Constitution and laws of the nation

conviction the decision indicating that the accused is guilty of a criminal offence

councillors people elected to represent the residents in different wards in a municipality

counter-argument view that challenges the conclusions or supporting information of adversaries

culture the beliefs, language, customs, ceremonies, arts, institutions, social relations, and other human endeavours characteristic of a particular community, people, or nation

critical thinking examining the thinking process to better understand its significance and the reason behind it

Crown attorneys who represent the monarch and prosecute the accused on behalf of the community

democracy a system of decision making that uses a majority vote of members or of elected representatives to make decisions

dictatorship a system (in which) a single ruler seizes absolute power by banning all opposition

ethnic cleansing the systematic elimination of an ethnic group or groups from a region or society, either through deportation, forced emigration, or genocide

evaluation making a judgment about an idea's merit or value

executive branch the branch of the government responsible for daily government affairs, which includes introducing bills that may become law

fascist a system of government that is not elected, and in which property is privately owned, but in which all industry and business is regulated by a strong national government

federal government the level of government responsible for issues of national concern, represented by Parliament in Ottawa

federal system a two-level system of governing

free vote a parliamentary vote in which Members of Parliament are allowed to vote according to their conscience or to reflect the voters' views

genocide the systematic and planned extermination of an entire national, racial, political, or ethnic group

global citizenship the responsibilities, rights, and privileges of being a member of the global community

globalization a process accelerated by modern communications technology that multiplies and strengthens the economic, cultural, and financial interconnections among many regions of the world

government the rule or authority over a country, province, or district

grassroots organizations people working together at the local level to achieve a common political or humanitarian purpose

Gross Domestic Product (GDP) the annual total market value of all the goods and services produced within the borders of a nation excluding trade with other countries

Gross National Product (GNP) the annual total market value of all the goods and services produced within the borders of a nation

gun control limits or restrictions placed on who can buy and/or use guns, and for what reason

habeus corpus the right of the accused to know the nature of the charge, the right to a fair and speedy trial, and the right to be presumed innocent until found guilty

impact statement a series of paragraphs written by either the victim or relatives of a victim outlining how the actions of the convicted affected their lives

infrastructure the networks of transportation, communication, education, and other public services required to sustain economic and societal activities

internment camp camp for political prisoners or prisoners of war

interest group a group of individuals who join together to pursue common goals and to advocate for their cause

intifadas the ongoing and sometimes violent uprising of Palestinian Arabs who protest what they believe is the unfair occupation of their land by Israel

judicial branch the branch of government responsible for interpreting and enforcing the laws passed by the legislative branch

learning skills a set of skills assessed by all teachers and reported on provincial report cards

legislative branch the branch of government responsible for passing laws and representing the interests of the voters

lobby group a well-organized group intended to influence policy making by engaging in regular dialogue with government officials

lobbying trying to influence legislators

lobbyist a professional trained in the art of policy influence

local citizenship the responsibilities, rights and privileges of being a member of your local community

lower-tier municipality a municipality in which the community is a part of a group of municipalities that form a region or county; a regional/county government provides certain services to the region as a whole

mandate support given to a political party or government by the electors

majority government a government that has more than half of the total number of parliamentary seats

mediation a method of conflict resolution in which a neutral third-party helps two disputing parties arrive at a mutually agreeable resolution

middle power countries that are not considered superpowers but still have some influence internationally

minority government a government that has fewer seats in Parliament than the total number held by all other parties

multinational corporation a company that operates in several countries

Municipal Act a set of guidelines that reflects the responsibilities and powers that a community has as well as how the local government is to be structured

municipal government local government that includes a mayor and a council responsible for delivering services to its population as outlined in the provincial *Municipal Act*

negative argument view that exposes the weakness of the opposite position

negotiation the process of resolving disputes through direct communication between the disputing parties to reach a mutually agreeable solution

non-governmental organizations (NGOs) non-profit, independent organizations dedicated to making the world a better place

opposition the political party or parties not in power

outsourcing when a company has work produced or completed in another country because it can do so cheaply. Usually the company that outsources the work is in a developed nation and the company that receives the outsourced contract is in a developing nation.

pandemic a disease that thrives over a wide geographic area and affects a large proportion of the population

parole early release with conditions, such as reporting to a parole officer, not leaving a community, accepting a curfew

passive resistance a non-violent form of deliberate non-cooperation with government authority

perjury the criminal offence of knowingly making false statements in court while giving evidence under oath

pesticides any chemicals or other substances used to destroy plant or animal pests, often used to control insects in lawns

plea bargain a deal between the Crown and a defendant, whereby the defendant pleads guilty in exchange for a lighter sentence

popular will the wishes of the voters

positive argument view that uses evidence to support the position being taken

power the ability to direct others to achieve what you want

premeditated planned ahead of time

pressure group a group organized to persuade policy-makers to make decisions that favour their interests

private member's bill legislation proposed by an MP who is not in the Cabinet

probation a sentence that allows convicted persons, especially young or first offenders, to go free under the supervision of a probation officer

protest group people who use public demonstrations to influence public opinion or to pressure governments and other organizations to act

provincial government the level of government responsible for provincial issues, represented by Legislative Assemblies in provincial capitals

public policy issue a problem situation sparking public discussion and debate about the need for government action to address public concerns

question period the time set aside each day where members of the House can pose questions to the government

rehabilitation the process of restoring to former standing, rights, privileges, reputation

resolution when individuals or groups decide on a predetermined course of action

riding a political division represented by a Member of Parliament or a Member of the Legislative Assembly; a constituency

Royal Commission a government inquiry into an issue that includes extensive research, consultation with experts, public hearings, and a final report released to the public

rule of law the principle that no government or person is above the law

seat the right to sit as a member of a legislature, based on winning a riding in an election

sentencing circle a justice system used in some Aboriginal communities that involves a process of healing for both the victim and the offender

simulation a model imitating real or assumed conditions

single-tier municipality a municipality in which only one level of government provides all services to its population

social trade-off giving up personal freedom to achieve social harmony

speech from the throne a speech written by the government that sets out the legislative program the government will present to Parliament

stakeholder a person with an interest or concern in a particular issue or decision

suspended sentence a judgment that is not carried out, provided the offender meets certain requirements set out by the judge

sustainable development development (construction) that can be maintained over time without causing damage to the environment

sweatshop a workplace where workers are poorly paid, have poor working conditions, and are often exposed to physical and psychological abuse

synthesis tying information together to build meaningful conclusions

transfer payments a system of payments from provinces with stronger revenues to provinces with smaller tax bases; intended to ensure equality of services for all Canadians

upper-tier municipality name given to the group of lower-tier municipalities that form the region or county

veto power the ability to reject a resolution

vote the act of expressing an opinion by a show of hands or ballot; used to make a decision such as passing a resolution or electing a candidate to office

vote of non-confidence occurs when a proposed bill receives less than a majority of votes in the House of Commons, defeating the government and forcing it to resign

voter's list a list giving the names, addresses, and occupations of all those entitled to vote in a given riding

INDEX